A DOCTOR AT CALVARY

The Passion of Our Lord Jesus Christ
as Described by a Surgeon

By

PIERRE BARBET, M.D.

Translated by
THE EARL OF WICKLOW

ROMAN CATHOLIC BOOKS
P.O. Box 255
Harrison, NY 10528

A DOCTOR AT CALVARY

is a translation of *La Passion de N.-S. Jésus-Christ selon le Chirurgien* by Pierre Barbet, M.D., published by Dillen & Cie, Editeurs, Issoudun (Indre), France, 1950.

NIHIL OBSTAT : M. L. DEMPSEY, S.T.D.
CENSOR THEOL., DEP.
IMPRIMI POTEST : IOANNES CAROLUS
ARCHIEP. DUBLINEN, HIBERNIÆ PRIMAS
18 AUG., 1953

ISBN 0-912141-04-2

Contents

Preface

I HAVE for a long time been asked, but of late with more eagerness, to collect together in one book the results of my anatomical experiments, of my archæological and scriptural researches, finally of my reflections on the Passion of OurLord Jesus Christ. It is a subject which for more than fifteen years has in truth never been out of my thoughts, and at times has almost engrossed me. For has this world any more important subject for meditation than those sufferings, in which two mysterious truths have become materialised for mankind, the Incarnation and the Redemption? It is clearly both necessary and sufficient that mankind should adhere to these with the whole of their souls, and that they should loyally derive from them their rule of life. But, in this unique event, which is the culminating point of human history, the smallest detail seems to me to have an infinite value. One does not weary of examining the smallest particulars, even when the reticence of the Evangelists makes it necessary for us to build our structure on scientific bases, which, even though they may be neither scriptural nor inspired, are nevertheless reasonably solid hypotheses.

Theologians can imagine and describe to us the moral sufferings, which formed part of the Saviour's Passion, beginning with those in the agony of Gethsemani, when He was overwhelmed with the weight of the sins of the world, and ending with His abandonment by the Father, which drew from Him the cry on the cross: *"Eli, Eli, lamma sabachthani!"* One may even venture to say that He continued to recite to Himself in a low voice the magnificent twenty-first psalm, of which these words are the first verse; a psalm which continues in notes of hope, and ends with a triumphal chant of victory.

But when the same theologians or exegetes wish to describe to us the physical sufferings of Jesus, one is struck with the difficulty which they find in helping us to take part in them, anyway in thought. The truth is that they scarcely understand them; there is little on this subject which seems more empty than the traditional sermons on the Passion.

Some years ago, my good friend Dr. Pasteau, the president of the Société de Saint-Luc of Catholic Doctors in France, was visiting the Vatican with several high dignitaries of the Church. He was explaining to them, following on my researches, how much we now know about the death of Jesus, about His terrible sufferings, and how He had died, suffering from cramp in all His muscles and from asphyxia. One of them, who was still Cardinal Pacelli, and who, along with the others, had gone pale with grief and compassion, answered him: "We did not know; nobody had ever told us that."

And it is indeed essential that we, who are doctors, anatomists and physiologists, that we who know, should proclaim abroad the terrible truth, that our poor science should no longer be used merely to alleviate the pains of our brothers, but should fulfil a greater office, that of enlightening them.

The primary reason for this ignorance is to be found, we must own, in the dreadful conciseness of the Evangelists: "Pilate . . . having scourged Jesus, delivered Him to them to be crucified . . . and they crucified Him." Every Christian, no matter how little he may be liturgically-minded, hears these two phrases throughout the years, four times during Holy Week, in slightly different versions. But how much does that mean to him in the long reading of the Passion? The solemn chanting continues: one can hear the howls of the Jewish mob and the grave words of the Saviour, and unless it has prepared itself beforehand, the mind lacks the time to dwell on the ghastly sufferings to which these simple words refer.

The Evangelists certainly had no need to be more explicit. For the Christians who had listened to the Apostolic teaching, and who later on read the four Gospels, these two words, "scourging, crucifixion," were all too full of meaning; they had first-hand experience, and had seen scourgings and crucifixions; they knew what the words meant. But for ourselves, and for our priests, they mean scarcely anything; they tell, indeed, of a cruel punishment. but they paint no definite picture. And one watches the unfortunate preacher desperately trying to express his sincere grief: "Jesus has suffered; He has greatly suffered; He has suffered for our sins."

To the man who knows what this means, who suffers in consequence, to the point of no longer being able to do the Stations of the Cross, there comes a terrible temptation to interrupt the orator, to tell him how much He suffered and in what way He suffered, to explain the quantity and quality of His sufferings, and finally how much He wished to die.

For several years I have had the supreme joy of hearing that in many churches my little *Passion Corporelle*[1] has inspired, enlivened, and sometimes completely replaced the sermon on the Passion. During the

---

[1] Translation published by Clonmore & Reynolds, Ltd.

war I even experienced the great happiness of being able to read it, at Issy-les-Moulineaux, to three hundred seminarists and their professors; it was in a paradoxical fashion, and by reversing the rôles, a true example of the apostolate of the laity. I shall preach the Passion no more, but it is largely with a view to these clerics that I have wished to divulge my ideas, so that they may nourish their devotion to Jesus crucified and may bring it out in their preaching.

That is why I have decided to collect all these ideas together in one book, which will enable me to develop them more easily. My anatomical experiments took place in the years 1932 and 1935. I described the first to my colleagues of the *Société de Saint-Luc,* whose judgment I valued more than any other. They were generous in their enthusiastic support and gave me the hospitality of their bulletin: in this were published *les mains du Crucifié,* May, 1933; *les pieds du Crucifié et le coup de lance,* March, 1934; *la descente du croix et le transport au tombeau,* March, 1938; *l'ensevelissement de Jésus,* March, 1948.[2] I published the result of my first researches in a small book, *les Cinq Plaies du Christ,*[3] in January, 1935; its fourth edition, supplemented with a chapter on the descent from the cross, appeared in 1948. In 1940 I produced my brochure, *la Passion Corporelle,*[4] which appeared first of all in *La Vie Spirituelle.* The essay on the burial of Jesus appeared in March, 1948, as the result of a talk given to the Paris branch of the *Société de Saint-Luc.*

I can claim that since I finished my experiments the conclusions to which I came have never been reversed, though I remain open to any new discovery which may show me to have been wrong. It has always been my aim to look on this as a scientific question and to put forward my conclusions as hypotheses, in my opinion solidly established but capable of modification, anyway in their details. But I have never ceased to reflect on this form of torment and on the pictures of the Holy Shroud, the authenticity of which is to my mind assured by a closely-knit web of anatomical proofs.

From this long, continuous meditation there has emerged, without further experiment, a series of complementary explanations which seem to me as luminous as they are simple. We find, for instance, the double flow of blood from the wrist, due to the double movement of straightening and relaxation on the part of the Crucified, and the thoracic flow

---

[2] The hands of the Crucified, May, 1933; the feet of the Crucified and the blow with the lance, March, 1934; the descent from the cross and the journey to the tomb, March, 1938; the burial of Jesus, March, 1948.

[3] *The Five Wounds of Christ.* Translation published by Clonmore & Reynolds.

[4] *The Corporal Passion.*

on the back due to the method of carrying to the tomb. We shall meet with all this later on, and we shall also see how these scientific conclusions are fully in accordance with the Gospels.

May I reassure my readers that in this book I am making no claim that I can provide a complete and definite solution to the problem of the Holy Shroud. God forbid! My aim is more modest, to set out my views as to the actual state of the question, following on a long study of the subject, or at least to describe the reasonably homogeneous and logical view which I have been able to reach so far. I shall point out what I consider to be doubtful and what I consider to be definitely admitted as true. That is the spirit of the scientific and experimental method. But I shall never forget that the shroud, as H.H. Pope Pius XI used to say, is still surrounded by many mysteries. The future has no doubt many surprises in store for us.

Another thing which I learnt in the course of my publications, is the difficulty of explaining scientific conclusions to the uninitiated, for these presuppose a whole course of previous teaching. When writing for my colleagues, everything went easily, and I was able to make myself understood in a few words. My natural tendency to be concise had every advantage, since it made my demonstration more precise and compact. But how often have those who were not doctors asked me for further information or have stated objections, the answers to which, as well as the explanations, had already been printed in my work. Yes, it had all been clearly explained, but in sentences too short for one who was not initiated, and there had been no repetitions; I had not made my point strongly enough. In later editions I profited by this experience, and I shall do so even more thoroughly in this book.

As is perhaps known, my anatomical experiments were undertaken after the exposition of the shroud at Turin in 1931. My old friend, Father Armailhac, whom God has now called to heaven, visited the Laënnec conference of students of medicine in Paris, in order to show us the latest photographs, which I myself used. He wished to obtain the opinion of anatomists. It is thus quite natural, since my first aim was to verify the anatomical accuracy of these marks (this aim has since then been considerably enlarged), that I should try to give the reader a short account of this remarkable relic, and of the passionate arguments which it has aroused, even and indeed especially among Catholics.

My studies also led me to inquire into everything which, in pagan and Christian archæology, in the ancient texts (apart from the Scriptures) and in the history of art can give us some information about this form of punishment which was used by the Romans; in this case the executioners were the Roman legionaries and the judge was a Roman procurator. In a book such as this, which is not bound to be as compact and light as a brochure, I can explain the results of these researches and experiments; I shall not restrict myself but I shall try and avoid all pedantry.

I had kept out of my book on the five wounds everything dealing with the other sufferings of Jesus, previous to His crucifixion: the sweat of blood, the cruelties inflicted on Him as a prisoner, the scourging, the crowning with thorns, the carrying of the cross, astonishing traces of which are to be seen on the Holy Shroud. My aim here, as the completion of my work, is to try and deal with all these questions, always in the same medical spirit.

I shall also give the opinions I have formed in regard to the descent from the cross and the carrying to the tomb, and the results of my exegetical (I hope the exegetes will forgive me), historical and philological researches, on the subject of the shroud and the burial.

I often wonder, indeed, why I should have been chosen to make these researches. I am aware that for forty years I have taken a keen interest in biblical exegesis, and that I have eagerly pored over that magnificent harvest of works which is one of the glories of the Church in France, from those of Father Lagrange to those of Father de Grandmaison, to mention only two of our writers who are now dead. But there are so many others that one can consult, taking from each the fairest flowers in his garden. I have retained from the solid classical education which I received (according to the usual formula) the capacity to go over the Greek and Latin, but alas, not the Hebrew texts. I have always taken a passionate interest in archæology and in the history of art, and I have studied the manifestations of the Christian spirit, from the frescoes in the catacombs, which I visited over a long period, down to the elaborations of modern art. Finally, I am first of all a surgeon, and thus well versed in anatomy, which I taught for a long time; I lived for thirteen years in close contact with corpses and I have spent the whole of my career examining the anatomy of the living. I can thus, without presumption, write " the Passion according to the surgeon "; may we say the cultivated surgeon, since that is what it is his absolute duty to be.

The reader may smile, I think, when he reads this naïve *Apologia pro domo*. He should understand that it is not just a list of titles with which I am seeking to justify myself, but an attempt to excuse my boldness. For all this filled me with the desire to face these problems, with the hope that, God willing, I might arrive at their solution. Furthermore, I only undertook my experiments, when I had made sure that none of my colleagues were doing the same.

But I feel reassured, as I read over again the delightful chapter IX of the *Fioretti*, when Brother Masseo, in order to test the humility of his master, kept saying to St. Francis: "*Perche a tte; perche a tte?*—Why you, rather than anyone else?" And Francis answered Brother Masseo: "Because the eyes of God on high have not seen anyone amongst sinners who is any more vile or more unworthy than . . . I am. And for this reason. . . . He has chosen me to perform this marvellous work in order to confound the nobility and the greatness and the beauty and the strength and the wisdom of this world, so that it may be understood that all virtue and all good come from Him, and not from creatures, and that no person can glorify himself when in His presence; but if anyone would glorify himself, let him glorify himself in the Lord, to Whom be honour and glory for ever."

I would not finish this preface without thanking, as I should, the Missionaries of the Sacred Heart at Issoudun, and their publisher, my old friend, Dillen, who have between them printed and distributed my little books with a truly fraternal devotion. I cannot do better than confide this book to them, to whom it already owes so much!

PARIS, *All Saints' Day*, 1949.

Chapter One

THE HOLY SHROUD

T HE reader who wishes to form a general idea of the problem, should read a little book which is as precise as it is concise, *La Passion selon le Saint Suaire*, by my friend Antoine Legrand (Librairie du Carmel, 27 Rue Madame, Paris). Paul Vignon's second book is also of value, on account of its very rich iconography, *Le Saint Suaire de Turin* (Masson, 1938).

Let us, then, also study the shroud, since I started my experiments in order to discover whether its markings corresponded with the realities of anatomy and physiology. I undertook this study with a completely open mind, being equally ready to affirm that the shroud was an absurd fraud, or to recognise its authenticity, but I was gradually forced to agree, on every single point, that its markings were exact. Furthermore, those which seemed the strangest were those which fitted in best with my experiments. The bloodstained pictures were clearly not drawn by the hand of man; they could be nothing but the counter-drawings made by blood which had been previously coagulated on a human body. No artist would have been able to imagine for himself the minute details of those pictures, each one of which portrayed a detail of what we now know about the coagulation of blood, but which in the 14th century was unknown. But the fact is that not one of us would be able to produce such pictures without falling into some blunder.

It was this homogeneous group of verifications without one single weak link among them, which decided me, relying on the balance of probabilities, to declare that the authenticity of the shroud, from the point of view of anatomy and physiology, is a scientific fact.

A.—THE HISTORY

It is certain that on the day of the Resurrection Peter and John found the shroud of Jesus in the tomb. The synoptics, who, in regard to the burial, only speak of the shroud, on the Sunday found the *othonia,* the linen cloths (Gerson, in 1304, translates this as the shrouds); the shroud clearly formed part of these. St. John, who on the Friday only speaks of the *othonia,* on the Sunday found the *othonia* and the *soudarion.* In company with Monsieur Lévesque we shall see that this *soudarion* means the shroud, in the Aramean in which St. John thought. If we refused to admit this, we should be compelled to place the shroud among the *othonia.*

What did the Apostles do with these? In spite of the natural repugnance of the Jews, for whom everything which comes in contact with death is unclean, especially a linen cloth stained with blood, it is impossible to believe that they did not preserve with the greatest care this relic of God made Man. One is also led to think that they would have been careful to hide it. It had to be protected from destruction by those who were persecuting the young Church. Furthermore, there could be no question of offering it for the veneration of the new Christians, who would be deeply imbued with the horror of the ancient world at the infamy of the cross. We shall return later to that long period, during which the cross was concealed under various symbols. We shall find that it is not till the Vth and VIth centuries that one comes across the first crucifixes, which in their turn were very much toned down; not till the VIIth and VIIIth centuries do they become rather more widely diffused. It is not till the XIIIth century that the devotion to the Passion of Jesus becomes general.

We would at this point add what is only a hypothesis, but we shall see, when studying the formation of the markings (E 2°, same chapter —the work of Volckringer), that it is the result of a mysterious biological phenomenon which has however been duly verified: it is possible that the markings of the body did not become visible on the shroud for a long period of years, though it bore bloodstains from the beginning. It is possible that they became distinct subsequently, in much the same way that a photographic film conceals its picture till it has been developed.

There is thus an obscure period when the shroud does not appear, indeed when *it cannot appear.* It may well have been carefully concealed, and thus have escaped all occasions of being destroyed. Romans, Persians, Medes and Parthians, each in their turn devastated Jerusalem and Palestine, massacring and dispersing the Christians, pillaging and demolishing their churches. What happened to the shroud? Nicephorus Callistus wrote in his ecclesiastical history that in the year 436 the Empress Pulcheria had built in Constantinople the basilica of St. Mary of the Blachernae and that she deposited there the burial linen of Jesus, which had just been rediscovered. It is there that we shall find the shroud in 1204 (Robert de Clari). Meanwhile, in 1171, according to William de Tyr, the Emperor Manuel Commenus showed the relics of the Passion to King Amaury of Jerusalem: the lance, the nails, the sponge, the crown of thorns and the shroud, which he kept in the chapel of the Boucoleon. Now, all these things were there, besides a veil of Veronica, said Robert de Clari, except for the shroud which was at the Blachernae, according to the same Clari. It is also worthy of note that Nicephorus, who died in 1250, wrote after the capture of Constantinople, in 1204, where the shroud had disappeared. There may thus have been some confusion.

But a long time previously, in 631, St. Braulion, the Bishop of Saragossa, a learned and prudent man, in his letter No. XLII (P.L.t. LXXX, 689), writes, as if telling of something which had been well known for a long time, " *de sudario quo corpus Domini est involutum,* of the *winding-sheet* in which the body of the Lord was wrapped." And he adds: " The Scriptures do not tell us that it was preserved, but one cannot call those superstitious who believe in the authenticity of this *winding-sheet.*" A winding-sheet which had been wrapped round the body of Jesus could only be a shroud; we shall see this in the chapter on the burial. Where then was it during this period?

If we turn to the three books written by Adamnan, the Benedictine Abbot of Iona, *About the Holy Places, according to the account of Arculphus, a French Bishop,* section III, chapter X, *de Sudario Domini,* (published by Mabillon—*Acta Sanctorum Ordinis Benedictini*), we shall find that Arculphus was a pilgrim in Jerusalem round about the year 640. He there saw and kissed *sudarium Domini quod in sepulcro super caput ipsius fuerat positum*—the winding-sheet of the Lord which was placed over His head in the sepulchre. This follows the words of St. John. Now, this *winding-sheet,* according to Arculphus, was a *long piece of linen* which gave the impression of being about eight feet in length. This was no small cloth; it was the shroud.

St. Bede the Venerable, at the beginning of the VIIIth century, also mentions the testimony of Arculphus, in his *Ecclesiastical History* (*de locis sanctis*). About the same period St. John Damascene mentions the *sindon* as being among the relics venerated by the Christians. We thus already find that *sindon* and *sudarium* are equally used as synonyms.

It would seem from this that in the VIIth century it was still in Jerusalem or had been brought back there, and that it was only taken to Constantinople at a later date. When? We do not know. Perhaps before the XIIth century, when the pilgrims spoke of the *sudarium quod fiut super caput ejus;* we have just seen that according to Arculphus this referred to the shroud. In any case, it was there in 1204, at the time of the fourth Crusade.

Robert de Clari, a knight from Picardy, who took part in the capture of Constantinople in 1204, leads us on to much firmer ground. (cf *La Conquête de Constantinople* in *Classiques français du moyen âge*, Ed. Champion, 1924). Robert is looked upon by historical critics as a man of moderate education, rather naïve, and whose views may be discounted in regard to the policy of the great barons, of which he knew little. But he was an observant and perfectly sincere witness, whenever he was able to see for himself.

Now, he gives a minute description of all the riches and the relics which he saw in the palaces and the *rikes kapeles* of the town, especially in the Boucoleon, which he rather amusingly calls *el Bouke de Lion*, and in the Blachernae. In the Boucoleon he saw two pieces of the true cross, the head of the lance, two nails, a phial of blood, a tunic and a crown. He also saw (described separately, with a long legend of how it was formed, after Our Lord had appeared to a holy man at Constantinople) what he speaks of as a *toaille*, a linen cloth bearing the face of the Saviour, like the veil of Veronica in Rome, and also a tile on which a tracing of it had appeared.

But it was at the Blachernae that he found the Holy Shroud. The whole account is written in the strange *langue d'oïl* of the XII century, which still lives on in Walloon dialects. It should be read out loud, with a northern accent, perhaps also with Walloon blood in one's veins, if one wishes to enjoy its full richness. He tells that: "And among the others there was a monastery known as Lady Saint Mary of the Blachernae, in which was kept the shroud in which Our Lord was wrapped; on every Friday this was held out, so well that it was possible to see the face of Our Lord. And neither Greek nor Frenchman knew what happened to that shroud after the town was taken."

The shroud was thus stolen, or to be more indulgent, it formed part of the spoils of war. Now, according to Byzantine historians, and Dom Chamard in particular, a shroud corresponding to de Clari's description was deposited in the hands of the Archbishop of Besançon, by Ponce de la Roche, a seigneur from Franche-Comté, the father of Othon de la Roche, who was one of the chief leaders of the Burgundian army in the crusade of 1204. And this shroud, which seems indeed to be ours, was venerated in the cathedral of Saint-Étienne down to 1349. I would note in passing that Vignon, in his book of 1938, has expressed some doubts as to its sojourn in Besançon; this is however very probable.

In the year 1349 the cathedral was laid waste by a terrible fire, and the shroud disappeared for the second time; only its reliquary was found. It had been stolen, and this fact is the true explanation of the false position which it was to occupy and the avatars from which it was to suffer during the following century. The memory of these still arouses prejudice against it in the minds of certain historians, whose number is steadily growing less, but who refuse to consider the intrinsic value of the sheet or to examine the markings, under the pretext that it can only be *a priori* a forgery—one might as well refuse to study the moon, because we can never see more than the half of it!

The shroud reappears eight years later, in 1357, in the possession of Count Geoffroy de Charny, having been given to him by King Philip VI. The latter must have received it from the robber, who is believed to have been one Vergy. Charny deposited it in the collegiate establishment at Lirey (in the diocese of Troyes) which he had founded a few years previously. Now, at about the same time there reappeared in Besançon another shroud, of which we have numerous copies, and which was clearly a poor and incomplete painted reproduction of the one at Lirey. The representatives of the Committee of Public Safety proved this in 1794, though this was no credit to them, and it was destroyed with the consent of the cathedral clergy.

The shroud at Lirey was also the object of the hostility of the Bishops of Troyes, first of all Henry of Poitiers, and thirty years later Peter d'Arcy, who objected to it being exposed by the canons of Lirey. They complained that the faithful were deserting the relics at Troyes, and were going in large crowds to Lirey. The Charnys quickly took back the relic, and kept it for thirty years.

In 1389 they presented their cause to the legate of the new Avignon Pope, that Clement VII who had just started the Western schism, and then to the anti-Pope himself. Both of these authorised the exposition in spite of Bishop Peter d'Arcy's prohibition. Then, when the latter complained, Clement VII ended by deciding (a somewhat unworthy solution) that the Bishop could no longer oppose the expositions, but that a declaration should be made at each one that this was a painting representing the true shroud of Our Lord.

In the memorandum which he presented to Clement, Peter d'Arcy made grave and malicious accusations of simony against the canons of Lirey. He further claimed that his predecessor had made an inquiry and had received the admission of the artist who had painted the cloth.

No traces have even been found of this inquiry or of these avowals; if there was a painter, it is probable that he was the one who copied the shroud of Lirey to make that of Besançon. The fact is that all the decisions were the result of private interests and were based on the argument that the Gospels remain silent in regard to the existence of the markings. It seems that no impartial examination was ever made of the sheet itself; had this been done, they would have seen, as one can see to-day, that there is no trace of painting. But the pseudo-Pope

Clement VII never seems to have concerned himself with this. It is not easy to summarise these rather squalid disputes. But it seems that the poor shroud was only guilty of one fault, it was without its credentials. How could it have had them, if its presence at Lirey was the result of a double theft, in regard to the second of which the King of France was compromised as a receiver of stolen goods. And it was this absence of an identity card which was held on all sides as an objection against the last owner, Marguerite de Charny, when she took it to Chimay in Belgium. In consequence, after a number of journeyings to and fro, she made a present of it in 1452 to Anne de Lusignan, the wife of the Duke of Savoy.

That is how it came to Chambéry, and became what it still is, the property of the house of Savoy which was formerly reigning in Italy. Please God it will one day come to rest in the hands of the Sovereign Pontiff, the successor of St. Peter and the Vicar of Jesus Christ, the only person on earth in whose custody it should be.

From then onwards the history of the shroud is well known. The Duke of Savoy had a chapel built for it at Chambéry. There was a series of expositions, and according to Antony de Lalaing the chronicler, it was made to undergo some strange tests in order to prove its authenticity. It was several times boiled in oil and also washed, but it was found impossible to remove the markings. A horrifying idea, if indeed the chronicle is to be trusted, but it anyway shows they had an obstinate determination to make themselves sure.

As if the ways of men were not enough, a fire broke out in the chapel in 1532, which narrowly missed destroying the relic. A drop of molten silver had burnt its way through the corner of the sheet where it was folded in its reliquary, and thus it is spangled with a double series of burns which we shall find equally spaced. These two holes are fortunately on each side of the central marking. The water used to put out the fire has left broad symmetrical rings along the whole length of the shroud. This was its second fire after its second robbery.

The fortunate result of this was a canonical inquiry so as to establish the genuine character of the damaged shroud; and the repairs made by the Poor Clares of Chambéry were accompanied by an official descriptive report which was drawn up by these holy women.

The shroud then made various journeys, following on the political vicissitudes of its proprietor; it finally arrived at Turin in 1578 where it was venerated by St. Charles Borromeo. The latter had taken a vow to go to Chambéry, but the Duke of Savoy spared him the labour of crossing the Alps, so that he went on foot only from Milan to Turin.

It was later deposited in the chapel adjoining the cathedral of St. John, where it is shown but rarely; exposition depends on permission being granted by the house of Savoy, who are not lavish in granting it. The last expositions took place in 1898 (when the first photograph was taken), in 1931 and 1933. Permission for the last one was obtained owing to its being the traditional centenary (though this is probably not exact) of the death of Jesus.

B.—THE HOLY SHROUD AND THE POPES

We have seen how the attitude of the anti-Pope Clement VII was as ambiguous as it was obviously political. The hypercritical historian Ulysses Chevalier seems to attach a special importance to his vacillating opinion, because he believes that this supplies him with an argument against the shroud, but he might, with more impartiality, have balanced this with the constant veneration shown by the later legitimate Popes. Once the shroud had found a home at Chambéry, Paul II attached a collegiate establishment, with twelve canons, to the church where it had been installed by Duke Amedeus IX. Sixtus IV, in 1480, bestowed on it the name of the *Sainte Chapelle*. Julius II, in 1506, granted it a Mass and an Office of its own, for its feast-day which was fixed for May 4th. Leo X extended this feast to the whole of Savoy, and Gregory XIII to Piedmont as well, with the further grant of a plenary indulgence to pilgrims.

And they all, in their solemn pronouncements, declare that this shroud is indeed the one in which Jesus was placed in the tomb. They all add that the relics of the Humanity of the Saviour which it contains, that is to say His Blood, deserve and indeed require to be venerated and adored. This is precisely that cult of *latria*, against which the two Bishops of Troyes protested with such violence, finally winning the approval of the anti-Pope Clement VII. And this is all the more important, because many decisions taken by the anti-Popes of Avignon were, once the schism was ended, approved by their legitimate Roman successors.

It would almost be necessary to mention them all, in order to tell of the many marks of veneration which they lavished, and of the indulgences which they granted and confirmed on its behalf. Pius VII solemnly prostrated himself before it in 1814, when he returned in triumph to the Papal States, and Leo XIII showed joy and emotion when he saw the first photograph of the shroud in 1898.

We then come, without speaking of our present Pope before he has himself made a pronouncement, to His Holiness Pius XI, of venerated memory. Those who came into close contact with him, and I had the honour to be among them, know how rigorous and exacting was the scientific precision which guided that surprisingly lucid mind; he would be content with nothing less than good reasoning based on solid facts. Mgr. Ratti had seen the exposition in 1898, and he remembered the supple quality of the material, the fineness of the lines, the absence of all colouring material, and the perfection of the anatomy of the body. But he had worked for many years at the Ambrosian Library, where the spirit of the Bollandists held sway, who are adepts at showing up false relics or fabricated legends; he had been well broken in by this at times very severe discipline. Now, from 1931 onwards he had the photographs of the shroud in his possession and made a careful study of them. He kept them within easy reach, according to his usual custom. He read everything which appeared on the subject, and my own *Five Wounds* (I know this from a reliable source, who was a friend of both of us). And as usual he did so with his pen in his hand, taking notes in the course of his reading. He did me the honour of wishing to see me. He went over the problem from every point of view, as he knew so well how to do, conscientiously, scientifically, slowly. He did not ignore any of the historical difficulties; this was his speciality, and he had at his disposal the Vatican archives, in which he was the supreme expert, as the Popes of the XVIth century already had the archives of Avignon.

But, as Father Armailhac has written: " Divine Providence ruled that it should be the best qualified of the Popes, the one least to be suspected of naïve piety, the one most expert in documents, who was to pronounce the verdict." This verdict, we must realise, was neither dogmatic nor infallible. It was no more than a personal scientific opinion; but it derives all its value from the eminent character of the man, combined with his pontifical dignity.

After five years of work and reflection, he formed his opinion, and as was his way, took the first opportunity of declaring it publicly: he would bring his allocutions, sometimes by an unexpected turn of thought, round to the subject which he had in mind.

On September 5th, 1936, he received a pilgrimage of young men belonging to Catholic Action, who were returning from the shrine of Our Lady of Pompeii. As souvenirs he gave them pictures of the Holy Shroud, and, after speaking to them of the Blessed Virgin, he said to them: " . . . These are pictures of her Divine Son, and one may perhaps say the most thought-provoking, the most beautiful, the most precious that one can imagine. They come precisely from *that object which still remains mysterious, but which has certainly not been made by human hands (one can say that this is now proved), that is the Holy Shroud of Turin (ma certamente non di fattura umana; questo gia si può dir dimostrato)*. We have used the word mysterious," he continued, " because that holy thing is still surrounded by considerable mystery;

but it certainly is *something more sacred than anything else;* and indeed (one can henceforth say that the genuineness of it is proved in the most positive way, *even when setting aside all ideas of faith or of Christian piety*), it is not a human work (*certo non è opera umana*)." (*Osservatore Romano*, 7-8 Sept., 1936.)

He was to preserve this conviction till his death. He expressed it in the same terms, on September 23rd of the same year, to the collaborators of the *Vie Spirituelle*. A short time before his death, on February 3rd, 1939, in a solemn audience, in which he was celebrating many anniversaries which had precious memories for him, he once again distributed pictures of the Holy Face on the shroud.

This learned historian, this man of science, had not only looked at the marks on the shroud, but had studied them carefully. He would not have countersigned a phrase which greatly distresses me, a remark of the good Father de Jerpharnion, whose splended work on the rock-hewn churches of Cappadocia I have read with delight: "*We deliberately avoid lingering* (my italics) before a series of developments by which we are shown how, on the shroud, all kinds of markings and tracings correspond with the smallest details of the Passion and the Burial of Christ." Such *a priori* scepticism has no scientific justification and can only lead to sterility.

Exactly the opposite position seems to me worthy of a man of learning, to whatever branch he may belong. All relics only draw the proofs of their authority from documents, from solemn attestations, from the certificate of authenticity which accompany them. Without these, they have no real value. I should like to know how many of these relics have certificates of authenticity which go back to their origins. On the contrary, there is but one in the world which would preserve its complete value, even if it was without historical backing, and that because it has intrinsic proofs of its authenticity. It bears them in itself. That relic is the Holy Shroud. Let us now spend a little time looking at the markings and tracings which it contains.

C.—General Description

1. *The Linen.*—The shroud is a piece of linen 40 inches broad, 13¼ ft. in length. Vignon put forward the hypothesis that formerly it was considerably longer, and that the shroud was shortened by cuttings made from the end by the Byzantine emperors for the purpose of gifts. It would seem, however, as has been stated in writing by Antoine Legrand and Father d'Armailhac (*Dossiers du Saint Suaire,* November, 1939), that there is nothing missing at the end of the shroud. A closer examination of the front of the picture of the legs shows that it is com-

plete and reaches to the end of the feet (cf. Chapter VI, end). On the other hand there has been a lateral cutting at this point, which has been filled in by a piece of stuff similar to that used by the Poor Clares to mend the burns.

It has been possible to make a leisurely study of the structure of this linen, thanks to Enrie's enlarged photographs, which show the surface enlarged seven times. One is able to examine it in all its details, better than with a magnifying glass, and this has been done by competent judges, both in France and in Italy. Expert investigation has found that it consists of a linen fabric with herring-bone stripes; to weave it a loom with four pedals would have been required. The woof of this, according to Timossi, an expert in Turin, contains 40 threads to two-fifths of an inch. It is a tissue of pure linen, close and opaque, made of coarse thread of which the fibre is unbleached. This is very interesting, for the photographic examination of the tissue has demonstrated that all the images on the shroud are the result of a simple impregnation of the threads; an impregnation which would have been facilitated by the fact that linen is an excellent absorbent. This examination definitely rules out the hypothesis which has been constantly repeated that it is a painting and therefore a fake. We shall return later to our opponents who would make out that it is a painting.

Such a material most certainly belongs to the age of Jesus. Similar fabrics have been found at Palmyra and at Doura Europos. It even seems that Syria and Mesopotamia were centres for this type of weaving, especially Syria. One would thus expect to find it among the wares on sale in Jerusalem round about the year 30. Pieces of linen have been discovered at Autinoé, of the same breadth but considerably longer (cf. the detailed study in Vignon, *Saint Suaire*, 1938).

2. *The Marks of Burning.*—Those who start studying the imprints are usually at first struck and disconcerted by the marks of burning which are ranged down both sides of the central picture. Their colour, which is more intense and blacker, eclipses to a certain extent the other markings, which are far less pronounced. The most important are in rows in two series of six, similar in form and dimension, except the four end ones which are merely partial. From this one can easily perceive where it was folded, by studying it in both directions, its length and its breadth; there must have been a series of 48 thicknesses. As the burning took place on one corner of the fabric which was folded rectangular-wise in the reliquary, it has entered into all the folds, thus producing the two series of holes. The corner was fortunately near the two outer edges, so that almost the whole central rectangle has thus been left intact, and only the shoulders and the arm in the frontal picture have been injured.

The burns are surrounded by reddish colouring such as would be left by an iron that was too hot, and in their centres portions of the fabric have been destroyed. These have been replaced by fresh pieces, the work of the Poor Clares of Chambéry. The water which was used to quench the fire has spread out across the fabric, leaving a dark ring like charcoal, and producing a number of other encircled areas, also in a symmetrical series, but running through the middle.

On the same lines as the large ones there are other less noticeable burns, in a series of small round reddish stains. They must have been caused by an earlier fire. These are indeed to be found on a copy which was made in 1516, and is now at Lierre in Belgium, so would have been made by an earlier fire than that at Chambéry (perhaps the one at Besançon).

3. *The Folds.*—Apart from the burns, one can be led astray at first sight by a certain number of transverse marks, which are black on the positive print, and white on the reproductions of the plate, and which stretch like bars across the picture. They are the folds in the material, which could not be straightened out by stretching in its light frame. The dark marks are their shadows.

4. *The Bodily Impressions.*—Down the central part of the shroud, one can see two impressions made by the body, with the two marks made by the head near to each other but not touching. One is the front picture of the body, the other the back one. When one remembers that the pictures were made by a corpse, the explanation is simple. The body would have been laid on its back on half the length of the shroud, which would then have been folded over the head to cover the front, reaching right down to the feet. A miniature by G. B. della Rovere (XVIIth century) gives a perfect presentation of how this would have been done. One can also see that, as the body imprinted its image on the shroud, the two impressions would each be inverted.

One must get this clear in one's mind: if a man is standing facing you, his right side will be to your left and vice versa. If he has his back to you, his right side will be to your right side and vice versa. This will be found on the facsimile of the photographic plate, which, as it inverts the picture of the shroud, gives the picture of the corpse itself. But in the impression on the shroud, and the positive print, the picture of the front appears as if one were looking into a glass; the right side, and the wound, will be to your right, and reciprocally. The same applies to the picture of the back.

The brownish colour of these impressions is due, as we have said, to the staining of each thread, which has been more or less impregnated.

The whole picture reveals a perfectly proportioned anatomy; it is well-made and robust and is that of a man about six foot high. The face, in spite of the strange effect of all these impressions, which when photographed give the effect of a negative, is beautiful and imposing. It is surrounded by two masses of hair, which seem to be rather pushed forward. It is probable that the bandage round the chin, which would be intended to keep the mouth shut, would pass behind these masses of hair; on the top of the head it must have pressed against the shroud, which would account for the space between the back and front pictures of the head.

The lower members show up very well in the picture of the back, and there is a perfect impression of the right foot. In the picture of the front, the lower part of the legs is not clear, as if the shroud had been held back from the insteps. But we shall see all these details when we study the wounds one by one.

The most striking thing in this ensemble of bodily impressions is the remarkable effect of relief which they give. Not one line, not one contour or shadow has been drawn, and yet the forms stand out strangely from the background. This receives further confirmation from a fact: never have I seen a copy, whether picture or drawing, which resembles the face on the shroud. On the other hand, the medal made of it in bas-relief by my friend Dr. Villandre evokes it in the most impressive fashion.

5. *The Marks of Blood.*—One finds these on all sides and we will study them in detail: there are the wounds of the scourging, of the crowning with thorns, of all the ill-usage that took place, the carrying of the cross, the crucifixion, even of the blow of the lance received after death, which drained the veins of their blood.

All the marks of blood have a special colour which stands out against the brownish tone of the body. They are carmine, a little bit mauve, as Vignon used to say. They vary in depth and intensity according to the wounds, and even in the length and breadth of each one, giving an effect of varying thickness which is at times astonishing, as if one saw the congealed blood in relief.

Another important peculiarity: while in the imprint left by the body everything is in light and shade, merging imperceptibly and without defined boundaries, the marks of blood have a far more precise outline. They even stand out very clearly in the reduced photographs. However, on the life-size photographs, while they preserve this clearness and give the impression of being thicker at the edges, here and there they seem to be surrounded by an aureole of a much paler colour, like a sort of halo. We shall see that this is produced by the serum which transudes from blood which has recently congealed on the skin.

I shall constantly revert to the principal fact regarding these images of blood, and I must insist on it from the beginning, because those who have not studied medicine and had to live in an atmosphere of blood, will find it hard to grasp. *The thing which immediately strikes a surgeon and which can be confirmed later by a more exhaustive study, is the definite appearance of blood congealed on the skin,* borne by all the blood-marks. You see! It is so definite to me, that unconsciously I am already speaking of blood-marks. It is thus, as we shall see, that these images of blood were formed.

When, in May, 1933, I was writing my first article on the wounds in the hands, my only documents, excellent as they were, were photographs. All the images were thus more or less black. Authors, especially Noguier de Malijay, insisted on the monochrome quality of the shroud, in spite of ancient and reliable witnesses, such as the Poor Clares of Chambéry. Therefore, having seen the shroud by the light of day in 1933, I wrote the following testimony in the first edition of *Les Cinq Plaies du Christ*:[1]

" At the last exposition, which took place in 1933, by special dispensation, on account of the jubilee year of the Passion, I went to Turin and on October 14th I was able to spend a long time studying the shroud, which was exposed in a monumental frame above the high altar, and was illuminated by strong electric projectors. The picture was just as it had been described, and brownish in colour; the wounds were simply darker than the rest, and stood out more or less from the whole human silhouette.

" But, on Sunday, October 15th, which was the closing day, the relic was taken out of the heavy frame in which it was exposed under glass, and twenty-five prelates bore it with all due solemnity in its light frame, out to the terrace of the cathedral so that it should be venerated by the vast crowd who were filling the square, behind a double line of foot soldiers. I was in front of them, on the steps of the terrace, and Cardinal Fossati, the Archbishop of Turin, was so kind as to have the frame placed for a few minutes on the edge of the terrace, so that we might have the chance of looking at it. The sun had just gone down behind the houses on the other side of the square, and the bright but diffused light was ideal for studying it. I have thus seen the shroud by the light of day, without any glass screening it, from a distance of less than a yard, and I suddenly experienced one of the most powerful emotions of my life. For, without expecting it, I saw that all the images of the wounds were of a colour quite different from that of the rest of the body; and this colour was that of dried blood which had sunk into the stuff. There was thus more than the brown stains on the shroud reproducing the outline of a corpse.

[1] *The Five Wounds of Christ.* English translation by M. Apraxine. (Clonmore & Reynolds.)

"The blood itself had coloured the stuff by direct contact, and that is why *the images of the wounds are positive while all the rest is negative.*

"It is difficult for one unversed in painting to define the exact colour, but the foundation was red (mauve carmine, said M. Vignon, who had a fine sense of colour), diluted more or less according to the wounds; it was strongest at the side, at the head, the hands and the feet; it was paler, but nevertheless fully visible, in the innumerable marks of the scourging . . . but a surgeon could understand, with no possibility of doubt, that it was blood which had sunk into the linen, and *this blood was the Blood of Christ!*

"I have a long experience of Italians, and I find their lively reactions very attractive; but I must own that on that day I was surprised: the crowd broke out in applause.

"As for me, my soul, both as a Catholic and a surgeon, was overcome by this sudden revelation. I was quelled by this Real Presence, the evidence for which was so impressive. I went down on my knees and I adored in silence."

I have been reproached in an ironical fashion which makes one grieve for the authors, on account of the phrase: "A surgeon could understand, with no possibility of doubt, that it was blood which had sunk into the linen." I may have erred on the side of conciseness, but I am not so naïve as I may seem. One might say that there are those who cannot read and those who do not wish to read. I have therefore added this little paragraph in the second edition.

"It is fully understood that a rigorously scientific proof that these stains are due to blood would require (if they were allowed) physical or chemical examinations; for example, the search by means of the spectroscope for rays of hæmoglobin or its derivatives. But, as it has been proved that the other images are not the work of the hand of man, that this shroud has contained a corpse, *can the marks of these wounds, which are so rich in details as genuine as they are unexpected, owe their colour to anything but blood?*"

As I have more space in this book than I would have in a brochure, I propose to develop my thought, and this will lead me to insist on a highly important point if we would understand these images of blood. It is that of their formation. We shall study this shortly, in section E of this chapter.

D.—The Photographs

On this subject I shall only state the essential facts. I cannot too strongly advise any reader who is interested to obtain the book by my friend Giuseppe Enrie, the official photographer of the shroud (to whom we owe much precious work), *La Santa Sindone rivelata dalla fotografia*. There is a good French translation by my dear friend, now dead, M. Porché (Librairie du Carmel, 27 Rue Madame, Paris VI). The proofs of the photographs can only be obtained from Enrie, Via Garibaldi 26, Turin. (There is a depot for France at the above library.)

1. *Technique.*—Enrie has produced twelve photographs, nine of which are of the shroud taken out of its frame and exposed to a high-power and carefully arranged light. Three of these are of the whole fabric. The others are photographs of the various details: two of the Holy Face, one of which is on a scale of two-thirds of the original, and the other life-size; one of the Holy Face with the upper part of the bust, also to a scale of two-thirds, and one of the back. There is finally one of the wound in the hand, enlarged seven times, which enables us to study the state of the tissue in every detail. The twelfth one shows us the complete exposition.

All these were taken on orthochromatic plates. Technicians will find all the details in Enrie's book. I need scarcely add that these photographs have received no touching-up, and have undergone no process other than that of normal development. Apart from the scrupulous conscientiousness of my friend Enrie, this fact has been certified before a notary public, by a commission of expert photographers. The authenticity of all the reproductions has been vouched for by the Archbishop of Turin, Cardinal Fossati. Besides, all the details of these official photographs are confirmed by the numerous snapshots taken by amateurs during the expositions of 1931 and 1933, some of them in full daylight, on the closing day; I know something about this. But let us return to what is to be seen in these photographs.

2. *Results.*—In a word, everything in the photographic plates connected with the images of the body is positive, as should be the case in a reproduction on paper when a body has been photographed. In this case, on the contrary, it is the reproduction on paper which gives a negative image of the body, because of the fact that this is how it is on the shroud itself. The marks made by the body on the shroud are thus like a negative; they have all the characteristics of an ordinary photographic plate; everything is inverted, black is white, and white is black. The only difference is that the negative image on the shroud shows no shadow, as is always the case when a normal object is photographed.

On the other hand, and this is of the greatest importance, the burns (as is obvious), but also the marks of blood, are clearly positive on the shroud: on the photographic plate they come out white. These then are positive, normal images on the shroud. The linen background, as would be expected, comes out black on the plate.

This leads us to a most important conclusion: the marks of the body have been produced by a process, which, if, as we believe, it was a natural one, bears a certain likeness to the phenomenon of photography. The marks of blood, on the other hand, can only have been made by direct contact; they are the marks of congealed blood; we shall return to this later.

It is impossible to give a clear summary of all Enrie's considerations; his book must be read. A word is needed however to explain that the facsimiles of these photographic plates, those which give a normal, positive portrayal of the Holy Face, for instance, have all the impeccability of the original plates. There has been no interference with them. The plates have been reproduced, not on paper, but on a sensitive plate.

3. *Conclusions.*—I will give here only the conclusions reached by Enrie himself:

(a) The negative marks are absolutely exact; the characteristics of this strange image, which has not been made by the hand of man, are to be found at every point, apart from the stains of blood.

(b) There are certainly no traces of colouring, of marks made by a paint-brush, or of other artifices such as would be employed by a draughtsman or a forger.

(c) The light and shade has no contours, it is without lines or stippling, but there are scarcely perceptible gradations, which remind one of a photographic process.

(d) The marks of blood, which are positive on the negative image of the Redeemer, are on the contrary strongly marked, and show the characteristics of an impression made by contact; there are also irregularities in their structure, which point to their natural origin.

(e) The anatomy and the pattern are true to life: the physical characteristics reveal both the personality and the race; they have not been altered by serious swellings and by a fracture of the nose, as was imagined after the photographs were taken in 1898, when the fabric had not been carefully stretched out.—(Enrie will please forgive me; but, apart from the abrasions and the wounds, there is a swelling in the right zygomatic region, and there is a fracture of the posterior nasal cartilage.)

(f) The parts corresponding to shadows are absolutely devoid of impression, for they allow the fabric to be seen intact.

(g) The facsimile of the photographic negative of the face displays with marvellous exactness some negative qualities of the imprint, for it reveals, not only a form, but also a spiritual content: the expression.

I do not wish to insist on this last conclusion. I will leave it to the reader to look at the images; they are more eloquent than I could ever be. In that face, which is definitely Semitic, one finds, in spite of the tortures and the wounds, such an effect of serene majesty that an unspeakable impression is left. If one would understand it a little, one must remember that if the Sacred Humanity had just died in that body the Divinity is always present with the certainty of the coming Resurrection.

No artist has ever imagined a face approaching this one. And I would not be so cruel as to remember the copies and the imitations which people have tried to make, nor even the after-touches which do away with the furrows. As Virgil said to Dante in his *Inferno*: *"Non ragionam di lor, ma guarda e passa*—Do not let us speak of them, but look and pass on!"*

E.—The Formation of the Impressions

1. *Bloodstained Impressions.*—We shall begin with these because, to speak the truth, they are the only ones of which we can imagine the formation in a way that is both certain and complete. As a Christian will have guessed, this almost raises the question of the circumstances of the Resurrection, which are a mystery. Even the hypercritics will not demand that I should supply them with a scientific explanation.

The marks of blood on the shroud are not graphic pictures, as are the bodily impressions. I do not say photographic, for as we do not know the way in which these latter were formed, we do not know if light played a part; anyway, as we have seen, they are very like photographic negatives. The bloodstained impressions are not pictures; they are counter-drawings and they are made by blood. But in what form? Liquid or congealed blood? Are they from clots which had dried already or recently formed clots, which were still exuding their serum?

We may start by dispelling a false idea, which is expressed in words that I have too often heard used by one of the oldest and firmest defenders of the shroud: "A flow of clots." Although I knew what to expect, I could not help giving a start each time. No! A clot which has been formed on the skin sticks to it and dries.

Another point: a clot is never formed in the body, or more exactly in the veins, in which the blood always remains liquid. The "thrombus" which appears in veins afflicted with phlebitis is an entirely different thing anatomically, and it is only to be found in unhealthy veins, with which we are not concerned here.

Blood remains liquid in corpses; we shall return to this when dealing with the wound of the heart. It becomes concentrated in the veins; at death the arteries empty themselves into the capillaries and into the veins, owing to the final contraction of the ventricles and to their own elasticity. It remains liquid in the veins for a very long time, usually till putrefaction sets in. It even remains *alive* for *several hours* and is capable of being transfused into a living man.

When blood leaves the veins owing to a wound, if collected in a receptacle it can be seen coagulating rapidly, that is to say it becomes a sort of red jelly, which we call a clot. This clot is formed by the transformation of a substance which is dissolved in the blood, fibrinogen, into another solid substance, fibrin; this latter contains within its meshes red blood cells, whence its red colour. Coagulation takes place in a very short time, never longer than a few minutes. Secondly, the clot grows smaller, and exudes its liquid content, the serum. It then gradually dries.

Thus, if blood should issue from a dead or a living body through a wound in the skin, a considerable amount of this will flow in liquid form along the skin, and, by reason of its weight, can fall to the ground. A part, by reason of its viscosity, will adhere to the skin (in larger quantities if this should be horizontal), and it will there coagulate rapidly. If the flow of blood continues, fresh levels of liquid blood will spread over the previous ones, and in their turn will coagulate. If the blood meets with an obstacle during its downward flow, it accumulates above it; the clot at this point will thus be thicker.

The clot grows smaller on the skin as in a receptacle, owing to the expulsion of the serum and the drying process which follows. But, when the surface is broad and shallow, this drying up will clearly take place more rapidly.

It will be understood that I am only giving these elementary explanations for those who are not doctors. They seem to me to be indispensable, for I have so often come across serious misunderstandings even among highly cultivated people. We thus see that the shroud may have been stained, either by liquid blood, or by clots which were still fresh and moist, or by dried clots. We also see that around the clot, if this was still fresh, it could be stained by the serum which had been exuded. To which category do our blood-marks belong?

Liquid blood is an exception and almost unique. I can only find traces of the blood which flowed from the holes in the feet, on the way to and within the tomb, in the direction of the heels. The greater part coagulated elsewhere on the soles of the feet, and these clots left their traces on the shroud when they were still fresh. One part, however, flowed beyond the feet into the folds, crossing these folds from one side to the other, forming symmetrical images which we shall meet with again.

Some of the clots must still have been fresh enough to remain moist.

One of these *may be* the large original clot of the heart wound, by reason of its thickness. The clots of the large flow of blood across the back of the body certainly form part of this group (cf. C. VIII), clots which were formed in the hollow of a sheet twisted beneath the loins into a band for the purpose of bearing the body to the tomb. The greater part of this abundant flow of blood, which issued from the inferior vena cava, and found its way out through the gaping wound of the heart, must have fallen to the ground on the way. Only a small part of it, which was able to reach the skin between the folds of the band and to adhere to it on account of its viscosity, became coagulated in the form of numberless windings, such as are characteristic of the flow of blood at the back. These clots were clearly quite fresh, when the body was laid down on the shroud; they left their trace very easily, with an abundance of serum around the marks.

Most of the clots were more or less dry at the time of the burial. How were they also able to leave their trace? We must understand that once the corpse had been installed, it was hermetically enclosed in a shroud and in linen cloths, all of which were impregnated with thirty kilograms of myrrh and of aloes; its wrappings would be practically impervious. We must also remember that the corpse would continue to give out moisture for some time. One tends to forget that all the cells of a corpse continue to live, each one on its own, those of the skin like the others, and that they die individually after different lengths of time. If the higher-grade and the nervous cells are the most fragile, yet the others last for some time; total death only sets in with putrefaction. Now our Faith tells us that Jesus never knew corruption; and every part of the shroud confirms us in this certainty. On the other hand all the wounds, all the abrasions with which the body was covered continued to exude a more or less infected lymph as when it was still alive, but in liquid form.

The result of all this was that the body was bathed in a watery atmosphere, which made all the clots on the skin and in the various wounds damp once more. And this brings us back once again to the fresh clots, *apart from the serum.*

Now, by this I do not mean that the fibrin became liquid again, which would be something quite different. Vignon, who was completely imbued with his aloeticoammoniacal theory of vaporographic impressions (a theory which he, however, found much less satisfactory from 1938 onwards) thought that it was ammonia which had again dissolved the fibrin and had liquefied the clots. He made an experiment by placing some clots on a substance which had been soaked in a solution of ammonia. In any case it would no longer have been normal, living blood, but a coloured liquid, susceptible of flowing, incapable of recoagulating. Such flows, taking place in a horizontal position in the tomb, would have been disastrous for our blood-stained images; in fact, there is no coloured flow on the shroud; there are only counter-drawings of clots.

Vignon's hypothesis is thus unable to account for our blood-stained images; on the contrary, it only makes for confusion. More than that, it has no basis in fact, nor has his theory of ammoniacal browning by the aloes. It is true that the fibrin will dissolve in a solution of ammonia; but I find no signs of ammonia on the shroud.

There is certainly a little urea, which may have been left by the sweat drying on the skin; there is also some in the blood and in the lymph which was exuded by the wounds. In no case would the amount of urea be considerable. But anyway, this urea has none of the properties of ammonia. It would need to be transformed into carbamate, and then into carbonate of ammonia. Now a transformation such as this would take a long time, much longer than the length of the period spent in the tomb. The presence of a special micro-organism, the *micrococcus ureae,* would also be needed. There is no reason why this should have existed on the surface of the body. My friend, Volckringer, who was pharmacist at the Hôpital Saint-Joseph, experimented by placing some urea on the skin of an animal; the vapours of ammonia did not appear for twenty hours. The reaction is delayed and even *held up* by all antiseptics, even mild ones, such as *aloes* for example! There is thus scanty encouragement for Vignon's hypothesis.

The two necessary conditions for the formation of ammonia, time and ferment, are absent, and for this reason I have always remained sceptical about this theory.

On the other hand it seems to me quite possible that clots which had become more or less dry, would, without liquefying the fibrin, in a damp atmosphere become sufficiently moistened to form a fairly soft kind of paste. Thus transformed they would be well able to impregnate the linen with which they came in contact and to leave counter-drawings on it with fairly definite outlines, which would reproduce the shape of the clots.

The colour of these counter-drawings would vary in intensity according to the thickness of the clots. Vignon saw clearly that when a drop of congealed blood grows smaller, its thickness is greater in the circumference than in the centre. And that is why many of these counter-drawings are highly coloured at the circumference and have in their centre a zone of milder colour.

And this is how, in my opinion, almost all the blood-stained images were formed—but I must return to the images produced by the flow of liquid blood, and to the possibilities which this blood would have offered an ingenious forger. Everyone who has had any experience knows that the stain made by blood on linen does not remain always the same, in particular if the linen has not been specially prepared. On a compress, when used in an operation, a drop of blood can be seen diffusing itself rapidly, the stain enlarges as it spreads into the tissue, but it does so with more speed in certain directions, following the threads of the material. If, for instance, it consists of plain twill, as is usually the case, around a central zone which is more or less round, one can see four little prolongations following the threads of the wrap and the woof, which thus forms a little cross.

The phenomenon is even more striking if, instead of blood, one uses a few drops of some more volatile liquid, such as tincture of iodine; the material becomes spangled with little brown crosses. This *irregular* and guided diffusion is all the more noticeable in proportion as the thread is capable of absorbing liquid. Now, as we have seen, the thread from which the linen of the shroud was woven, which is coarsely spun from unbleached fibre, is an excellent absorbent.

It is in fact noticeable that the edges of the two liquid flows which are on the shroud on the outside of the soles of the feet, instead of having the clear outline of the clots on the hands or the forehead, for example, are *irregular* and *inverted*. It would be interesting to have a photograph which had been directly enlarged in order to compare it with the one which Enrie made of the wrist. In the latter one can see that the coloration of the blood-stained imprint is solely the result of each thread being impregnated, each of which preserves its form and its separate existence. There is no clogging, not the slightest thickness of colouring matter between the threads of the material.

By reason of this detail a forger would have had the greatest difficulty in imitating blood-stained imprints, if he used blood as his colouring matter. Never would he have succeeded in producing those stains with clearly marked edges, which with such outstanding truthfulness reproduce the shape of the clots as they were formed naturally on the skin. May I say, in parenthesis, that this demolishes beforehand certain theories which will be put forward by opponents of the shroud, on the day when the physical examination, which would have taken place long ago were it not for the inertia of the proprietors, will perhaps have demonstrated scientifically that the stains were made by blood.

As I lacked the chance of making such decisive experiments, it was precisely the study of these pictures of the clots which led me to the conclusion that they really were counter-drawings of congealed blood. I shall describe these at greater length, for instance in connection with the crowning with thorns (see C. IV, D). But I could repeat the same demonstration in connection with all the blood-stained pictures. In the eyes of a surgeon they possess a most striking realism, which I have never yet seen in any painting.

All painters, apart from those who portray wounds that have no relation to reality, paint flows of blood with more or less parallel edges, and are well content as long as they follow the laws of gravity, as for example, in making them flow from the hand towards the elbow. But these are flows of liquid blood, of blood which is not clotted. And they imagine that they are thus being realistic.

There is no flow of blood on the shroud; there are only the counter-drawings of clots; these clots represent that part of the blood which has congealed on the skin, while flowing over it. If I sometimes refer to flows of blood, when describing the shroud, it is because these clots tell us of the past when that blood *flowed on the skin*: in the same way beautiful writing, though now motionless, evokes the movement of the pen by which it was traced.

Actually, those pictures which are meant to be the most realistic are the ones which contain the most blatant physiological errors. We shall find that this is specially the case in regard to marks of blood. When a crucifix is designed to stir our emotions by displaying to us the atrocious nature of the torture, so much the further is it from the truth. I know I shall be attacked for this, but still, it has to be said; if from the artistic standpoint I am able to appreciate the pictorial values of a Grünewald, the contorted way in which he paints the Crucified seems to me purely grotesque. I can assure you that the Passion was both *more simple* and infinitely *more tragic* than that.

After the exposition of 1933 I wrote *les Cinq Plaies*.[2] I already *knew*, after studying the marks of blood, that it really was blood which had formed these images of clots. I had recognised them, just as one recognises the image of a familiar face. I had a mistaken conviction that these marks were of the same colour as the remainder, and I had actually seen monochrome images on the linen by electric light. And suddenly, by the light of day, I saw that they had this carmine colour, which added one more note to the conviction which I had already formed. I thus had the right to state, without abandoning any scientific precision, that " the surgeon *understood,* without any shadow of doubt, that it was blood by which the linen was impregnated, and that this blood was the Blood of Christ." In this I was certainly being more scientific than those who refuse to look at the shroud.

And have we finished with this study of clots? Alas! We are far

---

[2] *The Five Wounds of Christ.* Translated by M. Apraxine. (Clonmore & Reynolds.)

from this and there will always be immense difficulties to be resolved. Spectroscopy, photography in all the zones of the spectrum, infra-red in particular, radiography, and everything else that we could imagine—since it seems impossible to achieve a chemical examination, all this research will perhaps tell us one day that a corpse covered with wounds lay for some hours in this shroud. Nothing will explain to us *how it left it,* while leaving on the shroud a fine and unblemished impression of the body and the marks of its bleeding. A man would not be able to remove the body of another, without destroying them.

It is certain that this Body, in its glorious Resurrection, could leave the shroud with the same ease as when it entered the cenacle *januis clausis*—"when the doors were shut." This final difficulty brings us to what is, humanly speaking, more or less a physical impossibility. Science at this point can do no more than keep silence, for it is outside its domain. But the man of learning at least has a glimpse that here is a palpable proof of the Resurrection.

When I had published the first edition of *les Cinq Plaies,* I went to the *École pratique* to read it to my old friend, Professor Hovelacque. He was devoted to the subject of anatomy, which he taught to the faculty in Paris, but he was far from being a believer. He approved of my experiments and conclusions with growing enthusiasm. When he had finished reading he put down my booklet, and he remained silent for a short while in a state of meditation. Then he suddenly burst out with that fine frankness on which our friendship had been built up, and exclaimed: " But then, my friend . . . Jesus Christ *did* rise again!" Rarely in my life have I known such deep and happy emotion as at this reaction of an unbeliever when faced with a purely scientific work, from which he was drawing incalculable consequences. He died a few months later, and I dare to hope that God has rewarded him.

2. *The Bodily Impressions.*—May we say at once, that if we know full well what these impressions are not, we have no precise idea of how they came to appear. To this we may add that we do not know when they appeared. One is reminded of that negative knowledge of God, which has been so well expounded by St. Bonaventure.

What exactly are they not? Either a forgery, a piece of trickery, or the work of human hands—this, I think, can no longer be affirmed. If this were a painting, it would have been done at the latest in the 14th century, when the shroud reappeared at Lirey. Need one go over again all the impossibilities underlying this hypothesis? Such a painting would contain a negative image, an unimaginable conception before the invention of photography. And nobody need say that the shroud was reversed by the Poor Clares of Chambéry; the Lierre copy, which dates from before their day, already shows the wound of the heart on the left. This negative presents so much difficulty that all the ancient copyists tried to interpret it in a positive image, which misrepresented all the details. Even modern artists, such as Reffo and Cussetti, who have copied the shroud having full knowledge of the subject, have not succeeded; their copies, which seem to bear a resemblance to the original, show on photographic plates positive images very different from those on the shroud. This is because the lights and shades on the shroud, when reproduced negatively, have an absolute perfection such as no painter can achieve, and which one only finds in nature or in objective photography.

There is not a trace of painting to be seen, even in Enrie's highly enlarged direct photographs. (To make this clear, one should explain that this is not just a matter of enlarging a photograph, but of an apparatus which produces on the plate an image enlarged seven times, such as a magnifying glass of the same power would supply to the eye.) These images, as shown by Viale, the director of the civic museums in Turin, have no style of their own; they are impersonal. They have nothing in common with any medieval French or Piedmontese style.

How could an artist, who was painting a shroud destined for public exposition, have dared to do an unheard-of thing, that of portraying a Christ who was entirely naked? How would he have come to contradict the traditional iconography, with a nail in the wrist, with a thumb hidden in the palm of the hand (which has often been repeated by those who have copied the shroud), with a Crucified Being who only shows one pierced hand and one pierced foot, with that curious flow across the back? How could he, while knowing nothing of the physiology of the blood, conceive of clots so true to life and how was he able to paint them on linen which had not been specially prepared? All artists have painted flows of blood for us; not one of them has thought of painting clots.

I will waste no time on the objection that the painting became negative owing to the weakening of the colours; this has been disposed of in a learned manner by Enrie. The darkest parts of the plate are those which correspond to the parts of the shroud which consist of bare linen; a colour which does not exist cannot be reversed. I have furthermore on twenty occasions seen the Assisi Cimabue; this is quite different from a negative like that of the shroud.

We can say, then, that there was no painting. Images of clots such as those on the shroud could not be produced with any colouring matter. But there are still some disappointments and uncertainties ahead of us. A corpse must have lain in that shroud—why should it not have been that of Christ 'and not of some other man? Let us deal quickly with an objection which I have often heard brought forward. This body bore all the stigmata of the Passion. All those, I shall be asked, which one would find on a crucified man? Yes, in fact including those of the scourging and of the wound in the heart from the lance. (The body would in this case have been returned to the family, as we shall see, Chapter II, c, 6°.) But only one crucified man was, to our knowledge, crowned with thorns, and that was Our Saviour. And then, if this was not the shroud of Christ, why was it so faithfully preserved? Finally, what man condemned to death could show in his face such nobility and such divine majesty? I will not insist on this last point; let the reader decide for himself when he has in all humility contemplated the face.

According to Vignon's theory, which is the oldest, the markings are due to a browning of the aloes which was spread over the linen, owing to the exhalation of ammonia by the body. These vapours would act in inverse ratio to the distance between the outlines of the body and the surface of the shroud. (The future will perhaps tell us whether there is any truth in this last phrase; I certainly do not see how it can apply to the image produced beneath the corpse; but let us pass on!) These vapours would be due to the decomposition of the urea (formed by the sweat and blood which had accumulated on the surface of the corpse?) At this point I refuse to follow him. We have recently seen, in regard to the clots which are supposed to have been liquefied by dissolving fibrin, how this transformation of urea into carbonate of ammonia was both problematic and a slow process. Vignon's theory, which seems so attractive at first sight, raises yet further difficulties; its foundations especially seem to be unsound. Vignon himself during his last years, and from 1938 onwards, does not seem to have had the same confidence in it.

My good friend Don Scotti, a Salesian, is a doctor of medicine and also an excellent chemist. He has made considerable researches in aloes since 1931, in regard to its components and its derivatives, of which I am not in a position to give a clear résumé. For example, *aloetine,* when it comes into contact with water or with alkaline, takes on a dark brown colour, as it becomes transformed into *aloeresinotannol.* Linen, which has been plunged for a few minutes in a solution of aloine, of which the chief colouring matter is *aloemodine,* as a result of simple contact with the air will in the space of two months take on a colour of rose carmine. The subsequent action of the light of the sun will make these colours yet more vivid. We can thus already see the possibility of a slow and progressive disclosure of the marks on the linen.

Judica and Romanese have, since 1939, obtained markings from corpses. What brings them together and also connects them with Scotti, is that they rule out ammonia. Both of them work by light contact. But Judica obtains his markings by spreading blood on the body and impregnating the linen with oil and with essence of terebinth. The images are brought out by exposition to steam. Romanese merely sprinkles the body with powdered physiological serum (solution of chloride of sodium) and sprinkles the linen with powdered aloes. The images obtained by these two processes are, it must be owned, far from the perfection of the face on the shroud. But they are something quite new, which should greatly encourage further researches along these lines.

I would now end up with an extremely stimulating work, which was published in 1942 by my friend Volckringer, the chief apothecary in the Hôpital Saint-Joseph, whose experiments with urea we have already considered. He has also made researches into the formation of colours, much on the lines of those made by Scotti. In this work (*Le problème des empreintes devant la science*—Librairie du Carmel, 27 Rue Madame, Paris, 6°), he has produced something quite original, combined with a fine collection of pictures, the only ones which can be said to approach the perfection of those on the shroud. It is a fact that these were also formed *naturally* and, as we shall see, without ammonia, without aloes, and some of them without direct contact. He is not dealing, it is true, with animal tissues; he is dealing with vegetable tissues; but they are living tissues, and one knows the analogies that there are between the two kingdoms. One can for instance say that urea, uric acid, allantoine and allantoic acid are to be found in plants. Desgrez has even shown how vegetable chlorophyl and animal hæmatoporphyrin will, under the action of ultra-violet rays, become transformed into the same urobiline.

By examining old herbals Volckringer has established the presence on the paper of quite special types of images, representing the plants which have been preserved. Once it was well and truly dried, the plant would soon lose most of its external characteristics. Being fixed, as it is, on a sheet of paper between two other sheets, we frequently find one upper and two lower images, the second being formed on the enveloping sheet, *through the sheet supporting* the plant. The presence or absence of chlorophyl was noticeable, and similar images were produced by the roots.

None of these images were to be found in recent herbals. They were, for instance, very clear in a herbal of 1836, while there were scarcely any markings in a herbal of 1908, which at the time was 34 years old.

These images seemed to resist all reagents, except ammonia; this latter greatly weakened the colouring, which it threw back in a brown circle on the edge of the area to which it was applied.

These images were " like a light design in sepia, perfect in continuity: examination under a magnifying glass revealed no fine lines, but a collection of stains without clearly defined boundaries." They would seem to be like the impressions on the shroud, and this is not all. "One could distinguish on the impression, which is sepia in colour, the veins of the leaves, in their smallest ramifications, and where the stalk had been cut . . . the folds and the reciprocal positions of the various parts of the plant, thanks to the comparison of the upper and the lower impressions. . . . The whole plant is faithfully reproduced in the two images."

And now we come to the most interesting point. Volckringer photographed these impressions and he found that on the photographic plate " in the reversed image the most prominent part of the plant came out light, while the more distant parts came out dark." The whole image gives an extraordinary effect of relief, and stands out naturally against a black background.

The plate thus gives us a normal, positive image of the plant which was formerly placed between those sheets of paper. Now, this plant has been reduced to the condition of a corpse, " a uniform and more or less crumpled mass," brown or blackish in colour; all relief has more or less disappeared, the veins are scarcely visible and the details have been greatly weakened. The negative of this corpse gives the same crumpled effect, the same absence of relief." And *this plant already had this appearance, a long time before the first marks of this excellent impression appeared, an impression which resembles that on the shroud.*

Volckringer ends by apologising that he has provided another problem for solution, instead of a solution for the problem of the shroud. However, this fresh fact makes it possible for us to say with some confidence how the impressions on the shroud were formed, and this is most important; we know we are dealing with a natural phenomenon, nature having spontaneously furnished us with a similar example.

Furthermore, may we not infer from this that the shroud, when found in the tomb, perhaps only bore marks of blood? Is it not possible that the bodily impressions only appeared gradually, after long years? This hypothesis, which was first derived from a French photographer, M. Desgranges, was already being pointed out in 1929 by Noguier de Malijay.

As can be seen, much still remains to be done to elucidate the question of the impressions on the shroud. We are always being asked why we have not carried out such-and-such researches or experiments—this would end by being rather irritating, were it not at the same time rather ridiculous. We did not wait for those who oppose the shroud's authenticity to suggest that we should ask for permission to make scientific experiments. We asked for these before they did; indeed, we asked for more. May I state once and for all: had the shroud been our property, this would all have been done at least seventeen years ago, for a programme had already been completed by 1933, and since then we have merely been trying to perfect it.

While waiting for that happy day one may perhaps conclude with the words of an obstinate opponent of its authenticity, Father Braun, in his article in the *Nouvelle Revue de Théologie* (November-December, 1930, p. 1041). The italics are mine and it is with joy that I have underlined the words, for all roads lead to Rome: "Certainly the *striking* impression which has been left on the *venerable strip of linen of Turin*, its astonishing *realism*, its *impersonal* and almost sculptural character, which is certainly something quite foreign to medieval painting, remain a mystery."

And to complete my thought, I would add, in company with our Holy Father Pope Pius XI: "There is still much mystery surrounding this sacred object; but it is certainly sacred as perhaps no other thing is sacred: and assuredly (one can say this is an acknowledged fact, even apart from all ideas of faith or of Christian piety), it is certainly not a human work—*certo non è opera umana.*" (September 6th, 1936.)

Chapter Two

CRUCIFIXION AND ARCHÆOLOGY

I T is certainly not without interest, before studying the actual sufferings of Jesus, to investigate what archælogy, in all its forms, literary texts and artistic documents, has to tell us about crucifixion. For this chapter I am specially indebted to Father Holzmeister, S.J., who has published a masterly and almost exhaustive study on the subject, in *Verbum Domini*, the review of the Pontifical Biblical Institute (May, July, August, September, 1934), under the title *Crux Domini ejusque crucifixio ex archæologia romana illustrantur*. The abundance and the precision of his sources have enabled him to reach conclusions, most of which seem to be irrefutable. As I do not propose to give all his references here, apart from a few of those which I have verified, and others which did not come from him, I would strongly recommend anyone who can obtain the articles, or the booklet which was made up from them, and who can read Latin, not to be content with the extracts which I have made. I shall, however, venture to point out the very few questions on which I disagree with him. I shall reserve the causes of the death of Jesus for a special chapter; medical knowledge is, indeed, required for this chapter, which was not possessed by the ancient authors, nor by exegetes in general, nor by this special author.

I shall also deal with certain information which we can obtain from the history of art. But, out of respect for the value of this work, I wish on the whole to keep to its order and to its divisions.

A.—THE PRACTICE OF CRUCIFIXION

It seems that the Greeks, who had a horror of crucifixion, did not practise it. We do not find its entering Hellenic history till the conquests of Alexander, when he borrowed it from the Persians. It was inflicted under the *diadochi*, under the Seleucids, such as Antiochus Epiphanes, in Syria, and in Egypt under the Ptolemies. In Syracuse, which was a Greek town, it had perhaps been borrowed by Denis the Tyrant from the Carthaginians.

It seems that the Romans adopted it following the example of Carthage, where it was frequently practised. As we shall see in section B, with them it was the final point of an evolution which started with a simple and reasonably harmless punishment, which was in ancient days inflicted on slaves. At Rome they started, during the wars, by crucifying deserters and thieves, but above all conquered rebels. Nowhere was this last reason resorted to so much as in the land of Israel, from the 2,000 seditious Jews who were crucified by the Legate to Syria, Quintilius Varus, after the death of Herod the Great, down to the hecatombs of the siege of Jerusalem, when the Romans crucified as many as 500 Jews a day, according to Josephus, a Jewish historian who was, however, not unfavourable to the masters of the world.

In times of peace it was the punishment meted out above all to slaves. A number of authors refer to it (Livy, Cicero and Tacitus). The comedies of Plautus, which teem with slaves, are full of direct allusions to what they seem to consider as their natural end: " My father, my grandfather, my great grandfather, my great great grandfather thus ended their career." (*Miles gloriosus.*)

This was first reserved for their organised revolts, such as that of Spartacus; after its repression there were 6,000 crosses marking out the road, the whole way from Capua to Rome. Later, proprietors were given the right of life and death over their slaves, who were looked upon as cattle. The death order was: " *Pone crucem servo*—place the cross on the slave," and not place the slave on the cross. We shall return to this important question of the *patibulum,* when we come to study the cross. (B, 2°, C, 3°, D, 4°.)

If this order was first given because of the flight of the poor man or for other serious offences, it ended by being issued for lesser reasons. We should also remember that, in accordance with an old and horrible custom, if the master of a house was assassinated and the criminal could not be found, all the slaves of the household were executed.

Even Roman citizens were on occasion crucified, and this not only by Caius Licinius and Labienus, on whom Cicero heaps bitter reproaches for this reason. From a series of texts it seems that this was done with some regularity, but that the victims were mainly humble citizens, who were either emancipated slaves or provincials. Cicero's invective would seem to claim that citizenship brought with it exemption from this. But in his time this was not an absolute guarantee, and one could cite, even according to him, a number of *cives romani* who were legally crucified.

B.—THE INSTRUMENTS OF CRUCIFIXION

The cross, according to the general rule, the regulation cross, if one may so express it, was made of two distinct pieces. The authors of the Septuagint already call them *" xulon didumon—*the double wood " (Josue VIII, 29). The one, which was vertical, and was a permanent fixture, was the *" stipes crucis ";* the other, which was movable and was fixed horizontally on the first, was the *" patibulum."*

1°. *The stipes crucis.*—In ordinary language, the trunk of the cross, for *stipes* can mean a trunk (of a tree), a stake and even a pale. This was what in early times was meant by the word cross. *" Crux,"* like *" stauros "* in Greek, meant no more than a stake fixed vertically in the ground, much the same as *" skolops "* which means a pale; indeed the words *stauros* and *skolops* could be interchanged, so that certain authors have used the word *" anaskolopisein "* (to empale) in regard to the crucifixion of St. Peter and that of Our Lord Jesus Christ.

The word *" crux "* then came to mean the combination of the two pieces of wood, as we understand it to-day. But as we shall see, a stranger thing yet, the words *crux* and *stauros* were used, by synecdoche, in reference to the movable *patibulum* only: *Crucem portare—stauron basatsein—*To carry one's cross.

As for St. Andrew's cross, in the form of an X, it is unknown in the ancient authors.

How high was this stipes? Father Holzmeister distinguishes the *" crux humilis,"* which would have been low, from the *" crux sublimis,"* which would have been high. But all the examples he quotes show clearly that the *crux sublimis* was reserved for personages whom it was specially desired to display, such as Regulus or Bomilcar at Carthage, or the Spanish assassin to whom it was ironically granted by Cæsar Galba, because he had claimed to be a Roman citizen.

On the contrary, most crosses were low, *humilis.* This allowed the wild beasts who were let loose in the arena to attack the crucified easily, and also the wolves of the Esquiline who used to devour the corpses (on the slopes of the Esquiline at Rome there were a large number of *stipites* permanently fixed). Suetonius gives a horrible account of Nero, who used to enter the arena disguised as a wild beast, so as to satisfy his sadism.

We should also note that crucifixion would be greatly simplified for the executioners by the use of low crosses, especially when work was pressing and there was a large number of condemned men. One should never, when studying a form of punishment which was practised almost daily, forget this idea of convenience, perfected by long use. One has to try and enter into the attitude of the executioner.

2°. *Patibulum-Furca.*—The horizontal piece of wood had a rather curious origin, anyway in Rome; it started by being a "*furca.*" The *furca* was a piece of wood in the form of an inverted V on which the shaft of the two-wheeled carts was rested when they were in the stables. When a slave was to be punished, the *furca* was placed astride the nape of his neck, his hands were bound to the two arms, and he was marched through the neighbourhood, while he was made to proclaim his offence.

This march of expiation was before long combined with the stripping and scourging of the man under sentence during its whole length. It was then found more convenient to hang the *furca* to a vertical stake, which made it possible to give even severer floggings. In the time of Nero (cf. Suetonius, the death of Nero) this was known as the punishment "*more majorum,*" according to ancestral custom. "*Nulla causa est,*" wrote Plautus, "*quin pendentem me virgis verberes*—I give you the right to have me beaten with rods, hanging from the cross" (*Casina,* v. 1003). "*Verberibus cædere pendens*—you shall be broken with blows whilst hanging" (*Mostellaria,* v. 1167).

But as a *furca* was not always obtainable, they began to use a long piece of wood, which was used for barring doors and was called the *patibulum* (from *patere,* to be open). It is thus that the horizontal part of the cross, which was no longer taken from a door, as can be imagined, became a rectilinear beam, which was borne by the condemned man from the tribunal to the place of the *stipites.* He usually bore it against the nape of his neck, with his arms stretched out and bound to it, so that he could give no resistance. One thus understands why the words of the death sentence were: "Place the cross on the slave." It was this *patibulum* which Tertullian compared to the great single main-yard of the Roman ships.

Under Constantine and his successors, when crucifixion had been abolished, another *furca* is to be found. It is a fairly tall stake, ending in a fork, like the letter Y. The condemned man was hung from it by the neck, and was quickly strangled. This was completely different from the lingering death of the cross.

3°. *The joining of the two pieces of wood.*—The two pieces of wood were thus separate; we shall find further proofs of this when dealing with the carrying of the cross (Chapter IV, E). How was the *patibulum* fixed on the *stipes*? It would seem that this could be done in two ways, either by inserting it into one of the faces of the stipes, or by placing it on its upper end; one would thus have either a † or a T, like the capital *Tau* of the Greek alphabet. There seems to be no ancient text to shed light on this problem in a definite way, and it is not till one comes to Juste Lipse (XVIth century) that one finds the two methods being named; he refers to the † as the *crux immissa* or *capitata*, and to the T as the *crux commissa*.

Almost all modern archæologists think that the Roman cross was a T. (See Dom Leclerc, *Dict., d'Archéologie.*) In Christian art both forms are to be found in every century, though the *Tau* seems to be the most ancient; we shall return to this in regard to the cross of Christ (D, 5°). It is certain, if one thinks of it from the point of view of the executioners, that the T was far easier for a carpenter to make. It was only necessary to hollow out a mortice in the middle of the *patibulum*, and to fine down the top of the *stipes* so as to form a tenon. With a medium-sized cross, not more than two metres high, the fixing could easily be done at arm's length. May I be so bold as to add that the *patibulum* which is shown at Santa Croce, on the stairs leading to the chapel of the relics, as being that of the good thief, has just such a mortice.

4°. *The Sedile.*—It is possible that, *in certain cases*, there was fixed on the front of the *stipes*, about half-way down, a kind of horizontal hook of wood, which would pass between the thighs and support the perineum. The reason for supposing this is to be found in three phrases of Seneca's (*Epistolæ morales*), in which he speaks of " *sedere cruce—* to sit on the cross," and even of " *acuta sedere cruce,*" as if this hook had a sharp edge like the wooden horses used for the punishment of medieval wrong-doers. The third text speaks of " *patibulo pendere, extendi, et sustineri—*to hang from the *patibulum*, to be stretched and supported." St. Justin also speaks of " *crucis lignum, quod medium est infixum, sicut cornu eminet, in quo insident crucifixi—*this wood of the cross which is fixed in the middle, which sticks upwards like a horn, on which those who are crucified are seated." St. Irenaeus says that the cross has five extremities; it is on the fifth that the crucified man rests. Tertullian also speaks (*Adv., Marcionem*), of the " *sedilis excessus,*" which recalls the horn of the unicorn. The word " *sedile* " simply means some sort of seat, and it is probably following this passage that modern writers apply it to this piece of wood; I have never, to my knowledge, seen it called by any other name.

We shall see, when we come to study the causes of death in crucifixion, that the object of it was to prolong the agony, by diminishing the dragging on the hands, which was the cause of tetany and asphyxia. It is more than probable that all crosses did not have it, and that it was only added with the intention of prolonging the torture. One can easily imagine, when there were hundreds of crosses to be made, that the carpenters were not eager to make their work more complicated, by an addition which they knew to be useless.

We shall find elsewhere, when we study the wounds in the hands (Chapter V), the reasons by which I am convinced that this support was absent in the cross of Jesus. Furthermore, this partly explains the relatively short duration of the agony.

The *sedile* has scarcely ever been represented by artists, painters or sculptors. This fact is no argument against its historic existence, even in the Passion of Christ. It is clear that the reason for this is the question of reverence. It is for quite other reasons that I would rule it out.

5°. *Suppedaneum.*—However, artists have frequently represented, and modern artists almost always represent, the feet of Jesus as resting on a horizontal or oblique bracket, to which they are nailed. I shall return later to this " *suppedaneum*," which Father Holzmeister claims was *unknown to every ancient author*. It is first mentioned by Gregory of Tours (VIth century—*De Gloria Martyrii*). We shall see, when we come to study the nailing of the feet (Dr, 6°, this chapter), how this product of the artistic imagination came to be developed.

6°. *The instruments for fixing.*—One has to acknowledge that the nailing of the hands and feet was the habitual method of fixing the body to the cross, whatever may have been the reasons for condemnation or the social status of the condemned. Slaves were nailed as were freemen, Jews as were Romans.

The initial error, which attributes to Jesus the monopoly of the nails, may be attributed to Tertullian, who wrote that: " He alone was crucified in this remarkable fashion " (*Adv. Marcionem*). This error was revived in our day by Mommsen, who was certainly an eminent historian, but many of whose theses have since then been very much questioned. This is not the first time that the growth of knowledge has inflicted some bitter defeats on the Germanic claims to infallibility. It is owing to Tertullian that Christian iconography so often represents Jesus as nailed between two thieves bound with ropes.

In fact the two methods of fixing (nails and ropes) were in use among the Romans from the beginning. But they were used separately. One must insist there is no text which suggests or leads one to believe that two methods were ever used at the same time, on the same crucified being. The experts knew well that three nails, or four at the most, were quite enough to achieve a rapid and firm crucifixion. All else is pure imagination.

I even believe that nailing was the most usual method. In a large number of texts not only is there a definite reference to the nails, but also to the flow of blood which would spread from the wounds over the cross. One thus finds in the *Golden Ass* of Apuleius: " Those witches who go to collect the blood of murderers fixed to the cross, so that they may practise their shameful magic." More striking still, the technical term which is most frequently used in Greek for crucifixion is " *proshèloun* " or its synonym " *kathèloun*," to nail; they both have the same root, the noun " *hèlos,*" which means a nail. And when Xenophon of Ephesus records that in Egypt the crucified were bound by their hands and feet to the cross, he expressly notes that it was a local custom, which proves that elsewhere nailing was more usual.

And let it not be said that the use of ropes was the special manner for slaves! Plautus, to whom one must always refer for the customs of the slave world, speaks of " *adfigere* " and " *offigere.*" " *Te cruci ipsum propediem adfigent alii*—Others will soon nail you to the cross " (*Persa,* v. 295). " Who will let himself be crucified instead of me?" says the slave Tranion; " *ego dabo ei talentum, primus qui in crucem excucerrerit, sed ea lege ut offigantur bis pedes, bis bracchia*—I will give a talent to the first man who shall have run to the cross, but on condition that his feet are nailed twice, and his arms twice " (*Mostellaria,* v. 359, 360). The use of the word *bis* (twice), according to the context, simply means that he asks ironically for two nails for each of the four members, so as to be the more certain that his substitute shall not escape. The last word, *bracchia* (the arms), already brings out (exaggeratedly) what we will demonstrate experimentally: crucifixion was not through the palms of the hands but through the wrists.

C.—The Accompaniments of Crucifixion

The details of these seem to have been clearly laid down in a series of laws and interior regulations. This, however, did not prevent certain sadistic vagaries on the part of the executioners.

1°. *The preliminary scourging.*—We are not dealing here with scourging ordered as a separate torture, nor even with a method of killing condemned men, but only with the scourging which was a *legal preliminary* to every execution. Everyone punished with death as a preliminary was always scourged, whether he was to die on the cross or otherwise; by beheading (Livy) or at the stake (Josephus). Only those were exempt, according to Mommsen, who were senators, soldiers or women who had the freedom of the city.

However, in the case of beheading, the scourging was done with the rods from the bundles of the lictor: " *Nudatos virgis cædunt secutique percutiunt*—They strip them and beat them with rods and strike them with an axe." (Livy.)

As we have seen, scourging was an ancient custom in Rome. It was also inflicted under Alexander and Antiochus Epiphanes and at Carthage. One keeps on coming across the formulæ " *proaikistheis anestaurothe—verberatos crucibus adfixit*—crucifying after scourging."

This scourging, which as we have seen was formerly inflicted on the cross, now took place in the area of the tribunal. The condemned man was bound to a column (probably with his hands above his head). As Plautus wrote: "*Abducite hunc intro atque astringite ad columnam fortiter*—Take him inside and bind him firmly to the column" (*Bacchides*).

The scourging was preceded by the stripping of the condemned man, who began his journey to the place of execution naked and scourged, and carrying his *patibulum* (Valerius Maximus—Cicero).

With what sort of an instrument was the scourging carried out? We have seen that those who were to be beheaded were beaten with the lictor's rod; for the other form of scourging a distinctively Roman instrument was used; the *flagrum*. It had a short handle, to which were attached several long, thick thongs, usually two of them. At a little distance from the end balls of lead or the small bones of sheep were inserted, "*tali*," such as were used for playing at knuckle-bones; these were the ankle-bones of the sheep.

The thongs would cut the skin and the balls and the little bones would dig deep contused wounds into it. There would be a good deal of hæmorrhage and considerable lowering of vital resistance. We shall have all too many chances of verifying on the shroud of Jesus the wounds which this terrible instrument could inflict, and the blood-stained marks which it left on the skin.

In Hebrew law the number of strokes was strictly limited to 40. But the Pharisees, who were scrupulous people, wishing to make sure that this number was not exceeded, had reduced the quantity to 39. The Romans imposed no limitation, apart from the necessity of not killing the victim; he had to be able to carry his *patibulum* and to die on the cross, in the regulation way. Sometimes, as Horace tells us (Epode IV), he was "*sectum flagellis—præconis ad fastidium*—so torn by the whips as to disgust those in charge."

2°. *The carrying of the cross.*—The condemned man, having first of all been scourged, went on foot and without clothes, but carrying his *patibulum*, from the tribunal to the place of execution, where the *stipes* awaited him, among a number of others like it.

We should state at once that the expression "*crucem portare*—in Greek *stauron bastazein*—to bear one's cross," is only to be found in the Greek or rabbinic texts (Plutarch, Artemidorus, Chariton, in the Jewish commentaries on Genesis and in the New Testament). In Latin it is only to be found in the Latin versions of the Bible: *Crucem portare, ferre, bajulare*. It is by syndoche, as we have seen, that the word cross means its horizontal part.

Among the Latins one never finds this phrase "*crucem ferre*," though we have noticed the formula used in the sentence, "*pone crucem servo.*" But we do find "*patibulum ferre*"—to carry one's *patibulum.* The details of how this was done are told by Denis of Halicarnnassus in his Roman history. The *patibulum* was placed on the shoulders and on the two arms outstretched, after which it was bound with cords to the chest, the arms and the hands. The condemned man thus only carried the *patibulum.*

Once again we find, among all the texts to which we could refer, that Plautus sums it all up in a concise phrase:

"*Patibulum ferat per urbem, deinde affigatur cruce*—Let him bear his cross through the town, then let him be nailed to the cross " (*Carbonaria*). The "*patibulatus* " was the condemned man bearing his cross (Plautus, *passim*).

The "*stipes crucis*," on the other hand, was awaiting the condemned man at the place of execution, Cicero (*pro Rabinio*) inveighs against Labienus that "*in Campo Martio . . . crucem ad civium supplicium defigi et constitui jussit*—In the Field of Mars he had the cross permanently set up for the punishment of citizens." One finds references to this "setting up permanently " in the Verrines and in Josephus.

In Rome, the Montfaucon[1] was in the Esquiline Fields, which have been made famous by Horace, and where, according to Saglio (Dict., Daremberg), there was quite a forest of crosses, a great plantation of *stipites.* It was outside the Esquiline Gate. For those who know Rome, this was near the Piazza Vittorio Emanuele, a short distance beyond the church of Santa Maria Maggiore, as one goes out from the centre of the city.

There is a final argument that this was the established custom, which is that the *patibulum* already weighed about 125 pounds so that the complete cross would have weighed more than 250 pounds. It must have required great effort to carry the *patibulum,* for a man who had been subjected to a severe scourging, which would have caused considerable loss of blood and a decline in his strength. How could he have carried a complete cross weighing more than 250 pounds? For it was not just a question of dragging it. One finds in all the texts " *portare, bajulare, bastazein,*" to carry, but never " *trahere, surein,* to drag."

May we end by saying that the bearer of the cross was preceded by an inscription on wood, the " *titulus,*" giving his name and stating the crime for which he was condemned. The *titulus* was later fastened on to the cross.

3°. *The method of crucifixion.*—All that we have said so far in regard to the carrying of the *patibulum* only and of its being fixed on to the *stipes crucis* on the spot, points to the method of crucifixion set

---

[1] The ancient place of execution in Paris.

out in the formula of Firmicus Maternus (*Mathem.*): "*Patibulo suffixus in crucem tollitur*—(The condemned man) having been nailed to the *patibulum* is raised up on to the cross."

If the crucifixion is done by binding with ropes, all that needs to be done is to affix the *patibulum*, to which the victim is already bound, and then to bind his feet to the *stipes* with a few turns of the rope. If he is to be nailed, the victim is unbound and then laid down on the ground, with his shoulders on the *patibulum*. His hands are held out and nailed to the two ends of the *patibulum*. The man is then raised up with the *patibulum*, which is fixed on to the top of the *stipes*. After this his feet are nailed down flat against the latter.

This raising up should be fairly easy to do, especially if the cross was not more than two metres high. Four men could easily hold up at arm's length the *patibulum* and the condemned man, both of which together would not weigh more than 325 pounds. If need be the victim could be lifted backwards up a little ladder placed against the *stipes*. If the cross was higher they would either have to use two forks for lifting the *patibulum*, or two ladders leaning against the sides of the *stipes*. In neither case would there be any great difficulty to overcome.

This technique is also suggested by the expressions used when referring to crucifixion. They all speak of an act of elevation: in Greek it is "*epibainein ton stauron, anabeinein eis ton stauron*—to go up on to the cross"; in Latin we find "*in crucem ascendere*," which means the same—"*in crucem agi, tolli, elevari*—to be lifted up on to the cross," and even "*in crucem salire*," as in an untranslatable pun of Plautus', when he makes Chrysalus the player say: "*Facietque me Crucisalum ex Chrysalo*—From being Chrysalus I shall become one who rises up on to the cross." It seems then that we must abandon any idea of crucifixion on the complete cross, whether lying on the ground or vertically against an upright cross.

May we not say that Jesus Himself described the true method, when He predicted to St. Peter: "*Extendes manus tuas et alius te cinget et ducet quo non vis*—Thou shalt stretch forth thy hands, and another shall gird thee, and lead thee whither thou wouldst not" (*Jn. XXI,* 18). The stretching forth of the hands went with the placing of the *patibulum* on the shoulders of the condemned whilst before the tribunal. They were then bound with a cord before they started out for execution.

We may add that the imagination of the executioners sometimes varied the regulation method of crucifixion. Occasionally, for example, they changed the standard position, and crucified them head downwards (*katô kara proshèlôthentes*), as was done under Diocletian and in Palestine (Eusebius). Everyone knows, as Origen says, that St. Peter was crucified thus.

4°. *The military guard.*—Every execution was carried out legally, under a completely military staff, who took their orders from a centurion, as Seneca says: "*Centurio agmen periturum trahens*—the centurion dragging along the crowd of those doomed to die." The army, which had already been in charge of the scourging, provided the escort from the tribunal to the place of execution, and the executioners of the crucifixion were recruited from its ranks; it would also be responsible for providing a guard to watch at the foot of the crosses. This was in order to prevent the friends of the executed men rescuing them; the guard had thus to be permanent until the condemned men were certainly dead. Its duties even continued after death, as Petronius adds: "*Ne quis ad sepulturam corpus detraheret*—Lest anyone should take the bodies away for burial." What then happened to the corpses of the crucified?

5°. *Burial and the lack of burial.*—The usual course was for corpses to remain on the cross and to be devoured by birds of prey and by wild beasts. Horace replies to an innocent slave: "*Non pasces in cruce corvos*—you will not feed the crows on the cross" (*Ep.* I, 16). And in *Epode* V he writes: "*Post insepulta membra differeni lupi et Aexquilini alites*—And then your unburied members will be dispersed by the wolves and birds of the Esquiline." And other texts take up the same theme (Petronius, Seneca, Artemidorus).

However, the bodies could be asked for by families who wished to ensure for them a decent burial; it seems that the law authorised this final grace without hindrance or demand for payment. Even the ashes of those condemned to the stake were returned to their relations (Pandectes). That such clemency was the rule is proved by the fact that the cases when free authorisation was refused are pointed out as exceptions. Cicero, in the *De Suppliciis*, bitterly reproaches Verres that he extorted a heavy payment for giving up the bodies of those who had been executed to families who did not wish to see them become the prey of wild animals. Such a financial extortion, says the orator, is against the law.

On the other hand the judge, since it depended on him, could refuse the authorisation in certain cases, and for various reasons, in which hatred for the condemned man usually plays its part. Such a refusal came to an increase of punishment; the crime of high treason entailed it. Vespasian added to the condemnation of certain conspirators that their bodies should be cast into the common sewer without burial (Suetonius). Augustus, after the battle of Philippi, had already refused permission for the burial of a notable prisoner, replying, when the request was made, that it would soon be the business of the vultures (Suetonius). In the same way Flaccus, who was Prefect of Egypt in the year 38 A.D., did not authorise the burial of certain crucified Jews (Philo—*In Flaccum*).

6°. *The blow with the lance.*—Later, we find the same provisions in the Digest: " The bodies of those condemned to death shall not be refused to their relations. . . . The bodies of those who have been executed are not buried, except when permission has been asked and been granted, and sometimes it is refused, especially in regard to the bodies of those who have been condemned for the crime of high treason " (Ulpian). The Digest belongs to the VIth century, but it is a compilation of all the ancient laws, which, when one takes into account the traditionalist spirit of Roman jurists, certainly gives a true picture of the customs and legislation of the period in which we are interested.

Elsewhere Quintilian, who belongs to the Ist century, writes: " *Percussos sepeliri carnifex non vetat*—the executioner does not forbid the burial of those who have been pierced." This word " *percussos*," unless I am mistaken, introduces a new idea which has a special bearing on our subject. What exactly does " *percussos* " mean? It does not refer to the execution itself, nor to the scourging; as however it refers to those who have been condemned to death, we know quite well that they have been scourged and crucified. It refers then to a special blow, given after the execution and which reminds us irresistibly of what is known as the " *coup de grâce* "; it seems to be similar to the revolver shot which is fired into the ear of a man who has been shot, even when he is clearly dead. One could then interpret Quintilian's phrase as meaning the executioner allows those who have been executed to be buried, after they have received the *coup de grâce*.

Of what did this regulation *coup de grâce* consist, which alone authorised the executioner to give up the body to the family? Origen speaks, as Father Holzmeister reminds us, of the " *percussio sub alas* " (*Comm. in Matth.*), which is evidently a blow delivered to the heart. But, when one comes to examine the context, one finds that it refers to the blow which was sometimes given immediately after crucifixion, in order to kill the condemned man quickly. He says that Jesus had not received it, and that this explained Pilate's astonishment that death had been so rapid.

But at this point we are confronted with a text of Sextus Empiricus, a philosopher and a learned medical man of the IIIrd century, who explains to us that " *è tès kardias trôsis aition estin thanatou*—the wound in the heart is the cause of death." It seems then that it was to this *coup de grâce* that Quintilian was alluding.

Thus, when the family asked for the body, the executioner had first of all to strike a blow at the heart. As he usually was a soldier, this blow would be inflicted with the weapon which he was carrying in his hand, probably a lance or a short javelin. We shall see that this blow at the heart, which was struck from the right side of the chest, was certainly studied and well known, on account of its mortal quality, in the fencing schools of the Roman armies. It gave complete security that the condemned man was really dead . . . and if need be was the cause of this.

D.—THE GOSPELS EXPLAINED BY ARCHÆOLOGY

1º. *The condemnation.*—A reason was necessary which would come within the scope of *Roman* law. In Jerusalem Pilate alone possessed the " *jus gladii,*" the power of life and death, which was bitterly grudged him by the Jews. The members of the Sanhedrin obviously could not produce the reasons for their hatred before a Roman official. And that is why they started by accusing Jesus of encouraging the people to revolt. But a brief inquiry and Herod's indifference soon brought this major accusation to nothing in Pilate's mind. He repeated three times: "I find no cause in this man" (*Lk.* XXIII). The Jews then alleged that He had made Himself the Son of God, and that this, according to their law, entailed the supreme penalty. But this failed to move the Procurator, and on the contrary had a vaguely disturbing effect on his superstitious soul; in the eyes of a pagan, the son of a god is a hero. It is clear that Pilate was doing all he could to release this man whose innocence was obvious and who called forth his respect. It was only after all these windings and gropings that the Jews were at last able to discover a reason which would compel Pilate to condemn Him: "He has made Himself a King. . . . If you release this man you are not Cæsar's friend" (*Jn.* XIX, 12). There was a satanic astuteness in this, for it contained a count of indictment, that of "rebellion against Cæsar," and it stirred up all the selfish anxiety of this poor colonial official, lest he should displease the central government, and even become involved in some subversive attempt against the emperor. From then onwards all the desire he had to be benevolent, all his concern for justice, which were surprising enough in a Roman brute (and which have won for him a certain indulgence, well expressed by St. Augustine), all this vanished before a serious count of indictment, which could gravely compromise any judge who refused to admit it. And from then onwards the condemnation was a foregone conclusion, and the application of the law meant death by crucifixion: *rebellion against Cæsar.*

He would have his revenge on the Jews by writing on the *titulus*: Jesus of Nazareth, *King of the Jews,* and by maintaining it in spite of their objections (O *gegrapha, gegrapha*—What I have written, I have written). This was only the expression of his resentment and ill humour.

2°. *The scourging.*—The question is whether this scourging was that which legally preceded an execution, or whether it was a punishment on its own. Matthew and Mark offer no solution to this problem, for they merely write: " Having scourged Jesus (he) delivered Him unto them to be crucified." This is a simple account of the succession of events, and this was what took place following every condemnation to death.

In St. Luke's Gospel Pilate already twice repeats to the Jews: " I will chastise Him therefore, and release Him." This reveals to us his intention to inflict the scourging as a special punishment, but does not yet tell us that he has done so. But St. John, who is often more explicit, when he considers he should complete, without contradicting, the Synoptics, in his quality of an eye-witness describes in detail what took place. Pilate had declared to the Jews that Jesus, whom he had questioned, was innocent; he offered to deliver Him because of the pasch, but the Jews called for Barabbas. " Then therefore Pilate took Jesus, and scourged Him." (*Jn.* XIX, 1). We have the scourging, the crowning with thorns, the *Ecce Homo*, the accusation that He had made Himself the Son of God. Pilate, in his anxiety, returned to question Jesus on this subject. When he went out once for a final attempt, the supreme accusation burst forth: He has made Himself a king; you are not the friend of Cæsar. And then came the condemnation.

We then see that the scourging had preceded the sentence of death and even the most important part of the " *actio* " of the trial; an unworthy trial, more like a riot than a judicial proceeding. Alas! The result was no different.

3°. *The crowning with thorns.*—We have said that it was the custom to submit the condemned to every kind of mockery and ill-treatment which depended merely on the imagination of the executioners. In the case of Jesus, the excuse was ready to hand: He was accused of having made Himself the King of the Jews, and this count of indictment would entail His condemnation to death. We may be sure that this royal Jewish title would have seemed to these legionaries of the empire to be a great piece of buffoonery, which they would at once have the idea of turning into a cruel masquerade. Hence the crowning with thorns, using an old chlamys as the purple mantle and a reed serving as a sceptre.

Philo gives us another example of this deep contempt of the Romans for Jewish royalty (*In Flaccum*): A few years after the death of Jesus, when the Jewish king Agrippa was passing through Alexandria, the populace got hold of a poor idiot, crowned him with the bottom of a basket as a diadem, wrapped him up in a mat, placed a reed in his hand, and supplied him with a mock bodyguard, surrounding him with derisive honours. The whole of this improvised masquerade was intended as an insult to Agrippa's Jewish royalty.

We shall return to the details of the crowning of Jesus when we come to study the wounds which resulted from it.

4°. *The carrying of the cross.*—We must first of all admit, in company with Father Lagrange and Father Huby, that Jesus, having been condemned by a Roman to the death of the cross, "*more romano*," according to the Roman custom would only have carried the *patibulum* and not the whole cross as depicted by most artists. We have seen that the expression " to carry one's cross," which one only finds in Greek texts, or those which have been translated from Greek into Latin, is the exact synonym of the Roman " to carry one's *patibulum*."

Was this *patibulum* fixed with cords on the two outstretched arms, as was the custom in Rome? Or did He carry it balanced on one shoulder? As the Gospels do not tell us explicitly, it is at first sight difficult to give a definite answer to this.

St. John's expression, however: " *bastazôn autô ton stauron— bajulans sibi crucem*—carrying His own cross " (Mgr. Knox's translation), would seem to suggest the active gesture of taking up His cross personally.

The episode with Simon of Cyrene would also point to the cross being carried balanced on the shoulder, without cords. According to the four Evangelists, Jesus, anyway when leaving the prætonium, was carrying His own cross (John does not mention Simon). Then the soldiers, seeing that in this way He would not reach Calvary, according to the Synoptics compelled the Cyrenean to carry the beam. This would seem to indicate, though without certainty, that it was resting on His shoulder, unbound by cords; as for Simon, there was no valid reason for binding a free man who had merely been called in. Luke alone adds that he was carrying it behind (*opisthen*) Jesus. This would mean that Jesus was walking in front, led by the soldiers; Simon followed Him, carrying the *patibulum*. We have thus travelled far from the most usual iconography, with Jesus carrying an immense cross, and Simon holding up the post behind Him. This is purely artistic imagination; it is not without beauty and mystical content.

We shall see that the marks of the wounds to be seen on the shroud and the stains on the coat of Argenteuil can only be explained by the scraping of the beam against the back which it was galling (unless we admit the carrying of the whole cross, which would certainly be inexact), at the time of the falls, when Jesus sank beneath it.

Finally, the Gospels bear witness that Jesus was not subjected to the Roman custom, according to which the condemned walked to execution completely naked. " They took off the cloak from Him, and put on Him His own garments, and led Him away to crucify Him " (Mt. XXVII,

31). This could be easily explained by the habit preserved by the Romans of respecting native customs. We find in Josephus (*C. Appionem*): "*Romani subjectos non cogunt patria jura transcendere*—The Romans do not force their subjects to break the laws of their country."

We would add that the binding of the arms to the *patibulum* was done specially with the aim of preventing any violent reaction by the condemned man. The soldiers must have become aware that Jesus was perfectly inoffensive. Their only problem was to make sure He reached Calvary alive.

5°. *The cross.* (1) *The height of the cross.*—Father Holzmeister thinks that a high cross (*sublimis*) was used. I would here venture to disagree with him. His one argument does not seem to be entirely convincing. He thinks, in fact, it would have had to be very high for it to have been necessary to fix the " sponge filled with vinegar " (the vinegary *posca,* which was the normal drink of the Roman soldier) at the end of a reed, in order to reach the lips of the Crucified.

Let us start by eliminating the word hyssop, which, even in Palestine, is a frail little tree, and let us, along with Father Lagrange, read not "*hussopô*" but " *hussô,*" which means a short javelin (Matthew and Mark speak of a reed, " *kalamos,*" but the short javelin had much that appearance). This " *hussos,*" the Roman " *pilum,*" was three feet long, about 90 centimetres, including the metal part which was about a foot long. When held at arm's length this would hold the sponge to a height of about 2·50 metres.

I think then that the *crux humilis* was used. There was no reason for setting up a special *stipes* of a higher kind, merely so as to mock the " King of the Jews." They had not the time for this, and the usual stakes were always ready at Golgotha, where most of the executions were carried out. Besides Jesus, who had been condemned unexpectedly, they had to receive on that day two brigands who had been condemned in the regular course of justice. These executions were thus quite normal and according to the regulations.

I should imagine that the stakes were about 6 feet 8 inches high, which would allow the *patibulum* to be fixed quite easily. The feet could without difficulty be nailed on to the *stipes* (with the flexion of the thighs and the legs, which we shall calculate exactly), at about 1 foot 8 inches from the ground. The mouth would thus be scarcely any lower than the *patibulum,* after the sinking of the body, and would thus be at a height of about 7½ feet. It would thus be more convenient to hold up the sponge on a *pilum,* to get it to that height, rather than to make the effort of holding it up in the hand.

Another fact should be taken into consideration, which is not mentioned by Father Holzmeister, the blow with the lance. It is certain, anatomically speaking, that the blow was given obliquely, but not far from the horizontal. According to my hypothesis of 6 feet 8 inches, the wound was about 5 feet from the ground. A foot-soldier would thus find it easy to give this blow, simply by lifting his arm. This would be impossible, if the cross were higher. Now, it is certain that the soldiers were legionaries, and therefore foot-soldiers. They were commanded by a centurion, who would have been an infantry officer, and would also not have been mounted. Only a horseman would have been able to give the blow with the lance had the crucifixion been at a higher level. It is clear that this will dismount many of the fine cavalcades which some of our painters have portrayed so impressively, but it seems to me to be far more in conformity with historical truth.

I venture to recall the text from Eusebius, which was quoted by Father Holzmeister himself, at the beginning of his work—St. Blandina " was exposed (on the cross) to be the food of wild beasts." The ordinary low cross must then have been used, that of the arenas: " And being hung on the cross, she bore a likeness to Him who for their sakes (the martyrs) had Himself been crucified." Did this likeness extend to the dimensions of the cross? I do not wish to read too much into the text, but it would seem to suggest it.

Finally, attempts have been made in favour of a high cross, to make capital of the verb " *hupsousthei—elevari*—to be lifted up," which we find Jesus applying to Himself three times in St. John's Gospel, alluding to the crucifixion. The third time, for instance, He says: " And I, if I be lifted up from the earth, will draw all things to myself "[2] (Jn. XII, 32). It is quite obvious that a cross of the dimensions we have in view would fully comply with the meaning of this verb.

(2) *The form of the cross.*—Was the cross of Jesus in the form of a T or a +? Father Holzmeister would seem to hold that the Fathers of the Church opted for a +, but he only deduces this opinion from certain comparisons which they make with the cross; for instance Jacob blessing Ephraim and Manasses with outstretched arms. One text only is a little more precise, that of St. Irenaeus, who counts five extremities (*cornua*) on the cross, including the *sedile*. All things considered, we find no definite affirmation of this in patrology. On the other side, Dom Leclerc quotes three texts from Pseudo-Barnabas, Origen and Tertullian, which undoubtedly have the T form in mind. Tertullian recalls the passage in Ezechiel, in which the Lord orders the latter to mark the foreheads of the men of Jerusalem with a Tau (the name of the Geek T), adding that it was a forecast of the sign of the cross, which Christians trace on their foreheads.

[2] Mgr. Knox translates this verse:—
" Yes, if only I am lifted up from the earth, I will attract all men to myself."

"The Gospels," writes Father Holzmeister, "give no indication as to the form of the cross. The *titulus* which was, as St. Matthew says, '*epanô tès kephalès autou*—above His head,' does not prove that the *stipes* was higher than the *patibulum*."

In fact, this raises no difficulty. The *titulus* was fixed to the *patibulum* of the T by a piece of wood and by four nails, as I have been able to demonstrate on a number of crucifixes; it could even have encroached a little on to the front of the *patibulum* and have been nailed directly to it. Both these methods are to be found in the work of several painters, especially Roger van der Weyden.

It may well be that the projection of the *titulus* above the *patibulum* was the source from which the form of the Greek and Latin crosses was derived. (These two adjectives have no geographical significance in this context.) The true classical Greek cross has, above the *patibulum* and crossing the middle of the *stipes,* a second oblique bar, which represents the *titulus*. The upper horn of St. Irenaeus would then be the *titulus*.

It must also be remembered that when the first crucifixes appeared (and they were still very rare), at the end of the Vth century (one of ivory in the British Museum), VIth century (the door of St. Sabina, the Gospel Book of Rabula), almost two centuries had passed by since crucifixion was abolished by Constantine (315 A.D., or at the latest 330), and none of the artists had ever seen a crucified being. St. Augustine, at the dawn of the Vth century, declares that nobody had been crucified at Rome for a long time. The form, then, was chosen by artists for æsthetic reasons, unconnected with reality; it was easier to place the *titulus* where it would be clearly seen, above the head of Jesus. The two forms will always be portrayed in every age, according to the choice of the artist.

From the VIth to XIIth century the productions of the East were the most important. These include many small objects, such as *ampullæ* (Bobbio, Monza), and censors, and are often marked with a +. This is also to be found in frescoes, as in Santa Maria Antiqua, or in the Forum (VIIIth century). However, the great compositions which are found on a wide scale from the XIth century onwards, often have in them a T. We find this in the church of St. Luke in Phocis, at Daphni, at Aquilea, and at Santa Maria in Vescovio. I place the Byzantine crucifixes in a separate group, occupying as they do a small space in the middle of a large cruciform frame, of which the extremities and the sides broaden out into a number of small subordinate pictures; such is the crucifix in the church of San Damiano at Assisi.

When the art of painting was revived in Italy in the XIIth and XIIIth centuries, the primitives usually have a +, as for instance, in the work of Duccio and Cimabue. But in the XIVth and XVth centuries, the T, begins to appear again in the work of Pietro Lorenzetti, in the lower church at Assisi; Giotto, in the Arena at Padua; Fra Angelico, in San Marco in Florence. All three fix the *titulus* on a narrow stem of wood on the *patibulum*.

In France, the Gothic sculptors are more inclined to use the +. But the T is definitely dominant in the XVth century in all schools of painting, whether they belong to Provence, Burgundy, Paris or the North; Bréa, Bellechose, and Fouquet generally employ it. In the Walloon country the great Roger van der Weyden never paints anything else. Albrecht Dürer also prefers the T. The same is true of Hieronymus Bosch in Holland and Memling in Flanders. In the XVIth century a few artists remain faithful to the T, such as Quentin Metsys. But, in the XVIIth, the Latin cross holds the field in every country; it is usually very high, amid stately and high-flown productions, which become further and further removed from piety and from the truth. One still finds an occasional T, however, in the work of Lebrun (at the Louvre) and in Rembrandt. Our modern artists are readily returning to it. But we must once more study the origins.

It would be most interesting to know how the Christians of the first centuries depicted the cross. This was unfortunately such an object of horror and infamy in the whole Roman world, that nobody dared to shew it, even for the eyes of the faithful. The apostolic catechesis was above all things a triumphant preaching of the Resurrection. The first crucifixes (Vth and VIth centuries) will be triumphal images of the living Christ, placed *in front of* the cross. It was not till the Middle Ages that the imagery and the cultus of the Passion developed, the mystical idea of the Divine Compassion.

One does, however, find very rare representations of the crucifix engraved on gems of the first centuries. In one of these Jesus is holding His arms in the form of a cross, but the latter is invisible. On two others the cross seems to be a T. On a cornelian in the British Museum, the Christ is standing, with His arms outstretched; there is a transverse bar behind Him, above His shoulders and His hands. He has the appearance of a condemned man carrying his *patibulum* in the Roman style, rather than one who has already been crucified. Finally, there is the famous *graffito* of the Palatine, a coarse satirical design, which represents a Christian adoring a crucified being with the head of an ass (this was a common calumny among the pagans), and shews a cross in the form of a T, drawn with clear lines.

The cross is extremely rare in the catacombs. About twenty have been mentioned and recent excavations have scarcely added to that number. They are plain crosses, skilfully expressed with lines similar to those in the letters of the neighbouring inscriptions. Almost always, and constantly in the first two centuries, the cross is symbolised by images which would be less easy for those who were not initiated to understand.

Chief among these, perhaps, is the anchor, the symbol of hope; for Jesus is our greatest hope. This anchor is frequently fastened to or covered by a fish. As everyone knows, the Greek word for the latter is "*ichthus*," the letters of which are the initials of the Greek words meaning " Jesus Christ the Son of God the Saviour." The fish stretched out on the anchor, and sometimes on a trident, is thus the perfect image of the crucifix. The anchor is in shape like a cross in the form of a T. However, but later and rarely, the rectilinear branch of the anchor has a cross-bar running through it, which stresses its crucial aspect, and is perhaps a figure of the *patibulum*.

The cross is to be found under the two forms T and +. The + is always alongside the name of some dead person. The T is also sometimes to be found in the same position; but more often it is in a very special place, in the middle of a name, usually of the same breadth as the other letters, but reaching beyond them at each end. For example in the catacomb of St. Peter and Marcellinus, *ad duos lauros*, we find △IONTYCIOY (Dionusiou). Curiously one finds the same arrangement with a bar above it, $\overline{\text{M}}$, which all archæologists believe to be an abbreviation for Martyr: thus VERIC$\overline{\text{M}}$VNDVS (Vericundus). These inscriptions with the T are ancient, belonging to the IInd or IIIrd century. I have not found any explanation of these among the archæologists. Would they also be the mark of martyrdom, like the little crosses which they hold in their hands in the fresco in Santa Maria Antiqua? Could it even be the mark of a crucified martyr?

As we have seen, information about the cross of Jesus is scarce and indefinite. But I can see no reason for believing that a special cross was made for Him. The cross which was waiting for Him was just one of those on Golgotha. It would then have been not only a cross of medium height, but also a cross in the form of a T, which, according to the opinion of archæologists, was the normal form of Roman crosses.

6°. *The nails.*—The two hands and the two feet of Jesus were nailed to the cross. It was not merely the fulfilment of David's prophecy:— "*Foderunt manus meas ea pedes meos*—They have pierced my hands and my feet " (Ps. XXI), but it was also affirmed by the Saviour Himself, who said to ten of the apostles when they had assembled in the Cenacle, at the time of His apparition:—"*Videte manus meas et pedes meos, quia ego sum*—See my hands and my feet, that it is I myself " (Lk. XXIV, 39). Two or three patristic texts, which only speak of nails in the hands, do not tell against this affirmation in the Gospels.

The only problem to be solved is as to the number of these nails: were there three or four? In other words, were the two feet nailed separately or one above the other? Roman archæology seems to be absolutely silent on this point. Ecclesiastical writers share the two opinions, but unfortunately they are unable, on either side, to produce any reasons in support of them.

St. Cyprian, St. Ambrose, and Gregory of Tours speak of four nails. On the other hand Nonius, in the IVth century, speaks of the feet crossed one before the other: " *Pedibus positis mutuo percomplicatis.*" St. Gregory of Nazianzus writes: " *Triclavi repositum ligno*—Placed on the wood with three nails," and St. Bonaventure: " *Illi tres clavi sustinent totius corporis pondus*—These three support the whole weight of the body." We may note that St. Bonaventure would seem to imply there was no *sedile*. St. Brigit, in her revelations, and Mgr. Paleotto, who was Archbishop of Bologna in the XVIth century, make things more complicated by saying the feet were crossed, but that a nail went through each foot. This is the method depicted by Giotto in the Arena; but it is very complicated. We shall find that the anatomical solution is much simpler and rests on a firmer foundation.

Aesthetic questions may be involved, since oral tradition is not, as might be expected, unanimous on this point. It is thus of interest to study the evolution of the crucifix on this particular point. A long study could be written about this, but we propose to give a brief outline *grosso modo* as follows: —

The first crucifixes do not represent one who is being put to death. Our Lord is standing, in a majestic attitude, in front of the cross, against which He extends His arms horizontally. The hands display the head of a nail, but the feet are not nailed (the door of St. Sabina). In the ivory crucifix in the British Museum, Jesus is lifted up on to the cross, with His arms extended and hands nailed, but the feet are hanging vertically and are not nailed. The arrangement is the same in the Gospel Book of Rabula, but the legs are nailed to the *stipes*, a little above the ankles, and separately, the feet are hanging freely, obliquely.

This posture later on led artists to imagine the *suppedaneum*, which they first placed in a horizontal position beneath the feet, the latter being nailed on to it, side by side; we find it thus in the Church of St. Luke in Phocis. But these horizontal feet were not aesthetic, and the *suppedaneum* rapidly assumed the form of an oblique bracket, which it preserved almost down to our own day; the feet thus resumed an oblique and far more natural position. We first find this in the Byzantines, at Daphni, Aquilea and elsewhere, and then among the painters and sculptors of the Middle Ages. This does not prevent our frequently finding the feet nailed flat against the *stipes*, especially in France during the XIVth and XVth centuries.

The oblique *suppedaneum* also brings about another transformation, the crossing of the feet. At first the lower members are portrayed as vertical, but then we find a slight bending at the level of the knees, in order to raise the feet in a vertical direction and to nail them side by side on the bracket. But soon the knees became more bent owing to the sagging of the body, and the feet were crossed one before the other on the support. This was already done as early as 1270, and can be seen in Santa Maria in Vescovio. This tendency does not seem to have been at all widespread in Italy before the XVth century, but was already to be found in France in sculptures of the XIIth century. After this, we still from time to time find two feet nailed side by side with two nails, but it becomes increasingly the rule to cross the feet. Nearly always, as we shall see (ch. VI), the left foot is behind the right, which is contrary to what one sees on the shroud.

From all this it is clear that the choice among artists of three or four nails rests on purely aesthetic preoccupations, and that their concern for form led them steadily back to historical truth. They will only have to do away with their imaginary *suppedaneum*, and they will conform to it completely, like their predecessors of the XVIth century.

7°. *Was Our Lord naked on the cross?*—At first it seems clear that before crucifying Him they removed His clothes, since the soldiers shared them and drew lots for His coat (Jn. XIX, 23). The question remains whether He was allowed a linen cloth round the loins. According to Father Holzmeister, the Fathers are unanimous in asserting this nudity. But it would seem that they usually base this opinion on reasons of symbolism drawn from the Old Testament (as for example, that Adam was naked when he sinned, and that Jesus was naked in order to redeem us), and they are content to refer to the " Roman custom," without their being any special historical tradition in regard to Jesus. Opposed to this opinion is an apocryphal passage in the *Acts of Pilate*, according to which, after removing Our Lord's clothes, they placed on Him a " *lention*," a Greek word meaning a linen cloth.

It has specially been objected that it would be surprising if the Romans, who had placed Our Lord's clothes on Him once more for the carrying of the cross, contrary to their own customs, but no doubt as a concession to Jewish ideas of decency and to their national customs, would not have left Him, when on the cross, this last piece of clothing.

The Jewish custom, writes Father Lagrange, was as follows: " When they were within a distance of a few arm's lengths, the condemned person was undressed; if it was a man, he was covered in front; if a woman, she was covered both in front and behind " (*In Marc* and *Sanh.*, VI, 14).

The whole question, however, remains affected by " Roman custom." Did the Romans crucify the condemned naked? According to Dom Leclerc, Artemidorus (*Onirocriticon*) says: " *Gumnoi gar staurauntoi.*" But what is meant by this word " *gumnos,*" naked? All the men of old wore under their clothes, whatever they were, what was known as the *subligaculum*. It was like a pair of drawers, consisting of a band of linen, which was wound round the loins and the thighs, and was worn the whole time.

St. Mark tells us (XIV, 51) that after the arrest of Jesus a young man (probably himself) followed the procession, having only his *sindon* on his naked body. The *sindon,* as we shall see, was a long piece of linen, which was wound round the body under the tunic, and which would be retained as a garment when asleep. Mark had just been sleeping in the Garden of Olives; he had then removed his tunic, but would clearly have kept on his *subligaculum* under his *sindon.* Now, the guard seized hold of him, but he, leaving his *sindon,* " fled naked— *gumnos ephugen.*" But would he not, in this state of nakedness, have been wearing the *subligaculum* the whole time?

I will, if I may, compare with this text a similar story in the *Fioretti;* the custom was the same in the XIIIth century. St. Francis, so as to punish Friar Ruffino who had refused, on account of his unfitness, to preach in the town, ordered him to go to Assisi and to preach naked. Now, the title of Chapter XXIX contains the words " *ignudo nato— naked as at his birth.*" It is explained in the text, through the mouth of St. Francis, that this means " *ignudo, solo co'panni di gamba—*naked, wearing only his drawers." I shall be told that this was another age. By all means; but the custom was the same and the word " naked " was probably understood in the same sense.

The question remains an open one. Let us see what iconography has to say about it. One may say that no artist has dared to represent Christ naked on the cross; to do so would be hateful. (See Fig. I; and yet the artist had the shroud before his eyes, in which Jesus was manifestly naked.) Dom Leclerc points out that on the carved gems, of which we have spoken, and which probably belong to the first centuries, the body of the Crucified is naked. I should say that it is difficult to judge according to the drawings which have been made of them. In any case, in the first important sculptures which we have (at St. Sabina and in the British Museum), Jesus (and the two thieves as well) is wearing the *subligaculum*.

This tradition has been carried on from that date in the countries of the East. Most of the Byzantine crucifixes (St. Luke, Daphni, etc.) are of this type. In the West on the other hand, and throughout all the early Middle Ages, the crucified is to a large extent clothed, as in the fresco of Santa Maria Antiqua (VIIIth century). One of the most characteristic types is the *Santo Volto* at Lucca, a cedar-wood crucifix which is said to have been carved by Nicodemus, but which must date from the VIIIth century at the earliest. The body is completely dressed (the whole garment is carved in wood) in a long robe with sleeves, which only leaves the hands and feet uncovered. In other places one finds a similar sculpture wearing rich clothing made of stuffs. The legs are straight and the whole gives an impression of majesty and triumph rather than of torture.

The *Santo Volto* has given rise to quite a school, and imitations of it are to be found over almost all the West; there is for instance the celebrated Saint Saulve (Saviour) of Amiens cathedral.

It is not till the first Italian renaissance (XIIIth century) and the period of French gothic sculpture that we once again meet with naked crucifixes, wearing only the *subligaculum;* this usually consists of a fairly long linen cloth, skilfully draped.

For my part I should not have too much difficulty in admitting that the imprints of the pelvis were made through the *subligaculum*. Volckringer's vegetable images were made through the sheet which was supporting the plants on to the sheet which was enveloping them. Nor do the pieces of paper struck on to the plants for fixing them prevent the formation of images through them. But the *subligaculum* of Jesus would surely have been copiously stained with blood, and these clots would have left their counter-drawings.

In all this we must own that there is a combination of one's concern for the æsthetic, for decency and for reverence, with the desire to express in a real way the true nature of the sufferings of the Passion. Having to a certain extent pleaded the cause of the *subligaculum,* I feel bound to return to the general opinion of the Fathers, who are so neat to unanimity as to produce an impressive effect.

I have verified the texts quoted by Father Holzmeister. They all speak of " *nudus, nuditas, gumnos, gumnesthai*—naked, nakedness, naked, to be stripped naked." St. John Chrysostom, for example, writes: " He was led naked to death—*Epi to pathos ègeto gumnos.*" " *Eistèkei gumnos en mesô tôn ochlôn ekeinôn*—He remained naked in the middle of that crowd." I have also discovered a text of St. Ephrem the Syrian (Sermon VI on Holy Week, Latin translation by Father Joseph Leclerc) in which, like Alexander of Alexandria, he says that the sun hid itself before the nakedness of Jesus. (He exaggerates when he refers to the moon as well, for when it is full it does not appear in broad daylight.) Meanwhile he writes:—" *Quia vero nudatus erat ille qui omnia vestit, astrorum lux obscurata est*—The light of the stars was darkened, because He who clothes all things was truly stripped naked."[3] Finally, we meet with even greater precision in St. John Chrysostom (*Homily on the Epistle to the Colossians*). He speaks of Jesus who, before mounting on to the cross shed the old man as easily as His clothes, and he adds:—" He is anointed like the athletes who are about to enter the stadium." Now, the whole of Greek sculpture portrays these athletes as entirely naked.

Did, then, all these patristic affirmations rest on an oral tradition which has been lost? It is difficult to come to a conclusion.

In any case, I repeat, never has any artist wished to make an entirely naked crucifix. Now, this is just what we shall find on the shroud. Could a forger possibly have conceived such an abnormal idea, and one which is so shocking to all our artistic traditions of decency and reverence?

8°. *The placing on the cross.*—It seems that there were only three methods by which this could be performed:

(1) The cross, completely put together, would be laid on the ground. Jesus would be crucified by the hands and the feet. The cross would then be raised up, and the *stipes* placed in a hole already prepared in the ground. Such a method would be complicated, difficult and dangerous. Artists like Rembrandt have been attracted by it, but I very much doubt whether it would have satisfied the executioners, especially if there was a number of crucifixions to be performed. From the technical standpoint I would have great difficulty in accepting it. Furthermore, it is ruled out by all that we know, *as a certitude,* about the Roman cross. It is said that the idea probably had its origin in the apocryphal *Gospel of Peter.* It was restored to a position of honour in the Middle Ages by St. Anselm.

(2) The whole cross is already in position and the condemned man is crucified standing up. This thesis has had its partisans and may come from the *Acts of Pilate,* another apocryphal work. There are the same archæological objections to this. I can discover only one merit; it inspired my old friend Fra Angelico to make a very touching composition, which I think nobody else has succeeded in doing. In that fresco of cell 36 of the convent of San Marco, in Florence, Jesus is

---

[3] The following description of St. Ephrem may be of interest here:—" If from *doctrine* we turn to *devotion,* we are confronted with the difficulty that with the single exception of the writings of St. Ephrem, nothing has come down to us from the first five centuries which gives us any clue to the popular devotions of the Faithful. St. Ephrem was a zealous mission preacher whose sermons and hymns brought him into direct touch with the feelings and religious habits of the people."
The Mother of Christ. By O. R. Vassall-Phillips, C.SS.R. p. 433. Trs.

standing with His back against the cross, at the top of a short ladder; He Himself is holding out His hands, which two executioners, whose ladders are leaning against the back of the *patibulum,* are about to nail.

(3) Jesus is nailed to the *patibulum* on the ground; He is then placed with His back to the *stipes,* and He is then lifted up so that the *patibulum* can be fixed on to the top of the stake. In order to make the lifting up easier, one may imagine Him going backwards up a ladder which is leaning against the *stipes,* like that in Fra Angelico's picture.

This is the simplest solution, and the one which would have made things easiest for the executioners, and this, as I have said, is an argument of the first importance. It is also in agreement with the texts of St. Athanasius, St. John Chrysostom, St. Ambrose and St. Augustine: " *Crucem ascendisse*—To have gone up on to the cross; *se permisit in crucem levari*—He allowed Himself to be lifted onto the cross." Finally it is the only solution which agrees with all that archæology has taught us about crucifixion according to Roman usage.

9°. *The blow with the lance.*—I have always wondered what was the reason for that strange gesture, which seems to be abnormal for a soldier who had just been present at the death of Jesus. The point of view of these guards had greatly changed during the three hours' agony, in the way of pity and of respect. The centurion, making himself the spokesman of the men (St. Matthew attributes the phrase to the whole group of men), had just solemnly proclaimed: " Indeed this was a just man," (Lk.) or following the Hebrew form of St. Mark and St. Matthew: " Indeed this was the Son of God."

Now, they were quite sure that Jesus was truly dead; they had spared Him the *crucifragium,* which was to bring the lives of the thieves to a rapid end by bringing on tetany and asphyxia, as we shall see. So it was the heart of a corpse which one of these soldiers was about to strike with a lance!

The fact is that, if we have interpreted the legal texts correctly, this wounding of the heart was the regulation act which had to be carried out, in order to be able to deliver up the body for burial.

According to St. John, it was after the blow with the lance that Joseph of Arimathea went to Antonia, to ask Pilate for the body of Jesus. But, since they reached Calvary, the whole platoon were able to see this important group (" and *makrothen* other women," adds St. Mark after naming some of them) who were surrounding Mary and John and who evidently made up the family. If these had all stood apart at first (*apo makrothen*), outside the circle of the sentries, they must have drawn in closer, after the departure of the insolent Jews. This is proved by the words of Jesus to His Mother and to His beloved disciple. Had the soldiers heard them speaking of their intention of asking for His body? In any case, it was clear that they intended to do so. The blow with the lance, once the death had been verified, was a natural and kindly gesture, a preparation for delivering up the body, in accordance with the regulations.

I must frankly own that I find relief in this idea and that I understand better.

Chapter Three

THE CAUSES OF THE RAPID DEATH

A.—THE PREPARATORY CAUSES

AFTER the death of Jesus and the blow with the lance which opened His heart, Joseph of Arimathea " went in boldly " (*audaciter*) and asked Pilate for the body of the Saviour. Now, " Pilate wondered that He should be already dead—*Pilatus autem mirabatur si jam obiisset —O de Pilatos ethaumasen ei èdè tethnèken.*" " And sending for the centurion, he asked him if He were already dead. And when he had understood it by the centurion, he gave the body to Joseph " (Mk. XV, 43-5).

Jesus had, in fact, only been in agony for about three hours, which for a crucified man is fairly short. The thieves had survived Him and in the end only died because, by breaking their legs, their asphyxia was hastened on. The Jews asked Pilate for this, because they wished to bury the three of them before nightfall. The Jewish rule was that crucified bodies should be taken down and buried on the same day. There was the further reason that this Friday was the eve of the Sabbath, and, even more, the eve of the great feast of the Pasch. It was the *Parasceve*.

Most of those who were crucified had a longer agony, more or less according to circumstances. It was not rare, according to Origen, to see them survive the whole night and the following day. There is an Arab text which affirms that in 1247 at Damascus a crucified man had lasted till the second day after. Even longer survivals have been mentioned, with less certainty.

It even happened that men who had been crucified were taken down, and survived. We are told of the case of one of Darius's magistrates (Herodotus) and that of Chéréas (Chariton). But the example quoted by Josephus is more interesting. During the siege of Jerusalem, in A.D. 70, three of his friends were taken prisoner by the Romans when he was absent, and were crucified. When he returned in the evening to the Roman camp, he immediately went to Titus and obtained their pardon; they were taken down from their crosses. The doctors were unable to restore two of them to life, but the third survived. Now, the first two had been nailed but the third had only been tied to the cross with ropes. One can thus see that a variation in the method of crucifixion could effect the length of the time which it took to cause death. Those who were bound with ropes, says Josephus, died less rapidly than those who were nailed, and could be more easily revived.

All the other authors who have referred to it are agreed in describing the cross as the most terrible and cruellest of tortures; *crudelissimum et teterrimum supplicium,*" wrote Cicero. But none of them have given the reason why, except that the torments lasted a long time. But why did Jesus succumb so much more rapidly than most of the condemned? That is what we must try and discover.

We can see that a whole series of circumstances, some of which have been brought forward as the causes of death, joined together in diminishing His physical resistance. And we know, through our psychological experiences, that a series of painful shocks do not just add up together, but in a certain sense, multiply each other. (A series of excitations lowers the level of resistance.)

Already, on the evening before, He had undergone, on the mount of olives, an appalling mental agony, produced by the foreknowledge of His physical Passion, and the knowledge of all the sins of men, the burden of which He was Himself assuming for their redemption. He Himself had said to the apostles: " My soul is sorrowful even unto death." He was sorrowful even unto death. Such deep distress can bring on a phenomenon which is known to medical men, and of which St. Luke, who was himself a doctor, gives a perfect clinical description, which is most striking in its conciseness. This phenomenon, which is also extremely rare, is provoked by some great mental disturbance, following on deep emotion or great fear. And St. Luke describes how there was, in Gethsemani, the struggle of the Humanity of Jesus when faced with the chalice of suffering which was offered to Him, and the acceptance of that chalice (Father . . . not my will, but thine be done). And St. Mark adds: " *Coepit pavere et tædere*—And He began to fear and to be heavy."

Then St. Luke adds: " *Et factus in agonia, prolixus orabat. Et factus est sudor ejus sicut guttæ sanguinis decurrentes in terram*—And being in an agony He prayed the longer. And His sweat became as drops of blood, trickling down upon the ground."[1] St. Luke's Greek text is more

---

[1] Mgr. Knox translates these passages as: —
" My soul is ready to die with sorrow."
" Father . . only as Thy will is, not as Mine is."
" And now He grew dismayed and distressed."
" And now He was in an agony, and prayed still more earnestly; His sweat fell to the ground like thick drops of blood."

exact: *"Egeneto o hidros autou ôsei thromboi aimatos katabainontes epi tèn gèn."* Now, *thrombos* means a clot. These clots have always presented translators with difficulty; they quite rightly say that clots cannot come out of a body. And thus they have set out to do violence to the words, because they do not understand the physiological phenomenon. Some ancient manuscripts have gone further still and have suppressed the passage, as if it was unworthy of the Divinity of Jesus. Father Lagrange, who was a most attractive exegetist, but not a doctor, translates it " like globules of blood, running right down to the ground."

Now, this phenomenon, which is known in the profession as *hæmatidrosis*, consists of an intense vasodilatation of the subcutaneous capillaries. They become extremely distended, and burst when they come into contact with the millions of sweat glands which are distributed over the whole skin. The blood mingles with the sweat, and it is this mixture which pearls over the whole surface of the body. But, once they reach the outside, the blood coagulates and the clots which are thus formed on the skin fall down on to the ground, being borne down by the profuse sweat. St. Luke thus proved himself to be a good doctor and a good observer when he wrote: " And His sweat became as *clots* of blood, trickling down upon the ground."

We can now conclude two facts from this phenomenon. There would first be an enormous fall in vital resistance after such a hæmorrhage, which would be a very serious one, on account of the extent of surface where it is produced. On the other hand, the abnormal state of this skin, which, having bled in close connection with its sudoral glands over the whole surface of the body, becomes tender and painful, makes it less able to bear the violence and the blows which it will receive during the night and during the following day, right on till the scourging and the crucifixion.

This sensitisation of the skin, which is a purely physiological phenomenon, causes us to reflect, by the way, about another fact which dominates the whole Passion; it must not be lost sight of, and it will help to explain, humanly speaking, why the agony was brief. All men have not the same resistance or the same defences in the face of physical pain. We doctors become aware every day that a rough type of patient is less sensitive to pain than one who is more refined and cultivated. And this is not merely a psychological phenomenon, for one often finds that labouring men, if their wills are weak, can bear quite ordinary pain very badly. On the other hand, individuals who are physically of a more refined type endure it with the greatest patience and in general put up a better resistance, under the influence of a more courageous soul and finer sensibility. It would seem, then, that there is some definite connection between the refinement of the sensitive nervous system and the intensity of even physical suffering, quite independent of purely psychical reactions.

Now, we are bound to believe that in the case of Jesus, the union of His divine with His human nature would have developed this physical sensibility to the highest degree. And then, as Our Lord had assumed this human nature, He had a firm will to endure the painful consequences to the utmost extent.

Under the same heading of the causes of general weakness we must also include the ill-treatment which He endured during the night, especially between the two examinations, when He was the prey and the object for mockery of a hateful mob of temple attendants, those "blood-thirsty dogs" as St. John Chrysostom calls them. To this we should add the blows which He received in the pretorium, after the scourging and the crowning with thorns; slaps on the face, blows with the first and even with a stick, for the word "rapismata," which St. Jerome translates as "alapas" (slaps on the face), means first and foremost blows with a stick.

The proof that this is the true meaning of "rapisma" is to be found in the comparison of St. John's with St. Matthew's Gospel, at the time of the scourging. Each of them tells us that having crowned Him, they said: "Hail, King of the Jews!" Then St. John adds: "Kai edidosam autô rapismata—et dabant ei alapas—and they gave Him blows" (with a stick).[2] But St. Matthew goes into greater detail: "Kai elabon ton kalamon kai etapton eis ten kephalén autou—acceperunt arundinem et percutiebant caput ejus—they took the reed (a stick) and struck His head."

We can find the marks of this ill-treatment on the shroud, for there is a large bruised wound on the right cheek and the septum of the nose is broken. But these blows, most of which fell on the head, could have produced quite a serious concussion, what we should call cerebral shock or even cerebral contusion; it would consist of a fairly widespread breaking of the small vessels in the meninges and in the brain itself.

The hæmorrhages would also have considerably weakened His vital resistance, by progressive stages. We have already spoken of the sweat of blood. But according to the bruised wounds with which we shall meet, it is above all the savage scourging and the crowning with thorns which He underwent in Pilate's pretorium, at the Lithostrotos, which would have caused the most serious loss of blood. The thongs, which as we know were barbed, would have covered the body with wounds

___

[2] Mgr. Knox translates this verse:—"They would come up to Him and say, 'Hail, King of the Jews', and then strike Him on the face." He translates the second quotation:—"They . . . took the rod from Him and beat Him over the head with it."

which continued to bleed long enough for us to find their bloodstained traces on the shroud, where they have left their counter-drawings, perhaps six hours later. I will pass over the wounds left by the carrying of the cross, which we shall study in detail. The crucifixion itself would only have caused a relatively small loss of blood.

But all these hæmorrhages, which would certainly have caused such extreme weakness that it was necessary to make Simon carry His cross if He was ever to reach Calvary, were not enough to cause death, or yet to account for the relatively short duration of the agony.

Hunger has been mentioned. It is true that He ate nothing from the Last Supper till His death. But one does not die of hunger in twenty hours. Nor is it very probable that during long agonies on the cross death was caused by hunger, as Eusebius maintains.

He was thirsty, violently thirsty, like all crucified beings. This thirst was due in the first place to loss of blood, and then to the profuse sweats which, as we shall see, went with the hanging by the hands and the cramps which this brought on. But this could not as yet be a cause of death. The exposure to the rays of the sun has also been suggested; the crucified died just as well in the shade and in all kinds of weather.

It is true that He experienced one of the most terrible forms of suffering which can be imagined, that caused by the rupture of a great nerve trunk, such as the median nerve. This rupture is accompanied by a sharp fall in arterial tension, even under a general anæsthetic, and it is our custom always to inject them with novocain before cutting them. This wound can cause loss of consciousness. But there is nothing in the Gospels to make us suppose that Jesus consented to benefit by such a fainting fit in order to interrupt His pain; and the nails would have continued to press upon these nerve wounds, when He struggled to speak. And these fainting fits are not mortal.

Some English authors, Dr. Stroud in particular, have produced the hypothesis of rupture of the heart, which would, in his opinion, account for the issue of blood and water (clots and serum!) at the moment of the blow with the lance. We shall deal with this last assertion at the end of Chapter VII. As for a cardiac rupture, this only takes place in an unhealthy organ, suffering from an infarctus or from fatty degeneration. We have no reason for thinking that there was any pathological condition in the heart of Jesus; the issue of clots and of serum, as we shall see, would be absolutely impossible in such a hypothesis. This can only be a pseudo-mystical fancy, which is indeed rather beautiful: that the heart of Jesus should break from excess of love for men. It cannot, however, be sustained scientifically.

There certainly was a hydropericardiac condition, which means that there was a serious effusion within the envelope of the heart; we shall study this along with the wounds in the heart (Chapter VII). It is possible, as Judica holds, that it was due to a traumatic pericarditis, which developed rapidly, and was the consequence of the various traumatisms undergone by the thorax, especially during the scourging. This effusion would have been the cause of terrible pain and anguish, but one cannot imagine it bringing about a rapid death.

In his article on *Le Supplice de la Croix* (The Suffering of the Cross), in the revue *l'Evangile dans la Vie* (April, 1925), Dr. Le Bec has brought forward the hypothesis, which since then has been fully supported by Dr. Louis (*Revue de la Passion*, November, 1936), that the swallowing of a little water by a crucified being brings on a mortal syncope. He cites the case of Kléber's murderer, who was impaled and died in this way. "He had scarcely drunk, when he cried out and died." It is certainly tempting to trace a connection between this fact and the sponge soaked in vinegar which was offered to Jesus. All modern exegetists consider that this vinegar was the *posca*, the ordinary drink of the legionaries. It consisted of water, with some vinegar and beaten eggs. There was always a pailful of it for the guards.

According to St. Mark and St. Matthew, it would seem that He died after receiving this drink. The phrase immediately following it in the text, which however stresses no relation between cause and effect, simply says: "And Jesus having cried out with a loud voice, gave up the ghost" (Mk. XV, 37). "And Jesus again crying with a loud voice, yielded up the ghost" (Mt. XXVII, 50). They do not say whether this great cry was a word. St. John is more explicit. He is also the only one to record the words of Jesus, "I thirst," and to describe the act of one of the assistants who offered Him a drink. And he adds: "Jesus therefore, when He had taken the vinegar, said: It is consummated.[3] And bowing His head, He gave up the ghost" (Jn. XIX, 30). He thus spoke after He had drunk (if He did drink) and this was not like the brutal swoon of the impaled man.

As for St. Luke, he passes over the episode of the sponge in silence. This is most astonishing on the part of a doctor, who was an excellent observer, and was most eager for information, for which he sought on every side. "Having diligently attained to all things from the beginning," as he says in his prologue.[4] He reads all these details in the works of his predecessors, and yet he overlooks them! Was this so-called swoon through swallowing really well known by the ancients, as Le Bec says?

[3] Mgr. Knox interestingly translates these words:—"It is achieved", a stronger expression.
[4] Mgr. Knox translates:—"having first traced it carefully from its beginnings".

He does not give his sources and I have been able to find nothing. How then can one explain a doctor such as St. Luke having overlooked such an important fact, which would have been the cause of death and would account for the shortness of the agony? This would be an unpardonable fault in a young student and is a most surprising act of neglect on the part of a fine clinician, such as our holy colleague was.

Now, he describes the darkness, the rending of the veil of the temple; then he continues: " And crying with a loud voice " (like St. Matthew, but now come the important words), " said: Father into Thy hands I commend My spirit. And saying this, He gave up the ghost " (*exepneusen,* the medical term).[5] No—I certainly do not find the hypothesis of this mortal swallowing satisfactory.

B.—THE DETERMINING CAUSE

All that we have so far examined constitutes the causes of weakness and pain, which would have only been able to accelerate the agony. We still lack the determining cause of death; that which certainly, and independently of previous circumstances, always ended by killing the crucified. This cause, may I say at once, was *asphyxia.* All the crucified died asphyxiated.

The work of Dr. Le Bec, my predecessor at the Hôpital Saint-Joseph (*Le Supplice de la Croix,* April, 1925, *loc. cit.*), contains some precise, exact and complete ideas on this subject. For him, the raised position of the arms, which were thus in the position for inspiration, would entail a relative immobility of the sides, and would thus greatly hinder breathing out; the crucified would have the sensation of progressive suffocation. Anybody will be able to verify that such a prolonged position, even with no dragging on the hands, already entails an extremely disagreeable dyspnœa (difficulty in breathing). The heart has to work harder; its beats grow faster and weaker. There then follows a kind of stagnation in all the vessels of the body. And " as oxygenation is not properly produced in lungs which are not working sufficiently, the additional burden of carbonic acid provokes an excitation of the muscular fibres and, in consequence, a kind of *tetanic condition of the whole body.*"

All this is perfectly accurate, physiologically correct, and logically deduced. Le Bec in 1925 had the immense merit of conceiving this theory, which is in strict agreement with reality. Happily for France he was not to have practical experience of this, but he worked out in theory everything which Hynek's sad observations were to confirm,

---

[5] Mgr. Knox translates:—" and yielded up His spirit as He said it ".

everything which the latter had already *seen* during the 1914 war, but which he did not publish till ten years after Le Bec's article.

It is indeed to Dr. Hynek of Prague that we owe the sad confirmation of Le Bec's thesis and this is the personal and important contribution to the study of the Passion which this author has made, for he saw with his own eyes that which Le Bec conceived with such fine intuition. (Dr. Hynek: *Le Martyre du Christ*, French translation. 1937. *The True Likeness*, English translation, 1951. Original Czech edition, November, 1935.)

Two facts put Dr. Hynek on the road of this explanation:

(1) The observation of the ecstasies of Theresa Neumann, who on almost every Friday lives through and reproduces the sufferings of the Passion of Jesus.

(2) The memory of a torture, or a severe punishment (call it as you will), which he had seen inflicted in the Austro-German army; as a Czech, he was called up in the 1914-18 war. This punishment, which was called "*aufbinden*," and which a later generation was careful not to forget, consists of hanging the condemned man by his two hands from a post. The tips of his two feet can scarcely touch the ground. The whole weight of his body, and this is the important thing, drags on his two hands which are fixed above him. After a certain time violent contractions of all the muscles are seen to appear, which end in a permanent state of contraction, of rigidity in the contraction of the muscles. This is what is usually called cramps. Everyone knows how painful cramps can be, and how they can only be stopped by pulling the afflicted limb in the opposite direction to the contracted muscles.

These cramps begin in the forearm, then in the arm, and spread to the lower limbs and to the trunk. The great muscles which produce inspiration, the great pectorals and the sternocleidomastöids and the diaphragm are invaded. The result is that the lungs are filled with air, but are unable to expel it. The expiratory muscles, which are also contracted, are weaker than the inspiratory (under normal conditions, expiration is done almost automatically and without muscular effort, owing to the elasticity of the lungs and of the thoracic framework).

The lungs being thus caught in a state of forced inspiration and unable to empty themselves, the normal oxygenation of the circulating blood is unable to take place and asphyxiation begins in the victim, as thoroughly as if he was being strangled. He is in the state of an emphysematous in a bad attack of asthma. This is also the condition produced by a microbial disease, tetanus, through the intoxication of the nerve centres. And that is why this combination of symptoms of general contraction, whatever may be its determining cause, and there are others, is called " tetany."

We must also note that this lack of oxygenation of the pulmonary blood causes a local asphyxia in the muscles, where it continues to circulate, an accumulation of carbonic acid in these muscles (Le Bec was right about this), which, in a sort of vicious circle, progressively increases the tetanisation of the same muscles.

The victim, with his chest distended, is then seen to show all the symptoms of asphyxia. His face reddens, and then goes a violet colour; a profuse sweat flows from his face and from the whole surface of the body. If one does not wish to kill the unfortunate man, he must then be cut down. This common punishment, says Hynek, might not last more than ten minutes. In Hitler's deportation camps it was extended to the point of murder.

Two former prisoners of Dachau have borne witness to this; they saw this torture inflicted on several occasions, and preserved a terrifying memory of it. Their testimony was taken down by Antoine Legrand, but I myself have not been able to see the witnesses.[6]

It would seem, from what these witnesses have described, as also from what was seen by Hynek but, *Deo gratias,* was less prolonged, that suspension by the hands brings on asphyxia, with generalised contractions, as Le Bec has foreseen—the crucified all died of asphyxia, after a long period of struggle.

How then could they escape for the moment from these cramps and this asphyxia, so that they survived for several hours, even for two or three days?   This could only be done by relieving the dragging on the hands, which seems to be the initial and determining cause of the whole phenomenon.

After crucifixion, as we have seen, the body sagged, and dropped to a considerable extent, while at the same time the knees became more bent. The victim could then use his two feet, which were fixed to the *stipes,* as a fulcrum, so as to lift his body and bring his arms, which in the general sagging would have dropped by an angle of about 65°, back to the horizontal. The dragging on the hands would then be greatly reduced; the cramps would be lessened and the asphyxia would disappear for the moment, through the renewal of the respiratory movements . . . Then, the fatigue of the lower limbs would supervene, which would force the crucified to drop again, and bring on a fresh attack of asphyxia. The whole agony was thus spent in an alternation of sagging and then of straightening the body, of asphyxia and of respiration. We shall see how this has become materialised on the shroud, in the double flow of blood issuing from the wound in the hand, where there is an angular

---

[6] Dr. Barbet gives an account, however, of what they saw. As it is extremely distressing I have made it an appendix, for some readers may prefer to leave it alone.

gap of several degrees between the two flows. The one corresponds to the sagging, the other to the straightening position.

One can see that an exhausted victim, such as Jesus was, would not be able to prolong this struggle for long. And then, if in His supreme wisdom He considered that the time had come to die, that "all was consummated," He could do so with no difficulty by abandoning the struggle. He did not have to deal with that vital instinct which makes a man who has decided to commit suicide struggle against drowning as soon as he has jumped into the water.

Special circumstances could make this struggle easier or lessen its necessity. We have seen how those who were bound survived longer than those who were nailed, according to Josephus. And Abdias, in his life of St. Andrew, states that he was bound and not nailed, so as to prolong his sufferings. It is possible that a strong rope wound several times round the feet and the insteps would provide a solid support and it would not slip on a roughly cut *stipes*. Resting on the cords would certainly be less painful than on the edges of a square nail which had been sunk into the metatarsals. It would be possible to hold oneself up for a longer time, without the excess of pain in the feet to bring one back to the sagging position. Here again Jesus was subject to the most terrible conditions.

Finally, when they wished to prolong the torture they made use of the *sedile* (I do not refer to the *suppedaneum,* which is mentioned by no ancient author, and is a pure invention of the artists). The crucified would be placed astride this, and it would soon cause great pain in the perineum and the thighs. But nevertheless the force of the dragging on the hands would be greatly lessened, and there would only be the difficulty in breathing, and the pain caused by the extension of the arms without the dragging on the hands. The body, however, even when supported in this way, would not be able to remain indefinitely in the same position; it would have to lean forward and to sag. The dragging on the hands would increase, and the cramps and asphyxia would set in. Nevertheless, the *sedile* would allow a considerable lengthening of the torture.

With the opposite intention, the executioners had a sure way of bringing about the death of the crucified, which was to break their legs. This method was often used in Rome and elsewhere. We find it mentioned in Seneca and in Ammienus Marcellinus. Origen states that this was done "according to the Roman custom." This was known as the "*crurifragium.*" The word was perhaps invented by Plautus:—"*Continuo in me ex Syncerasto Crurifragium fecerit,*" says Syncerastus the slave. "He would immediately change my name from Syncerastus to Broken Legs" (*Poenulus,* v. 886). It was for this *crurifragium,* as they wished to remove the bodies before nightfall, that the Jews went to ask Pilate. "*Ina kateagôsin autôn ta skelè, kai arthôsin*—That their legs might be broken and that they might be taken away" (Jn. XIX, 31).

The exegetists . . . and the doctors have had plenty to say as to how this *crurifragium* could cause death. They have spoken of the heart ceasing to beat owing to the pain. The pain of a fracture is certainly very severe, since we describe it by the word "exquisite," an adjective which may appear to be ironical; it is used, however, in its Latin sense, and means a special pain, one that is singled out, "*exqusita.*" This pain, which for the moment may be quite slight, may cause a loss of consciousness, but not a mortal swoon, a definite stopping of the heart. We must seek elsewhere.

Others, especially doctors, have spoken of a fatty pulmonary embolism, through the fat of the marrow passing into the open veins of the broken bone. These fatty embolisms have had a certain vogue for a long time; at least in theory, for one scarcely ever finds them in an autopsy. This point of view has been almost completely abandoned, and it is now-adays looked on as a very doubtful and unusual possibility. It cannot be the normal cause of death after a *crurifragium*.

On the other hand, what we now know of the tetany and asphyxia of the crucified sheds a very bright light on this method of dispatching them. Those who were being put to death could only resist this asphyxia by drawing themselves up with the support of their feet. If their legs were broken it became absolutely impossible to do so. From then onwards asphyxia seized them completely and finally; death came on very quickly. As for those who had been placed on the *sedile,* the breaking of their legs would also make it more difficult for them to draw up their bodies. But if the *sedile* was used, it was to make them suffer longer, and therefore I do not think that the *crurifragium* would have been for them.

In regard to Our Lord, we shall see, when we come to study the wounds in the hands (Chapter V), that there are anatomical reasons which convince me that He hung simply by three nails, with no other support.

Let us say at once, so as not to confuse this study with that of the wounds, that this asphyxia is specially borne out by the marks which it has left on the shroud. We might even say that tetany and asphyxia, of which for a doctor there can be no doubt, prove that the imprints on the shroud conform with reality; this body died the death of a crucified body.

We can indeed see that the great pectoral muscles, which are the most powerful inspiratory muscles, have been forcibly contracted—they are enlarged, and drawn up towards the collar-bone and the arms. The whole thoracic frame is also drawn up, and greatly distended, with a " *maximum* " inspiration. The epigastric hollow (the pit of the stomach) is sunk and pressed inwards, through this elevation and this forward and outward distension of the thorax; not through the contraction of the diaphragm, as Hynek writes. The diaphragm, which is a great inspiratory muscle, would also tend to raise the epigastrium in a normal abdominal respiration. With this distension and this forced elevation of the sides, it can only move back towards the abdominal mass; and that is why, above the crossed hands, the hypogastrium, the lower abdomen, can be seen protruding.

The sternocleidomastoïds, the other inspiratory muscles, can scarcely be seen, as they are concealed by the beard; but the head is distinctly fixed with a forward lean, as would be the case.

The long flows of blood, which descend from the wrists to the elbows, seem to follow the very noticeable furrows separating the long extensor muscles of the hand, where they are contracted on the forearm. The thighs show the marked muscular protrusion which, on a body which is otherwise perfect in its contours, also point to tetanic contraction.

On the posterior side, the cervical spine seems to be leaning forward, contrary to the normal curve, and this fits in with the frontal image. On the other hand the lumbar region, which should present a curve with a concavity behind, the lumbar lordosis, seems to be flattened out, with the spines of the vertebræ protruding, as Dr. Gedda saw so clearly. He deduced from this that the body was less rigid than was usually thought.

I am not altogether in agreement with his interpretation. The very clear protrusion of the knees, especially of the left one, shows a persistent flexion which would be incompatible with any slackening. This flexion of the knees always entails a certain flattening of the lumbar lordosis, and this would be the case on the cross. On the other hand, people have grown accustomed to thinking of the contraction of tetanus (the disease) as always ending in the curving backwards of the whole body, from the heels to the nape of the neck; that is what is called the " *opisthotonos.* " It is in fact what happens most frequently in an infection of tetanus. But one fairly often comes across the opposite, a bending forward, the " *emprosthotonos.* " We have no experience of what takes place in crucifixion. But it would seem to be fairly normal that, with the sagging of the body, from the fatigue of the head which would fall forwards, from the flexion of the hips and the knees, the body has a natural tendency to contract in a forward curve in " *emprosthotonos.* "

An attitude of body results from this, which is registered in its completeness on the shroud: the flexion of the head forwards, the flattening out of the concavity of the nape of the neck and of the lumbar lordosis, the presence of the lumbar spines, the protrusion of the femoral quadriceps and of the great muscles at the back of the hips, which have worked so hard in raising the body during the agony.

And thus it seems to me that the causes of the death of Jesus emerge quite clearly from the human and scientific point of view (and what is poor science but ignorance disguised!). Many predisposing causes brought it about that He was worn out and physically shattered, when He faced the most terrible torture that the malice of men has conceived. One cause was, however, the determining and final one, asphyxia.

Or, rathermore, these are the circumstances, all more or less harmful, amidst which He died, and owing to which He wished to die. For thus had it been foreshadowed in the prophecy of Isaias (LIII, 7): " *Oblatus est quia ipse voluit*—He was offered because it was His own will."

When one re-reads the Gospels with a medical eye, one is more and more struck by the way in which He dominates the whole proceeding. He has fully and freely accepted all the consequences of the human nature which He has assumed by His submission to the will of the Father, and has fully understood what havoc these traumatisms can cause in our poor battered flesh.

But it is evident with what serene self-control, with what supreme dignity He dominated this Passion which was foreseen and willed by Himself. He died because He willed it, when He was able to say to Himself in a state of full consciousness:—" It is consummated."—My task is accomplished (Jn. XIX, 30).[7] He died in the way that He willed.

In that human body, suffering and dying, the Divinity dwelt. It remained in this corpse. And that is why, unlike anything else in this world, the Face on the Holy Shroud shows us such serene and astounding and adorable majesty.

---

[7] Mgr. Knox's " It is achieved " is surely far more expressive. Trs.

Chapter Four

THE PRELIMINARY SUFFERINGS

LET us now begin to study all the wounds of the Passion of Jesus. My first publications, following on certain experiments made in 1932 and 1933, were deliberately restricted to the five wounds in the hands, the feet and the side. My essential aim was to localise these wounds and to determine what methods were employed in the crucifixion. This was thus a specifically anatomical work. Before, however, resuming this account, which in the course of the years has become very diffuse, it has seemed advisable, so that this book may be as complete as I should wish, to begin by studying the ill-treatment undergone by Jesus, before He was actually crucified.

This ill-treatment, of which a large part was inflicted during the trial by night and in the prætorium, and also the carrying of the cross, are the subject of a fine work by my friend Dr. Judica (*Le lesioni da traumi contusivi sul Corpo di Cristo. Medicina italiana, Nov.,* 1938) from which I shall borrow plentifully, and which I shall now and then discuss in detail. I shall add to this some information of my own in regard to the scourging and the crowning with thorns.

I hope to bring to this examination the same objective point of view from which I do not think I departed during my researches in regard to the five wounds. But it may, I think, be granted me, that when one has come across a large body of evidence which bears the stamp of truth, and which never once breaks down, one has more and more reason for believing in the marks of the shroud. While preserving an honest Cartesian doubt, which I have tried to do all through, one becomes increasingly confident that the document which one is verifying is authentic.

At the end of the study, when one has established the fact that *all* the images, even and indeed especially when at first sight they seem to be weird and contrary to traditional iconography, are in conformity with experimental truth, this collection of partial proofs will end by being equivalent to an absolute proof. If we calculate what the probabilities are, an infinitesimal possibility of error will be seen to be as good as a certitude. That is why, speaking from the anatomical standpoint, I ended by accepting the Holy Shroud as genuine. A forger would somewhere or other have made some blunder which would have betrayed him. He would not have contradicted all artistic traditions with such supreme unconcern.

A.—GENERAL REMARKS

As Judica has pointed out, traumatisms produce very varied injuries on the skin, the traces of which on the shroud differ considerably according to their nature and their depth. They produce ecchymoses (blue marks), and hæmatomes (an agglomeration of blood) under the skin, and deep visceral lesions. Not one of these lesions can leave a mark, unless it has led to a deformation of the surface, modifying the shape as we have seen in the case of the nose. For the shroud to show us anything else it is necessary that the skin should be broken, so that there would thus be a bleeding wound.

The cutaneous irritations caused by the blows, owing to their accumulation, produce little vesicles, which break and spread sero-sanguineous exudation all over the body. This leaves no mark on the linen; but this exudation could have contributed towards the formation of the bodily imprints, better than Vignon's urea derived from sweat. This problem, as we have seen, is still very obscure.

The excoriations remove the whole epidermis from certain surfaces, laying bare the papillæ of the dermis, which bleeds, and more or less destroying the chorion. This is what we shall see in the wounds left by the scourging and in the excoriations of the whole body, especially of the face.

Finally, the contused wounds break the continuity of the skin in all its thickness, and have contused, jagged edges. These are produced especially when the skin rests on a bony resistant surface.

B.—THE ILL-TREATMENT DURING THE NIGHT AND IN THE PRÆTORIUM

You have often read what the four Gospels tell us. Let us search for the marks of this on the shroud.

Excoriations are to be found almost everywhere on the face, but especially on the right side. This side is also deformed, as if there were hæmatomes beneath the bleeding surfaces. The two superciliary arches show those contused wounds which we now know well, and which form from within outwards, being caused by a blow with a fist or a stick, the bony arch cleaving the skin on its deep surface below the brow.

The most noticeable lesion consists of a broad triangular excoriation below the right eye-socket. The base is ¾ of an inch long; the point is directed upwards and inwards, and joins another excoriated area on the nose, about two-thirds of the way up. At this level the nose is deformed by a fracture of the posterior of the cartilage, near to where it joins the nasal bone, which is intact. All these lesions seem to have been caused, as Judica says, by a stick about 1¼ inches in diameter, and vigorously handled by an assailant standing on the right of Jesus. We have already said that "*rapisma*" means a blow with a stick. There are also excoriations on the left cheek, at the end of the nose and of the lower lip.

They are to be found in large numbers all over the body. We shall find that the most striking ones are due to the scourging and the carrying of the cross.

C.—THE SCOURGING

We know already what the instrument of torture was like, the Roman "*flagrum*," the thongs of which had two balls of lead or a small bone, the "talus" of a sheep, at some distance from their end. There are plenty of the marks of this on the shroud. They are scattered over the whole body, from the shoulders to the lower part of the legs. Most of them are to be seen on the back portion which proves that Jesus was bound with His face to the column, with His hands above Him, for there are no marks on the forearms which are quite visible. These could not have failed to receive some blows, if they had been bound lower down. A considerable number of marks are however to be found on the chest.

One must add that only those blows have left a mark which produced an excoriation or a contused wound. All those which only caused ecchymosis (a severe bruise) have left no mark on the shroud. Altogether I have counted more than 100, perhaps 120. This means, if there were two thongs, that Our Lord received *about sixty strokes apart from those which have left no mark.*

All the wounds have the same shape, like a little halter about three centimetres long. The two circles represent the balls of lead, while the line joining them is the mark of the thong.

They are nearly in pairs of two parallel wounds, which makes me think that each *flagrum* had two thongs, and they are laid out in the form of a fan, the centre of which would be the executioner's hand. On the thorax they are oblique, horizontal on the loins, and oblique once more on the legs. At this level, one can see in the frontal image long oblique furrows (similar to the halter-like wounds at the back), which must have been produced by the ends of the thongs. Having struck the calves of the legs with their leaden balls, they have turned round the outer edge of the leg and lashed the front with their points.

We may assume that during the scourging Our Lord was completely naked, for the halter-like wounds are to be seen all over the pelvic region, which would otherwise have been protected by the *subligaculum*, and they are as deep as on the rest of the body.

Finally, there must have been two executioners. It is possible that they were not of the same height, for the obliqueness of the blows is not the same on each side.

Painters have been content with, at the most, vague, formless excoriations; is there one of them who could have imagined and realised these minute details?

D.—THE CROWNING WITH THORNS

Artists soon formed the habit of surrounding Our Lord's head with a circular crown made of intertwined thorns. Byzantine painting never had this crown, and it is quite exceptional in the Italian primitives. Pietro Lorenzetti and Giotto placed nothing on the head. But from the XVth century onwards, in every country, this head-band of thorns appears and it has persisted right down to our own day. Why was this form of crown adopted and so faithfully maintained? No doubt for æsthetic reasons or owing to ignorance. Painters and sculptors have interpreted the Gospel texts according to their own ideas and have not had the slightest concern for archæology; I bear them no grudge for this.

St. Luke does not mention the crowning. St. Mark writes: " *Peritheasin autô plexantes akanthinon stephanon*—And platting a crown of thorns, they put it upon Him " (Mk. XV, 17).[1] This gives no indication as to its shape. St. Matthew and St. John are more precise: " *Plexantes stephanon ex akanthôn, epethèkan epi tès kephalès autou*— And platting a crown of thorns, they put it upon His head "[2] (Mt. XXVII, 29, Jn. XIX, 2). St. John says "tè kephalè," but with " epethèkan " it comes to the same thing.

St. Vincent of Lérins (*Sermo in Parasceve*) was to write at a later date: " *Coronam de spinis capiti ejus imposuerunt, nam erat ad modum pilei, ita quod undique caput tegeret et tangeret*—They placed on His head a crown of thorns; it was, in fact, in the shape of a *pileus*, so that it touched and covered His head in every part," and he affirms that Our

---

[1] Mgr. Knox translates:—" And put round His head a crown which they had woven out of thorns."

[2] Mgr. Knox translates:—" They put on His head a crown which they had woven out of thorns."

Lord's head received seventy wounds. The *pileus*, among the Romans, was a sort of semi-oval head-dress made of felt, which enveloped the head and was specially worn during work. It was also a mark of liberty, and the expression used for the liberation of a slave was: "*Servum ad pileum vocare*—To call a slave to the pileus." St. Brigit declared later on in her revelations that the crown tore the whole of the head of Jesus.

This states in precise terms what St. Matthew and St. John clearly insinuate: that the crown was a sort of cap made of thorny branches, and not just a head-band. This cap would have to be fixed round the head with some kind of band. A quantity of thorns are to be found throughout the world, said to belong to the crown, and which have been distributed throughout the centuries, so as to satisfy the devotion of the faithful.

It is generally admitted that they belong to a thorn-bearing tree which is common in Judea, the *Zizyphus spina Christi*, a kind of lote-tree. It is probable that there was a heap of its branches in the prætorium, used for firing by the Roman cohort. Its thorns are long and very sharp. The scalp bleeds very easily and very vigorously, and as this cap was driven against the head by blows with a stick, the wounds must have caused much loss of blood.

At the Cathedral of Notre-Dame, in Paris, we have the "Crown of Thorns." St. Louis obtained it from the Venetians, with whom the Emperor of Constantinople had left it in pledge for a loan, and he had the Sainte Chapelle built in order to provide a home for it. Now, this crown has no thorns; it is a circle of plaited rushes and this explains everything. After they had imposed the crown of thorns the soldiers must have fixed it on Our Lord's head with these plaited rushes, binding it all round. This explains why ancient authors since Gregory of Tours have said that the crown was made of sea-rushes. (Would these be prickly?)

Such a crown would have wounded the whole surface of the cranium and also the forehead. Now, let us have a look at the shroud. There is no mark left by the top of the head; this must have been covered by the classical bandage which was used to keep the mouth shut.

In the image, on the back portion, one can see flows of blood the whole way up the head, each one coming down from the wound made by a thorn and following irregular courses. They all stop at a rather concave line fairly high up, which must mark the place where the band of rushes was drawn tightly against the nape of the neck. And then there is another series of large flows underneath which seems to become lost in the mass of hair.

It is behind the head that most blood is accumulated. There is nothing surprising in this, since, during the whole time that Our Lord was on the cross, that was where the crown would come into contact with the *patibulum* each time He drew back His head and the thorns would be driven yet a little further into the scalp.

In front the flows of blood are milder, but also easier to discern. There are already some coming from the top of the cranium and there is a long trail on each of the thick masses of hair that frame the face. There are four or five which start from the top of the forehead, moving down towards the face.

One of these is particularly striking and so true to life that I simply cannot image such a one being portrayed by a painter (Fig. I). It begins with a thorn-wound, very high up, just where the hair begins. The flow then moves down to the medial part of the left superciliary arch, following a meandering course obliquely downwards and outwards. It broadens progressively, just as a flow of blood does on a wounded man when it meets with obstacles.

One must, in fact, never forget that we only see here a part of the blood which gradually coagulated on the skin. The flow is slow and continuous; several minutes are necessary for coagulation to take place. Only a small part, then, coagulates in the region of the wound. The further down one goes on the image, the greater is the quantity of blood which has reached that level, which arrives there when it is time for it to coagulate. The more also do the successive sheets of blood accumulate their clots in successive layers. The total mass of clots is thus broader and thicker the lower one looks; and this is because the blood has met with obstacles.

One should also point out that the blood has not moved downwards in a straight line. This error has scarcely ever been avoided by artists; when the course is irregular in their paintings, this is owing to caprice on their part, and cannot be accounted for by any obstacle or natural reason. But here the flow undulates a little both to left and right, and that is natural; the blood may be following for the moment a crease in the forehead, or maybe some little thorny branch which is lying obliquely against the forehead, and forces the blood to flow in an oblique direction.

Towards the base of the forehead the same flow, which really deserves this minute survey, stops just above the superciliary arch and spreads out horizontally towards the mesial line, increasing in height, while the thickness of the clot is visibly increased, which makes the colouring of the counter-drawing more intense. There are all the traces of something having halted its descent, as when a mill-race meets a dam. The blood has been forced to accumulate slowly, and has been able to coagulate at leisure, which accounts for the way in which it has spread out in breadth and increased in height, and for the way the clot has thickened.

An obstacle is there and it is evidently the place where the head-band of rushes was bound round the base of the forehead above the eyebrows. One of the sprigs must have been tied closely over the forehead, for there is a horizontal band without clots stretching right across. To right and left, near the sides, there are two clots which have stopped at exactly the same level, and one can follow the whole course of the band. Beneath it, the blood appears once more, in the vertical frontal flow which we have just analysed, below the point where it had begun to spread out horizontally and to thicken out in the direction of the mesial line. As the obstacle is always there, close against the skin, it must be that the blood managed eventually to filter through the sprigs of the head-band, and got past the dam. The clot which has been formed underneath is thin and narrow in the supra-orbital region, but it spreads out and progressively thickens out on the inner side of the left eyebrow as far as the eye-socket. There is always the same process of flowing and coagulation.

I would defy any modern painter, unless he is a surgeon, with a thorough knowledge of the physiology of coagulation, and has meditated for a long time on all the possible avatars of that thin thread of blood slowly coagulating in the midst of the obstacles, to imagine and to portray this image of the frontal clot. Even with such conditions, it is more than likely that here or there some blunder would betray the forger and the work of his imagination.

As for the hypothetical painter whom people have dared to claim was capable, having painted or stained these negative images in the Middle Ages, of imagining (whatever his genius may have been) all the minutiæ of this clot which is as pregnant with truth as if it was on a living man —it is enough to disgust a physiologist and a surgeon. Please do not talk of it! This image, and it alone, should be enough to prove that nobody has touched the shroud except the Crucified Himself. And it is one image among a hundred others.

E.—THE CARRYING OF THE CROSS

There are on the shroud clear traces of excoriations at the level of the back and the knees.

Let us first of all remember that there is a venerable tradition, which has been given sensible expression in three Stations of the Cross, that Jesus fell three times beneath His burden, before reaching Calvary. This would have decided the soldiers to make Simon of Cyrene carry the *patibulum* instead of Him, walking behind Him. On a rough uneven road, with many scattered stones, such falls would not take place without excoriation, especially at the level of the knees.

Judica, to whose work we will now return, with great exactness shows us the images of wounds on the front of the knees, especially the right. The right knee seems to be more contused, and shows in the region of the patella a number of excoriations which vary in size and shape, and have jagged edges. A little above and on the outer side, there are two round wounds, about a centimetre in diameter. The left knee also shows various contused wounds, but they are less evident and less numerous.

But it is specially in the dorsal image that we find marks of the carrying of the cross. On the right shoulder, in the outer part of the sub-scapular region, there is a broad excoriated area, which is in the form of a rectangle of about 10 × 9 centimetres. (One can also see in the frontal image that this area extends forwards into the outer clavicular region with broad patches of excoriation.) The area at the back seems to be made up of an accumulation of excoriations. They are super-imposed on the numerous wounds of the flagellation, which seem to be as it were bruised and widened by them, when compared with those alongside them. It would appear that some weighty body, and one with a furrowed surface and which was badly fastened, must have lain on this shoulder and have bruised, reopened and widened the wounds of the scourging through the tunic. (Fig. II.)

Further down, but on the left side, there is another area of excoriations of the same type, in the left scapular region. It is round, with a diameter of about 5 inches. (All this is exact, but if greater precision is required, it is the left sub-scapular region and at the point of the left shoulder blade.)

But it is in our interpretations that Judica and I part company, though in very friendly fashion. He supposes that Jesus must have carried a complete cross, with the *patibulum* and the *stipes* adjusted, and that this was a Latin cross (the T would anyway make no difference to his thesis). This cross would be carried as it is usually represented, on the right shoulder; one of the horizontal branches would be hanging down in front of the body; the other would be pointing upwards behind the head; the vertical part would be hanging obliquely behind the body. He imagines the cross would be about 9 feet in height (this would mean a weight of about 312 pounds!).

The wound on the right shoulder would then be produced by the rubbing of the angle formed by the vertical and horizontal pieces, a right angle into which the shoulder would be fitted, and also by the edges of these two pieces of wood. As for the left wound, this would be produced at the time of the falls; the transversal arm behind would fall back against the back when Our Lord was on the ground and would naturally strike the left shoulder-blade. I think, just as he does, that it is during the falls that the wood of the cross wounded the left part of the back.

But I also consider that the interpretation of these two wounds should be rather different from his. In Chapter II I studied the shape of the cross at some length, the methods of crucifixion and the place of the *titulus*, in agreement with archæologists and modern exegetists. In order to be positive I also furnished textual and documentary proofs. It is nowadays generally held that the cross was made of two separate pieces and that, even if it was a Latin cross (which I definitely do not believe), the condemned only carried his *patibulum* to the place of execution, where the *stipes* was permanently set up; it was all that He was able to do and He was not able to do it up to the end ! May I repeat once more the phrase of Plautus in the *Carbonaria*: "Let him carry his *patibulum* through the town and let him be nailed to the cross."

My friend Judica will forgive me if, in my preface, when mentioning some qualifications which I may have for the study of the Passion(!), I forgot one: In 1903, when I was 19 years old, I was a sapper in the 5th Regiment of Engineers, which was in charge of railways, and I often had to carry the sleepers that were to be laid under the rails. I can thus speak as one with practical knowledge. These sleepers are carried on the shoulder and, as they are heavy, two men are needed; now and then, however, one would see some sturdy fellow showing off and carrying one all on his own. I have, in any case, often carried on my shoulders beams which were a little less heavy and I know how it should be done.

The beam has to be balanced on the shoulder, on the right by the right-handed, on the left by the left-handed. One can tell at once to which group a man belongs, as his cheek will be scorched by the tar on the beams. One does not carry them exactly in the middle; one should have rather more behind than in front, which makes them hang backwards obliquely. This is because the right hand is pressing on the upper side of the forward end so as to stop it from jerking upwards. If the beam was exactly horizontal the smallest shaking would disturb its balance and it would tend to fall forward, while it would be impossible to hold it back.

On the other hand, when it is held forwards by the right hand, this hand will, by a natural movement, be guiding it outwards to the right, while the oblique back end will be pointing inwards towards the mesial line. All these details have their importance, especially as regards the consequences of a fall forwards. I have noticed this, for I was also regimental medical attendant (owing to being a medical student) at the

Polygon,[3] where the training was carried out. The man who stumbled against a stone, through not lifting his foot, would usually fall on his knees and, as Judica has pointed out correctly, would fall on the right knee if he was right-handed; he would tear his trousers and graze his skin. He would then sprawl forwards and leave go of his beam so as to fall on his hands.

Now, the beam would already be oblique behind, pointing downwards and to the left. It would thus overturn, rising up in front, and would slide obliquely down the back, flat against it. Having rubbed the skin off the right scapular region it would do the same on the left, but lower down near to the point of the left shoulder-blade, grazing the spinal column on the way, and would go on injuring the skin as far as the posterior part of the left iliac crest. In brief, it would tear the clothes and cause excoriations on all the bony protrusions which it would pass on its way, from the right shoulder down to the left sacro-iliac region, and sometimes even reaching the sacrum itself.[4]

These lacerations are not bruises caused by a blow. They are excoriations produced by the violent rubbing of a hard mass which is weighing against these parts which protrude and offer resistance. The skin is rubbed away by the beam as it passes roughly across the back, till it reaches the earth.

Does not this experience, which I have met with in my own life, give a most satisfactory explanation of the contused wounds on the shroud? Remember as well that the left scapular region may have begun to be excoriated before the falls, for Jesus was bent forwards owing to exhaustion. In fact, owing to its obliquity, as I have already described, the *patibulum* would already have been rubbing against the left shoulder blade.

Let us also add that the tunic of Argenteuil (which has its documents, O historians, dating at least from the time of Charlemagne) shows bloodstains in the same places. These stains stand out very black in the photographs made with infra-red rays, in 1934, by my friend Gérard Cordonnier, of the Marine Regiment of Engineers, who is an ardent upholder of the shroud. Judica mentions this elsewhere, but following Hynek, but his quotation is not quite accurate. This is what Cordonnier says (*La Passion et le Crucifiement*, Paris, 1934, Librairie du Carmel, 27 Rue Madame, 6°), and I have before me his photograph by infra-red rays: (1) There are several moderate-sized stains on the outer half

---

[3] An area in France specially used for military exercises.
[4] Iliac means " near or pertaining to the flattened upper bone of the pelvis ". The sacrum is " the triangular bone formed by the fusion of vertebrae at the lower end of the spine, and forming the posterior part of the pelvis ". Trs.

of the collar bone, the acromion and the right sub-scapulary region. (2) There are some small stains spaced out at regular intervals on the spines of the vertebræ, starting from the seventh cervical (which always protrudes). (3) There is a very large stain on the lower part of the point of the left shoulder blade, extending to the right a little beyond the mesial line. (4) There is an important mass at the back part of the left iliac crest. (5) Further down and on the inner side are to be seen a group of stains where would be the left sacral region.[5]

All these anatomical points have been marked, by reproducing the stains of the tunic on a linen tunic of the same dimensions (the tunic had been photographed, stretched out on a paper marked with numbered squares), and by placing this tunic on a normal man, about 6 feet in height.

When considering the shroud, we have only mentioned the wounds on the right shoulder and the left shoulder blade. Are there also any marks of excoriation on the left iliac crest like there are on the tunic? It is possible, but they would be veiled by the left extremity of the back transversal flow.

Does not this description justify the prophecy of Isaias (I, 6)?: " *A planta pedis usque ad verticem non est in eo sanitas: vulnus et livor et plaga tumens; nons est circumligata nec curata medicamine, neque fota oleo*—From the sole of the foot unto the top of the head, there is no soundness therein: wounds and bruises and swelling sores: they are not bound up, nor fomented with oil."

---

[5] Of the Holy Coats (of Trier and Argenteuil) the *Catholic Encyclopedia* says: " The possession of the seamless garment of Christ (Jn. XIX, 23), for which the soldiers cast lots at the Crucifixion, is claimed by the cathedral of Trier and the parish church of Argenteuil. The Trier tradition affirmed that the relic was sent to that city by the Empress St. Helena. . . . The Argenteuil tradition claimed that the garment venerated in that city as the Holy Coat was brought there by Charlemagne. . . . The modern advocates of the Argenteuil tradition now designate the relic honoured there simply as the seamless garment of Christ; they deny to the Church of Trier the right to call their relic by this name, conceiving however that the Trier relic is genuine, but that it is not the *tunica inconsutilis,* but the outer garment of Christ.

" Those who believe the Trier tradition claim on the contrary that the relic of Argenteuil, which is woven of fine wool and is of a reddish brown colour, is not a tunic, but a mantle. By this they do not seek to dispute the authenticity of the Argenteuil relic, but to assert that it is the *cappa pueri Jesu* and not the *tunica inconsutilis.*" The article is by Dr. Friedrick Lauchert of Aachen. Trs.

Chapter Five

THE WOUNDS OF THE HANDS

W E know that the usual custom of Christian iconography is to represent the nails as piercing the palms of the hands of the Crucified. One could, however, cite a number of exceptions to this rule. I found yet one more, after my audience of Easter, 1934, in the *Sala di Tronetto* of the Vatican. This is to be seen in a great ivory crucifix, given by the Knights of St. John of Jerusalem to Pope Pius XI. The nails are still a little too far down, but clearly in the centre of the wrists.

One can say as much, for example, of a Rubens in the Rijk Museum of Amsterdam and of the three Van Dycks of Antwerp, Brussels and Bruges. I have also before me the photograph of a crucifix of the early XVIIth century, made of ivory, which, besides having great æsthetic value, is also, to my mind, almost perfect from the anatomical point of view. The nails are exactly in the bend of the wrist, with the thumbs pointing down the palms of the hands and slightly bent. Furthermore, the two feet are nailed down flat on the *stipes* and the right is behind the left (Fig. XII). M. R. Grünevald, who is head of a department in the Ethnographical Museum in the Trocadero, has kindly sent me this photograph after reading the first edition of my *Cinq Plaies* (*Five Wounds*).

Crucifixion in the palms of the hands is simply the literal translation into art of David's words: " *Foderunt manus meas*—They have pierced my hands," and those of Jesus to Thomas: " *Vide manus meas*—See my hands." The artists have not searched further afield; for them the hands mean the palms. We shall see, however, that the Bolognese artists of the XVIth century were the first to recognise (maybe experimentally) that this crucifixion in the palms of the hands was an impossibility.

The stigmata have on several occasions been brought forward as an objection to my insistence on the wrists. I answered this beforehand in the first edition of the *Cinq Plaies* (p. 8). But, as often happens, I did this too concisely, in eight lines, forgetting how few readers are able to read, in this age of the cinema and the Digests (Indigests).

It is certain that most stigmatists (I am referring to those who have been recognised by the Church), from St. Francis of Assisi down to our own days, bear their wounds in the metacarpal region, in the palms of the hands—that is to say, in the front of the hands. Are these stigmata the exact reproduction of the wounds in the hands of Jesus? That is the question.

It is very unlikely. One should first of all point out that these wounds vary in appearance. They are more or less superficial or deep, varying from excoriation to a gaping hole.

Sometimes, as in the case of St. Francis of Assisi, one meets with a kind of fleshy excrescence, the anatomical nature of which I shall not try to define, for it bears no likeness to anything I have ever seen. It is, however, clearly affirmed and exactly described in the *Fioretti*, which I now venture to translate from its delightful XIVth century Italian, in Passerini's edition (Sansoni, 1905, p. 170): " And thus His hands and feet appeared nailed with nails, of which the heads were in the palms of the hands and in the *soles* of the feet, outside the flesh. Their points came out on the back of the hands and the feet, where they were twisted and turned back; this was done in such a way that it would have been possible to pass a finger quite easily, as through a ring, where this twisting and turning back had taken place, for it came out right above the flesh. And the heads of the nails were round and black." Another passage states that these nails could be moved in the grooves where they were lodged through the hands and feet; this was definitely ascertained after His death.

Can my question, then, be answered in the affirmative? No! These stigmata are not the exact reproduction of the wounds of the Saviour. They did not appear thus when He was laid in the shroud. It was not thus that He showed them to His faithful, in that glorious body, in which it pleased Him to preserve them. And I do not stress the flagrant improbability of the heads of the nails in the soles of the feet, since it is so obvious that the nails must have been driven in through the back of the feet.

I would add to this that the exact localisation of these stigmata is not always the same, but it varies throughout the whole extent of the metacarpal zone, as far as being very near to the wrists. We should come to the conclusion that the stigmatists can give us no information either as to the position or the form of the wounds of the crucifixion. (See also p. 113, the wound in the heart.)

Furthermore, that is the opinion of the stigmatists themselves; their wounds have only a mystical value for them. I will only quote one, Theresa Neumann, whose supernatural manifestations seem to be now-

adays well confirmed by the proper authorities. Theresa has said to one
of her friends: " Do not think that Our Saviour was nailed in the hands,
where I have my stigmata. These marks only have a mystical meaning.
Jesus must have been fixed more firmly on the cross."

And as we are dealing with the mystics, may I, with all the desirable
reserve and with the greatest reverence, recall this revelation of the
Blessed Virgin to St. Brigit (Bk. I, c.10): " My Son's hands were pierced
at the spot where the bone was most solid—*Perforatæ fuerunt Filio meo
manus in ea parte, in quo os solidius erat.*"

To conclude: without wishing to discuss the bodily mechanism of
the miracle, which we are indeed scarcely in a position to do (for I firmly
believe that these stigmata have a preternatural cause), it is permissible
to believe that the impression was usually made at the spot where the
stigmatists believed that Our Saviour received His wounds. This would
appear to be necessary and providential, so that the stigmatist should not
be bewildered at these manifestations and so that they should retain
their mystical meaning for his soul. And let us also own that we
understand nothing about this mystery. If, for example, such an ordeal
was imposed on me, I think that the stigma would be perhaps . . . not
in the wrists, but in the palms of the hands, just in order to teach me
humility!

In any case, the sacred texts, to which we must give our complete
submission, are not so explicit. They do not speak of the palms, but of
the hands. It is for anatomists to say what is meant by the word hand.
Those of every age and every country are agreed on this point: the hand
consists of the wrist, the metacarpus and the fingers.

Now, the wound we are studying is easy to see on the shroud; the
two hands are crossed—the right is extended as far as the outer edge of
the upper part of the right thigh; the left passes in front of the right
wrist, which it conceals completely, and goes a much shorter distance
beyond the mesial line. This would suggest that the right shoulder is
lower than the left, and this can be verified better on the dorsal image.

In passing, let us remember that the wrist is an area whose boundaries are not clearly defined, astride the hand and the forearm, and com-
prising the two rows of bone of the wrist, jointed among themselves,
in addition to the joints connecting them with the forearm and the metacarpus (radio-carpal and carpo-metacarpal). *The forearm comes to an
end and the hand begins at the radio-carpal above the wrist.*

One can only see the four fingers of the two hands. The thumbs do
not appear and we shall see why they are so fixedly turned back, concealed within the palms.

On the back of the right hand, the wrist of which is concealed by the
left, there is no trace of a wound. On the left, which passes in front of

the other, one can on the contrary see a very clear wound, which it is possible to study in detail. It has formed a rounded-off image, from which a broad flow of blood has issued, which mounts obliquely upwards and inwards (anatomically its position is like that of a soldier when challenging), reaching the ulnar edge of the forearm. Another flow, but one more slender and meandering, has gone upwards as far as the elbow. It would seem to have followed a furrow between two extensor muscular groups; here and there it has escaped towards the ulnar edge, by reason of its gravity.

On the cross the large principal flow was, as will be understood, vertical, following the laws of gravity. And one can calculate, by means of the angle formed by this flow and the axis of the forearm, what was the obliquity of the latter on the cross. With the vertical it must have made an angle of about 65°.

This fits in, furthermore, with certain experiments I have made in regard to the possible elongation of the upper limb, which cannot exceed two inches, and certain geometrical constructions which I have carried out. If one supposes that the arms were nailed more or less transversely (and this would happen naturally when the arms were stretched out in order to nail them to the *patibulum*), it would be impossible to lower the body beyond this angle of 65° with the vertical. This is the reason why: there has been a good deal of talk about the arms being lengthened by dislocation, and I have had some difficulty in convincing certain good friends of the shroud who are not, however, versed in anatomy; this is a matter that needs some understanding. Dislocation could only take place in the joints of the shoulder and the elbow. A dislocation of one or the other would shorten the arm and would not lengthen it. Besides, the elbow is a hinged joint which it would be impossible to dislocate simply by pulling it along its axis. In the shoulder, however, the two surfaces, the one, that of the humerus, which is spherical, and the other, that of the shoulder-blade, which is almost flat, can be separated a little if, by a violent pulling, one distends the ligaments of the joint (as one can see happening at the base of a finger when it is pulled and made to crack). This elongation can be increased a little if the shoulder-blade is moved to and fro, but all this will reach four or five centimetres at the most.

On the other hand, if one wishes to determine the necessary elongation of the arm, when the weight of the body moves it from 90° to the angle of its final position, it is only necessary to calculate the length of the hypotenuse of the triangle of which the two other sides are the length of the arm in its original position and the lowering of the shoulder with the body. If we take, as an average length, that there is just under

2 feet between the shoulder and the wound in the hand, a lowering from 90° to 45° would give a hypotenuse of just over 2 feet 6 inches. Then the arm, which began at just under 2 feet, would have been lengthened by about 8 inches. On the other hand, constructions show that between 90° and 65° the arm is only lengthened by 2 inches, and this I consider to be the maximum length. Nothing will be gained by supposing that the original position was oblique and not transversal, for the more the initial position is oblique, so much the more will the same lowering of the body imply a greater elongation of the arm. Thus, from 65° to 45°, with a sagging of about 10 inches, we have an elongation of 4 inches; and from 65° to 35°, with a sagging of just under 2 feet, the arm would be lengthened by 1 foot.

May I be excused for all these figures; I wished to view the problem from every side; anatomy and geometry seem to me to agree with each other; everything concurs in making me think that the arms were nailed more or less transversely and descended to an angle of 65°. And this is precisely the angle which I measured on the shroud.

If one examines the left wrist on the shroud a little more closely one notices that there are two principal flows of blood which have emanated from the same central zone, which is the wound of the nail. These two flows diverge slightly, forming an angle of about 5 degrees. I have given much thought to this strange image (it is the truest and the most instructive in the whole of this study) without discovering its import. I now think I have found it in the changes in the position of the body.

We have already seen in Chapter III, B (The Determining Cause of Death), that hanging by the hands causes a variety of cramps and contractions in the crucified which are described under numerous general headings, stretching to what we know as "tetany." Eventually these reach the inspiratory muscles and prevent expiration; the condemned men, being unable to empty their lungs, die of asphyxia. They can, however, escape for a few moments from this tetany, and from its consequent asphyxia, by lifting the body upwards with the feet as a support. At this moment the knees and the hips are extended, the body is raised, while as a result the angle formed by the forearms with the vertical decreased slightly, in the direction of the original right angle. The body thus alternates, during the agony, between a sagging position and a state of asphyxia and a raised position which brings relief. In each position the vertical flow of blood, which coagulates slowly on the skin, would make a slightly different angle with the axis of the forearm. The flow furthest from the hand, which is at an angle of about 65°, corresponds with the sagging position. The one nearest the hand corresponds with the raised position and gives an angle of from 68° to 70°.

We now come to the subject of my researches: where was the nail driven in? I am prepared to state my conclusion immediately: in the middle of the wrist.

The wound at the back of the left hand, which is the only one that is visible on the shroud, is certainly not at the level of the metacarpus, which would be the case had the nail been driven into the palm. This becomes obvious to an anatomist at the first glance. The beginning of the fingers, which is marked by the head of the metacarpals, is quite visible. The wound is some way off by at least the whole height of the metacarpus.

Neither is it on the forearm. I know well that there are those who hold that the nail was driven into the lower part of the space between the radius and the ulna. But this space narrows down into the angle leading to the lower radio-ulnar joint. This would certainly be a very solid spot to choose, for above the nail there would be the whole solid carpal mass, but one would have to go further up to find a space of $\frac{1}{3}$ of an inch between the radius and the ulna, for this is the breadth of the nail. And this would place the wound at a distance from the wrist which would be incompatible with the image that we have.

I experimented on a forearm which had been amputated from an adult man, completely splitting the radio-ulnar space: the lowest point where the nail could find its way between the bones was 2 inches above the bend of the wrist. This is, however, not in the hand but in the forearm, and the Scriptures will not allow us to place it there.

The great kindness of M. Vignon and of Father d'Armailhac, who both studied the shroud with equal devotion and scientific serenity, has enabled me to ascertain the exact level of the wound. They were able to lend me some life-size photographs of the frontal and dorsal images on the shroud. There is no shadow of doubt that the wound on the back of the left hand, while it is not on the metacarpus, nevertheless is still on the hand; it must therefore be in the wrist. I have measured the distance between the hole and the head of the third metacarpal, on these photographs and on other plates with the measurements marked; it is just over 3 inches.

I shall be brief in dealing with the palm. Were the nail driven into the middle of the palm in the traditional manner, between the third and fourth metacarpals, it would perforate the skin and the palmar aponeurosis, would perhaps injure the superficial arterial palmar arch, slip between the flexor tendons, traverse the interosseous muscles, and would emerge between the extensor tendons. The body when hanging drags on the nail. From what transversal organs can it obtain support? Some transverse fibres of the palmar aponeurosis; a thin transverse palmar ligament before the metacarpal heads; lower down, at the level of the commissure, another little palmar ligament. Those who have dissected hands know that is small enough. *All these organs are vertical.* There remains the skin which would probably tear as the result of the dragging of the body, as far as the commissure.

I have indeed performed the following experiment. Having just amputated an arm two-thirds of the way up from a vigorous man, I drove a square nail of about ⅓ of an inch (the nail of the Passion) into the middle of the palm, in the third space. I gently suspended a weight of 100 pounds from the elbow (half the weight of the body of a man about 6 foot tall). After ten minutes, the wound had lengthened; the nail was at the level of the metacarpal heads. I then gave the whole a moderate shake and I saw the nail suddenly forcing its way through the space between the two metacarpal heads and making a large tear in the skin as far as the commissure. A second slight shake tore away what skin remained.

Now, it was not a weight of 100 pounds but of nearly 240, which was dragging on each nail in the hands of the Crucified, for, as we know, the division of a weight between two oblique and symmetrical forces means that each one is bearing considerably more than half the weight.

I have been able to find the most valuable testimony in an old Italian book which my good friend M. Porché, who is a member of the Committee of the *Cultores Sanctæ Sindonis*, has been able to obtain. Mgr. Paleotti,[1] the Archbishop of Bologna, after he had seen the *Santa Sindone* in Turin in 1578, accompanied by St. Charles Borromeo, produced a detailed description of it, perhaps the first to appear (Bologna, 1598). Attached to it there is a very minute copy of the shroud showing the bloodstained images with their colours. It is the only valid copy that I know of. It is in places a work of the most marvellous intuition, for one has to remember that the author can have known very little about anatomy.

For instance, he demonstrates at some length that the nail emerged "in the joint which anatomists call the *carpus*." *Carpus* is most exact, but he is unaware of the fact that this *carpus* is a bony group made up of eight ossicles, jointed among themselves, the integrant part of the hand, or that the joint of which he speaks, the radio-carpal joint, is above the *carpus*. He then builds up a complete theory, according to

[1] Mgr. Gabriele Paleotti became a Cardinal and at the conclave which elected Gregory XIV he obtained the votes of an important minority. He is best known for the *Diarium* or journal which he kept at the Council of Trent, where he was sent by Pius IV, and which is considered one of the most important works for the history of the Council. He showed great zeal for the Tridentine reforms.

which the nail would have entered the upper part of the palm, but obliquely, pointing towards the arm, and would have emerged in the said "joint." This is anatomically impossible, and I have tested it by experiment. But it was already the *manus* which was disturbing the exegetist. I have lately noticed that certain of my contemporaries seem to be haunted by this concern to reconcile the Scriptures with a *false conception* of anatomy. He adds—and I find this of great interest—that it is certain that the nail was not driven directly into the palm, "because the nail would not have supported the weight of the body but, owing to this weight, the hand would have been torn, as *has been proved by the experiments carried out by talented sculptors on corpses with a view to making a picture.*"

Don Scotti, a Salesian, who is a doctor of medicine and of science, and who collaborated with me in producing the Italian edition of the *Five Wounds* (Turin, 1940), has pointed out to me that these experiments belong, not to the Middle Ages but to the Renaissance—to that very XVIth century which saw the flowering of anatomical studies. This is worthy of note in view of the constantly revived hypothesis that the shroud is the work of some mediæval forger. I thus find myself supported by well-advised and anonymous predecessors, so that I feel confident as to the good sense of humanity in general, and of these artists in particular. It is certain, then, that the nails could not have been driven into the palms without rapidly causing a tear; we must look for another place.

The objection will be made that the body of the Crucified was dragging entirely on the hands. I am not speaking here of the fixing of the feet, which could not appreciably relieve the dragging. The knees were bent and the nail in the feet only supported a negligible part of the weight; its main use was to prevent the feet from leaving the cross. But it has been objected that the arms could have been bound with ropes to the transverse beam of the cross, while the perineum might be resting on the *sedile.* Under these conditions the fixing of the hands would not need to be so solidly done; a part of the weight of the body would be supported by these contrivances. I have not waited to be contradicted, as Père Braun with fairness admits, before putting forward these objections and answering them. When we come to reason the matter out we shall find that we end by eliminating both these possibilities.

As we saw in Chapter II (B, 6°), nailing was the method most frequently used, even for slaves. Binding with ropes was more rare except, perhaps, in certain countries, such as Egypt. There is no text which suggests that nailing and binding with ropes were combined; and, as it was unnecessary, I think one may confidently assume that it was not done.

As for the *sedile,* the existence of which is implied by certain texts, and affirmed by St. Justin, its name is only to be found once, in Tertullian. We have already studied it in Chapter II (B, 4°), and we came to the conclusion that it was far from being regularly used. It was only added to the *stipes* when they intended to prolong the torture to the maximum; it would have just this effect. The crucified could, on account of it, put up a longer resistance to the asphyxiating tetany, as the dragging of the body would not bear entirely on the two hands.

We may then presume, when we take into account that the agony of Jesus was relatively short, that His cross was without this support. Had He been bound with ropes as well, were this not foreign to the history of crucifixion, the agony would have been prolonged.

But it is for another reason that we definitely do not admit that either of these methods was employed, and that is the sagging of the body on the cross.

From now on we can work out the details of the crucifixion exactly as it was carried out. The *patibulum* was carried to the place of execution by the Condemned and, having been dropped on the ground, He would stretch out His arms on it. The arms, as held out by the executioners, would naturally be outstretched parallel with the *patibulum,* making an angle of 90° with the body. The executioners take the measurements and, with some sort of auger, make two holes in the beam. They know that the hands will be easy to pierce but the nails enter less easily into the wood. They then nail one of the hands, hold out the other and nail it as well. The body of Christ already reproduces the T of the cross, with the arms and the *patibulum* at an angle of 90° to the body.

He is then placed once more on His feet, by lifting up the two ends of the *patibulum.* This they lift up and fix on the top of the *stipes,* thus making the cross into a Tau. At that moment the body sags, stretching out the arms, which go from an angle of 90° to 65°. All that remains to be done is to nail the feet, one above the other, as we shall see, with one single nail, bending the knees, which at once take up their sagging position. The angle behind these is of about 120° while the angle in front of the two ends of the legs is of about 150°.

When, in order to escape from asphyxia, the body is straightened out, using the nail in the feet as a support, the arms are raised up towards the horizontal but, according to the shroud, do not go beyond an angle of 70°. The angles of the knees and the ends of the legs open out at the same time. I calculated all these angles of the sagging position without making any experiment but relied on the body dropping 10 inches, which would correspond with a passage of the arms from 90° to 65° (assuming a length of 1 foot 10 inches from the shoulder to the wrist). Afterwards I made the experiment on a dead body and the measurements corresponded exactly to this.

The important thing in all this is the sagging of the body, which drops by 10 inches; it is clear that this sagging can only take place if it is not held up by any *sedile* or bound by any ropes. The sagging has taken place; there must, then, have been no ropes or *sedile;* the body was supported only by the nails in the hands, while the nail in the foot, in the sagging position, would be supporting nothing whatever. We, therefore, need to find a place in the hand where the nails would be able to hold firmly and to uphold this weight of nearly 240 pounds per nail. An executioner who knew his trade would know that the palm of a hand which was fixed by a nail would become torn away.

We must, then, find out where the nail really went. Certainly, according to the shroud, it was not into the metacarpus. It is worth noting as we go along that a forger would certainly have placed it there. In this case, as in that of so many strange images which contradict the ways of iconography, he would have had to conform to the normal customs, since this false shroud was destined for the contemplation of the faithful. It would seem that this forger appears to be more and more clumsy.

When one works one way upwards to the top of the palm, what does one find? A transversal projection consisting of the junction in their upper end of the thenar and hypothenar eminences, the short muscles of the thumb and the little finger. Behind this ridge, there is a small bundle of thick fibrous muscles, as high as the width of a finger, firmly inserted within on to the hamate and the pisiform bones, and outside on to the trapesium and the scaphoid bones. This crossed over the flexor tendons, which it holds firmly in place, closing the carpal canal and giving insertion to the muscles of the two eminences: that is, the transverse carpal ligament of the wrist.

Above this ridge, a hollow appears, which corresponds to the chief bending fold of the wrist; then we have the anterior surface of the forearm. It would therefore seem natural to drive the nail, not into the projection which forms the heel of the hand, but into the hollow lying above it. It is then in the chief bending fold of the wrist that the point is actually placed. This fold is opposite a hole which is marked on the shroud at the back of the wrist, a little more than 3 inches from the head of the third metacarpal.

Now, one can verify that this fold is exactly in front of the upper edge of the transverse carpal ligament, which already forms an extremely resistant transverse frenum; the surgery of the phlegmons of the sheaths teaches us to have a certain respect for it. On the other hand, this upper edge is projected on the wrist, barring the head of the capitate bone. The whole semi-lunar and a little of the triquetral go beyond and above it.

If one examines a frontal cutting of the wrist, and better still a radiograph taken from in front, one finds that in the middle of the bones of the wrists there is a free space, bounded by the capitate, the semi-lunar, the triquetral and the hamate bones. We know this space so well that we know, in accordance with Destot's work, that its disappearance means a dislocation of the wrist, the first stage of the major carpal traumatisms. Well, this space is situated just behind the upper edge of the transverse carpal ligament and below the bending fold of the wrist.

I did not appreciate the importance of all this till I had made the following experiment: having amputated an arm two-thirds of the way up, I took, immediately after the operation, a square nail with sides of ⅓ of an inch (like those of the Passion), the length of which I had reduced to 2 inches for convenience of radiography. The hand was laid flat with its back on a plank, and I placed the point of the nail in the middle of the bending fold of the wrist, the nail being vertical. Then, with a large hammer, I hit the nail, as an executioner would do who knew how to hit hard.

I repeated the same experiment with several men's hands (the first had belonged to a woman). Each time I observed exactly the same thing. Once it had passed through the soft parts, and the nail had entered fully into the wrist, I could feel it, in spite of my left hand which was holding it firmly, moving a little obliquely, so that the base was leaning towards the fingers, the point towards the elbow; it then emerged through the skin of the back of the wrist at about a centimetre above the point of entry, which I observed after removing the nail from the plank. Radiographs were taken at once. I had thought, *a priori*, that the nail would dig deep into the wrist, and would probably pass through the semi-lunar bone, crushing it on its way. The movements of the nail while it was sinking had, however, made me suspect that it had found a more anatomical path.

In fact, in the radiograph taken in profile, the nail, which is a little bit oblique, in a backwards and upwards direction, passes between the projections of the semi-lunar and of the capitate, which remain intact. (Figs. III and IV.) The radiograph taken from the front is even more interesting: the shadow of the square nail appears to be rectangular, on account of its obliquity. The nail has entered into Destot's space; it has moved aside the four bones which surround it, without breaking one of them, merely widening the space. (Figs. III and IV.)

The dissection of the hand confirmed my radiographic results. The point of entry, being a little outside and medial to Destot's space, the point of the nail reached the head of the great bone, slid along its mesial slope, went down into the space and crossed it. The four bones were pushed aside, but were intact and by reason of thus being pushed were closely pressed against the nail. Elsewhere the latter was resting on the upper end of the transverse carpal ligament.

Should one not, as St. John did when telling how Jesus was spared the breaking of the legs, remember the words of the prophet: "*Os non comminuetis ex eo*—You shall not break a bone of him*"?

The point of emergence is thus a little above and a little within the point of entry. If I had driven in the nail a little on the inner side of the bending fold I should have fallen straight into Destot's space, which is a little on the inner side of the axis of the wrist in the axis of the third intermetacarpal space.

The obliquity of the nail pointing backwards and upwards is solely caused by the arrangement of the bony surfaces around Destot's space, for this happened every time during my experiments and in spite of my resistance.

I have, in fact, repeated this experiment a dozen times since then on the hand of an arm which had just been amputated, moving the point of entry all round the middle of the bending fold. In each case the point took up its own direction and seemed to be slipping along the walls of a funnel and then to find its way spontaneously into the space which was awaiting it.

If one tries to drive the nail in further down, into the transverse carpal ligament of the wrist, the latter is not perforated, but one slips underneath and the nail takes an oblique position, whether upwards towards Destot's space or downwards towards the palm, where it disappears and where it cannot receive the weight of a body without tearing the hand.

The last time that I performed on a freshly severed hand I took a bistoury (a kind of thin scalpel) with a blade $\frac{1}{3}$ of an inch long. I pricked it into the bending fold of the wrist, and as I pushed I came through the wrist without effort, emerging at the back of the hand always at the same spot. This spot on the hand of a normal man is always about 3 1/5 inches from the head of the third metacarpal. This is the same distance that I have measured on the shroud.

There must, then, be an anatomical passage already formed, a natural road along which the nail passes along easily and where it is held solidly in position by the bones of the wrist, the latter being held firmly by their distended ligaments and by the transverse carpal ligament, on the upper edge of which it rests.

The effusion of blood would be moderate and almost entirely venous; the nail meets with no important artery, such as the palmar arches, which would have spread out a broad patch of blood on the whole back of the hand laid against the cross and might have brought on a serious hæmorrhage.

Is it possible that trained executioners would not have known by experience of this ideal spot for crucifying the hands, combining every advantage and so easy to find? The answer is obvious. And this spot is precisely where the shroud shows us the mark of the nail, a spot of which no forger would have had any idea or the boldness to represent it.

But these experiments had yet another surprise in store for me. I have stressed the point that I was operating on hands which still had life in them immediately after the amputation of the arm. Now, I observed on the first occasion, and regularly from then onwards, that at the moment when the nail went through the soft anterior parts, the palm being upwards, the thumb would bend sharply and would be exactly facing the palm by the contraction of the thenar muscles, while the four fingers bent very slightly; this was probably caused by the reflex mechanical stimulation of the long flexor tendons.

Now, dissections have revealed to me that the trunk of the median nerve is always seriously injured by the nail; it is divided into sections, being broken sometimes halfway and sometimes two-thirds of the way across, according to the case. And the motor nerves of the oponens muscles and of the short flexor muscle of the thumb branches at this level off the median nerve. The contraction of these thenar muscles, which were still living like their motor nerve, could be easily explained by the mechanical stimulation of the median nerve. *Christ must then have agonised and died and have become fixed in the cadaverous rigidity, with the thumbs bent inwards into His palms.* And that is why, on the shroud, the two hands when seen from behind only show four fingers, and why the two thumbs are hidden in the palms. *Could a forger have imagined this?* Would he have dared to portray it? Indeed, so true is this that many ancient copyists of the shroud have added the thumbs; in the same way they have separated the feet and shown their forward faces with two nail holes; but none of this is to be seen on the shroud.

But, alas, the median nerves are not merely the motor nerves, they are also the great sensory nerves. When they were injured and stretched out on the nails, in those extended arms, like the strings of a violin on their bridge, they must have caused the most horrible pain. Those who have seen, during the war, something of the wounds of the nervous trunks, know that it is one of the worst tortures imaginable; so bad is it that its prolongation would not be compatible with life, without some sort of suspension of the normal functions; this most frequently takes the form of a fainting fit.

Now, Our Saviour, the God-Man, who was able to extend His resistance to the extreme limit, went on living and speaking until the *consummatum est,* for about three hours! And Mary, His Mother and our Mother, was there, at the foot of the cross!

Let us, then, conclude with this thought, by which every Christian who is able to feel compassion must needs be overcome (but which is, nevertheless, no more than the result of strictly objective observation): the nails in the hands were driven into a natural space, generally known as Destot's space, which is situated between the two rows of the bones of the wrist. Now, anatomists of every age and land *regard the wrist as an integral part of the hand,* which consists of the wrist, the metacarpus, and the fingers.

We may then, in accordance with our experimental knowledge, with the shroud and with the Holy Scriptures, repeat after Our Lord, in the strictly anatomical sense, the words: " *Vide manus,*" and after David: " *Foderunt manus meas.*"

Chapter Six

THE WOUNDS IN THE FEET

W E have seen that it was very difficult to fix the place of the wounds in the hands. The question of the feet is a great deal simpler and more easy to solve (Fig. V).

One starts by observing that in the posterior image on the shroud the feet are crossed. The right foot has marked a complete imprint, to which we shall return later. One can see the heel and the middle part of the left; but it disappears obliquely behind the right (and must thus have been in front on the cross), crossing its inner edge, and its forward part is not visible.

It is clear that one must study this closely and study the different photographs, comparing them with each other, if one wishes to arrive at the details; but this crossing of the feet evidently took place from the beginning. The images are complicated by the flows of blood which spread out over almost the whole length of both the feet, in front of and behind the holes of the nail, and these stretch beyond the impressions. It would seem certain that the blood which on the cross had been moving down towards the toes continued to flow, but this time towards the heels, while the body was being carried to the tomb in a horizontal position. On the back half of the sole a part of this has formed clots which have made counter-drawings, but a part must have continued to flow till it reached the shroud, on the outer side of the heel. Furthermore, the linen has formed folds running lengthwise so that there are some clots, and some liquid blood has even transuded on the opposite face of the fold.

One can indeed observe, as regards the feet, that there are symmetrical and inverse images, of which one is entirely on the outside of the impression of the heel and which can only be accounted for by the mechanism of the fold.

Having sorted out these rather complex images we return to the fact that the feet, even in the sepulchre, remain partially crossed. When we take into account what we know about the rigidity of a dead body, this can mean only one thing: that this was even more so on the cross, the left foot being in front, with its sole resting on the upper part of the right foot. Once the nail was removed and the body was laid flat they would tend, owing to the force of gravity, to become parallel once more, but the rigidity would have kept them still slightly crossed. One can also see how, both in the frontal and the posterior image, the left knee and thigh are projected forwards and upwards when compared with the right side.

This cadaverous rigidity would certainly have come on quickly and have been considerable, for we must take into account the fatigues of the agony of Jesus and the contractions which He underwent. A certain effort would have been required to bring the arms back from the position of abduction to that of adduction, with the hands crossed as they are on the shroud. But there was no reason for modifying the position of the feet, since they could enter the tomb in their natural position of crucifixion, crossed and in a state of hyperextension.

This hyperextension, which was due to their being nailed flat on to the *stipes*, distinctly facilitated the very fine impression of the sole of the right foot, since this was lying naturally against the shroud. There has been some rather light talk about the dislocation of the ankles, which in medical terms we call subluxation or luxation. I was even surprised to find this in Hynek's book. It is, however, only necessary to lie down on a plank and to make the experiment *in vivo* to find out about this. The tibiotarsal and the sub-tarsal joints have normal movements which are wide enough to allow for this forced extension. One only has to bind the knees very slightly for the feet to be in natural contact with the ground, with no great difficulty and without pain.

This matter is further facilitated by the varus movement, which brings the point of the foot towards the mesial line, turning the foot over in an inwards direction. This movement takes place in the talocalcanean and the talocalcaneonavicular joints.

We have seen how, in the sagging position, the forward angle of the ankle was one of $150°$. This can be opened even wider by increasing the angle behind the knees to more than $120°$, which brings it nearer to the ground and corresponds with the straightened position.

In all this, I am taking for granted the well-formed foot of a man, with closely-fitting joints, being slack at no point. With the foot of a woman we could reach an even greater extension, but in the case of a man we must resolutely rule out any injury to the joints of the foot, any sprain or any dislocation.

It is worthy of notice that this crossing of the left foot in front of the right is contrary to the custom usually followed by artists; in the vast majority of crucifixes one finds the right foot crossed in front of the left. I have often asked myself what is the reason for this.

The reason is probably æsthetic, and is connected with the all too-frequent habit of depicting the head of Christ as bowed down towards the right. Attempts have been made to explain this attitude symbolically, which seem to me to be somewhat far-fetched: we are told that Jesus being crucified to the north-west of Jerusalem, and facing south (?), would have bowed His head towards the west where the new Church would grow up amongst the Gentiles, thus turning it away from the east and from the Jews who had rejected Him (!). It would be a waste of time to discuss what foundation there is for this symbolism, and we shall not try to do so.

But, looking at this from the point of view of the artist, it is certain that this bowing of the head to the right entails a curve in the whole silhouette of the body, which, in order to balance the whole body harmoniously, must lead to a bending of the right thigh, bringing the right knee forward and thus placing the right foot in front of the left. This was the impression which I received, and several sculptors and painters spontaneously expressed the same idea to me, when I put the question to them.

I would, however, take this opportunity to say that this bowing of the head to the right, as a translation of " *et inclinato capite emisit spiritum* —and bowing His head He gave up the ghost," rests on a physiological error. If the Crucified were still alive, it would be impossible for Him to bow His head to one side, unless He were in the straightened position. If He were sagging, tetany, which affects equally the two muscular masses of the neck, both left and right, would keep His head in a symmetrical position, leaning backwards or forwards, according to whether the sternocleidomastoïd or the trapezius muscles were predominant. After the death, " *inclinato capite,*" we should find that the same equality of the muscular masses, fixed by the cadaverous rigidity in the position of tetany, would keep the head central, symmetrically placed and leaning forwards towards the sternum, with the two sternocleidomastoïds, which are powerful inspiratory muscles, contracted in asphyxia. That is the position which my good friend Dr. Villandre has, acting on my suggestions, given Him in his fine crucifix, and it would seem that this can still be seen on the shroud.

It has also been affirmed that certain artists, from the beginning of the XVth century, among whom we may mention Rubens, had seen the shroud. (We have seen how he, among several others, placed the nails in the wrists.) They may have seen that on the relic the feet were crossed; but as the whole image of the body is in reverse, it gives the impression that the left foot is behind the right. And, if they had not considered how the image would necessarily be inverted, they might have copied the position of the feet, without giving the matter further thought. This is a simple hypothesis—but let us return to the study of the impressions.

The image of the right foot on the posterior image is the most interesting, because it is the most complete. One has to be careful because the markings are far less definite in the region of the heel, and one would, therefore, run the risk of making the foot a little too short. We shall return to this when we are dealing with the bearing to the tomb (Chapter VIII).

When, however, we compare the photographs in various formats and prints in different colours, we are able to trace the posterior outline of the heel. This being so, it is possible to make a counter-drawing of the image of the right foot, by means of which one obtains a very interesting impression of the sole.

Its inner edge is more light and soft half-way along, but shows everywhere a very clear concavity corresponding with the arch of the sole of the foot. The image becomes broader in front; further forward yet one can distinguish five toes clearly marked; the great toe with its long, broad oval, well above the four others, the three next with round outlines, the fifth more or less triangular with its base behind. In short, one is faced with a normal impression of the sole of the foot, such as we can take on a sheet of smoked paper, or which a wet foot would leave on a flagstone. The arch of the sole of the foot is normal, neither flat nor hollow. The toes are slightly spread apart from each other, as one would find in a foot which had never worn boots or shoes, and when walking had always been bare or merely wearing sandals.

On this imprint one can see the clots of flows of blood, spread about in no special order, carmine in colour and standing out against the dark brown of the foot. Half-way along there is a rectangular stain, rather nearer to the inner than to the outer edge of the impression, and this is where the flows seem to have their centre. Some of them go in the direction of the toes. The largest part spreads out towards the heel, and, as we have already stated, reaches beyond the image of the foot, as far as the fold in the shroud.

This four-sided image is certainly the mark of the nail, although Father Noguier de Malijay used to locate the crucifixion in the direction of the heel, and supposed that it was done through the tarsus " by analogy with that of the hand in the wrist." We are in full agreement as regards the hand, although this eminent religious was never able to fix the spot precisely, as he was not in a position to make experiments, but his views in regard to the foot cannot be maintained. In order to nail one tarsus in front of the other, a nail more than 4½ inches long would be needed. Besides, the bones and joints of the tarsus would resist penetration, especially if the two feet were crossed, thus greatly increasing the resistance. Finally, no image is to be seen in the tarsus corresponding with the piercing of the nail.

I have also tried to nail the front tarsus of a freshly amputated foot, which is the least thick part of the tarsal group: *for one foot alone,* I had to strike firmly twenty times with the hammer before I had made my way through the bony group, by going deep into it.

We then still have to locate the hole of the crucifixion. Operative surgery and our special master, Professor Farabeuf, will make this possible for us. Through him we know that Lisfranc's spaceline, which separates the tarsus from the metatarsals, is marked by an oblique line both outside and behind, the ends of which are situated in the middle of the inner edge and in the middle of the outer edge of the foot. Let us measure and trace this, and we shall find that the wound of the nail is immediately in front of Lisfranc's spaceline (Fig. VI).

On the other hand, it is in the axis of the space which separates the second and third toes; we know how, owing to the greater breadth of the first metatarsal, this axis more or less divides the breadth of the first into two equal parts.

We can then conclude with reasonable precision that the nail passed through the posterior part of the second intermetatarsal space. I made an experiment in regard to this. The passage was easy; the nail only met the soft parts, while pushing aside the second and third metatarsals. Behind, the artery of the foot has plunged into the posterior part of the first space. The nail managed to avoid the deep arch of the sole of the foot, which crosses the base of the metatarsals. In any case, the hæmorrhage was not mortal and the blood, which is venous, would have flowed especially after the removal of the nail, which explains the large flow towards the heel which has begun to slope downwards by the dorsal decubitus (Fig. V).

Try this on yourself; lie down, cross the feet, with the left in front of the right, and you will come to understand how things were, as I did. To bend the knees is enough; the flexion need not be very accentuated, thirty degrees from the extended position will suffice. The feet extended, with the toes stretched, can even remain flat, without there being any need for any contrivance such as an oblique shelf, the imaginary *suppedaneum.* As such a contrivance would serve no purpose and would only complicate the crucifixion, it is therefore more than likely that the executioners would not have used it; and they knew their trade. Above the nail was to be found the whole mass of the two tarses; through their strong intermediary, the Crucified was able to lean His weight on the nail when He wished to relieve the dragging on His hands and to lessen His cramps. The thickness which had to be pierced was not very great, and the greater part of the nail was driven into the wood; the nail went through the soft parts easily and without meeting any resistance; finally the hæmorrhage was not great and would not interfere with the prolongation of the torture.

In this chapter we have not yet dealt with the frontal image on the shroud (Figs. VII and VIII). This is because there is far less to be learnt from it. One can see the two knees clearly, at the level of the upper edge of the pieces of linen sewn in by the Poor Clares. The patellas are noticeable, and the left is clearly in front of the right. The legs come next, but the lower parts become less and less distinct, so that the region round the ankles is extremely difficult to decipher. It would seem that the shroud must have become separated from this region and have passed over it rather like a bridge, from the middle part of the legs to the end of the feet.

There is, however, on the back of the feet a large bloodstained image with the shape of an irregular trapeze, which is prolonged at the base by a kind of tail on the left-hand side. This has been explained in various ways. Vignon places it on the back of the left foot and even believes it to be the wound of the nail. I do not agree with this. If one compares the scarcely visible portion of the back of the feet with the image of the soles, it becomes quite clear that the feet, which on the cross were right across each other, have become diverted from this position while still remaining crossed, so that the left foot now only covers the back of the right foot in its forward part, near the points. The back of the right foot should be more or less visible on the forward impression.—Now this bloodstain is certainly in the axis of the right leg.

If one works this out by means of an anatomical construction (taking into account the contour of the thigh and the position of the patellas), or by working out the situation of the ankles on a living man of suitable height, as was done by Antoine Legrand, it would seem likely that this important clot was formed whilst Our Lord was still on the cross, issuing from the wounds in the sole of the left foot and on the back of the right foot. The pressure of the left foot would have spread this blood over the back of the right foot and it would have continued to flow down the furrow between the two feet. Once the nail had been removed, and the two feet had been slightly separated from each other, this clot on the back of the right foot would be completely visible; its trapeze would be prolonged in the furrow, coming to a point near the toes. As for Vignon's nail-hole, I fail to see it.

May I repeat, all this remains rather hypothetical. The weakness of the impressions makes them difficult to decipher, so that separate anatomical constructions are necessary. However, all that one is able to derive from them only confirms the conclusions one has reached from the images on the soles.

Our conclusion is: There was one hole, piercing the two feet crossed one over the other, through the second intermetatarsal spaces, with the right foot against the cross and the left in front. It would seem that one can obtain a symmetrical image of the nail in the impression of the back of the left foot, but much less clearly than on the back of the right foot. The front part not being visible, the marking is less precise; but when compared with the position of the heel, it would seem to be at the same level, both longitudinally and transversally.

Chapter Seven

THE WOUND IN THE HEART

I SAY "wound in the heart" and not wound in the side, because this is attested by tradition, and it has been confirmed for me by experiment. *The blow of the lance which was given to the right side reached the right auricle of the heart, perforating the pericardium.*

"Ad Jesum autem cum venissent (milites), ut viderunt *eum jam mortuum,* non fregerunt ejus crura, sed unus militum *lancea latus ejus aperuit, et continuo exivit sanguis et aqua* " (Jn. XIX, 33, 34).—" But after they (the soldiers) were come to Jesus, when they saw that He was already dead, they did not break His legs. But one of the soldiers with a spear opened His side, and immediately there came out blood and water."

In Chapter II we found the reason for this blow with the lance, in such strange fashion given to a corpse. The body of one who had been executed was legally delivered to the family, once this had been authorised by the judge. But the executioner could not do so till he had made sure it was dead (and if need be, have caused the death, which was not necessary in the present case), by a blow which would open the heart. This action which seems so strange was merely the carrying out of a legal regulation.

This flow of blood and water from the dead body has always deeply moved exegetists and theologians. We find Origen already replying to the idiotic sarcasms of Celsus (*contra Celsum,* II, 36): " I know well that neither blood nor water flows from a corpse; but in the case of Jesus it was miraculous."—This proves, incidentally, that Catholics would do well to rely on a well-established revelation, instead of letting themselves be carried away by the latest pseudo-scientific idea, for fear of appearing to be behind the times, as one sees happen all too frequently; the Church, with her responsible and inspired High Authority, on the other hand, gives them the example of prudence.

As regards the water, we shall see what caused this, without any shadow of doubt. One is, however, astonished to find the strange idea surviving throughout the ages that blood coagulates in a corpse, and that it is only by a miracle that liquid blood can issue from it. Those who were in charge of sacrifices and auspices, on the one hand, and also butchers, would be aware that anyway the greater veins, when opened, produced a flow of blood.

I do not wish to pile up texts, but I find this error confirmed by Mgr. Paleotto, the Archbishop of Bologna, in his *Description of the Holy Shroud* (1598) to which I have already referred. " Real blood and real water," he writes, " issued from the breast of the Redeemer . . . . and issued after death; this was an admirable thing, as St. Ambrose remarks, who holds that it was a miracle, saying . . . . that after death the blood normally coagulates in a corpse." And he quotes St. Ambrose (*In Luc*, cap. 23): " It was miraculous for blood to issue from a corpse . . . . for, to be sure, after death, the blood coagulates in our bodies— *Nam utique post mortem sanguis in nostris corporibus congelascit.*" In Mgr. Paleotto's eyes it was even more miraculous that blood and water could issue at the same time though distinct from each other, when they should have mingled very closely.

Father Lagrange, the eminent exegetist, to whom I owe the quotation from Origen, writes in his commentary on St. John the following remarks about this issue of blood and water:— " John also knew this (that it was miraculous) and that is why he insisted so strongly that it had been seen by an eye-witness. We shall, therefore, not try to provide a physiological explanation which would more or less meet the facts. But precisely because he regards the fact as miraculous and because he bears witness to its reality, we have not the right to say it only has a symbolic value. It is the reality which is important above all, as the foundation of the symbol."—May I be forgiven if I seem to lay down the law, but I fail to see that St. John declares that there was a miracle. He certainly seems to be astonished, but is not the issue of water alongside the blood the cause of this? Does he not mean: there issued blood, and also water? Perhaps he knew that blood can issue from a corpse; but the water would seem extraordinary to him, as at first it would even to a doctor in our day.

As for the symbolical explanations which all the Fathers have superadded to this real fact which has been so solemnly affirmed, these are too numerous for me to deal with them and would draw me away from my subject. They all have the redemption and purification in view. Let us content ourselves with a very beautiful one from St. Jerome, which is not quoted by Father Lagrange: " *Latus Christi percutitur lancea, et Baptismi atque Martyrii pariter Sacramenta fundantur* "

(Epist. 83, *ad Oceanum*). This double flow consecrates at the same time the Baptism of water and the Baptism of blood of the martyr.

What part of the side received the blow with the lance? There is a steady tradition that it was on the right side of the chest; this is all the more important in that there is a generally held opinion, even in our day, that the heart is on the left, which is not the case. The heart is mesial and in front, resting on the diaphragm, between the two lungs, behind the sterno costal mass, in the anterior mediastinum. Only its point is definitely to the left, but its base extends to the right beyond the breastbone.

Here are two examples of this tradition that the blow was on the right side. St. Augustine writes in his *City of God* (Lib. XV, cap. 26): "*Ostium in latere dextro accepit, profecto illud est vulnus, quando latus crucifixi lancea vulneratum est*—A door was opened in His right side, which is surely the wound when the side of the Crucified was wounded by the lance." Pope Innocent III (1190-1216) writes (*Lib. Myster. Evangel.*, Lib. II, cap. 58): "*Calix ponitur ad dextrum oblatæ latus, quasi sanguinem suscepturus, qui de latere Christi dextero creditur profluisse*—The chalice is placed to the right of the oblation (the Host), as if to receive the blood which we believe to have flowed from the right side of Christ."

But let us be content with the account in the Gospel: "One of the soldiers with a spear opened His side and immediately there came out blood and water" (Jn. XIX, 34). I sought in anatomy and in experiment for the explanation of this text, and this is what I found:

The shroud bears clear marks of this wound on the left side, and as the images are reversed, this means that it was on the right.

It is a curious thing that, in spite of the common prepossession which places the heart on the left, when in fact only its point beats there, nobody has ever quarrelled with me over this question of the side. Better still, nobody has ever brought forward the fact of the stigmatists as an objection. St. Francis, it is true, had his wound on the right. But since his day numerous stigmatists have had their wound on the left, as, for example, Theresa Neumann. The change of the side is more remarkable than the variation in the part of the hands used, and various explanations have been put forward . . . which explain nothing. Here is an example: the stigmatist in this case would place his wound on the side facing the wound of Jesus, whom he is contemplating. Rather than put forward such scientific theories I would prefer to own that this is beyond the domain of science and to respect the mystery of these phenomena. This supports the opinion which I have worked out in regard to the wounds in the hands: the stigmata have a purely mystical significance and in no sense can they be regarded as a more or less exact reproduction of the five wounds of the Passion.

On the frontal image of the shroud (Figs. I, VII and VIII) one can see on the left side (thus on the right side of the corpse) a very large flow of blood which is partly hidden on its outer edge by a piece of linen sewn on by the Poor Clares of Chambéry after the fire of 1532. It spreads out above to a breadth of at least 2¼ inches and comes downwards, undulating and narrowing, for at least 6 inches. Its inner edge is curiously cut about by some rounded indentments which, in a flow of blood on a motionless and vertical corpse, are at first hard to explain. It does not spread out in a homogeneous fashion and there are even some gaps.

No painter has thought of portraying such an irregular flow of blood. Nevertheless, this corresponds with reality and, once again, it is the imagination of the artists which is at fault. Only nature and in consequence the shroud could be so true and exact.

My friend Antoine Legrand had the ingenious idea, after he had traced the points of reference which we shall settle later in accordance with the shroud, of painting the wound of the heart, and the clot which had formed below it, on the muscular chest of a man of the same build as Our Lord. The painting was made, as will be understood, in the position of burial, with the hands crossed above the hypogastrium. He then made him take the position of crucifixion, with the arms at 65°. Now, in this position, he immediately saw the middle ribs protruding, and on each of these the anterior end of a digitation of the sarratus magnus muscle. Each one of these muscular protrusions, which are, however, well known by artists, corresponded with each undulation of the edge of the clot. Why did they not think of this? Because they were painting flows of blood; because they were ignorant of the physiology of coagulation; because they did not know that the blood would spread out, would become slower in its descent and would coagulate more easily into a larger clot at the level of each of these intermuscular hollows. Would I have thought of this myself, even knowing all that I do?

When the shroud is seen by the light of day the stain, like all the blood-stained imprints, stands out against all the rest of the impression, which is dark-brown in colour. There must clearly have been at this spot an important flow of blood, of which a large part would have fallen on the ground and the rest would have coagulated on contact with the skin, in successive layers. The upper part of the clot, that nearest to the wound, is the thickest, just as it is the broadest. This, as we have said already, is a normal fact of experience among surgeons. The contrary effect is produced when the blood is halted in its descent above some obstacle, as on the forehead after the crowning with thorns.

On the upper part of the blood-stained image, one can clearly distinguish, on the original as on the photographs, an oval stain with a main axis going slightly obliquely upwards and outwards, which is distinctly the impression of the wound in the side, from which the blood issued. The greatest axis of this wound is just under 2 inches in length, while it has a height of about two-thirds of an inch. It was the markings of this which were taken, so as to reproduce them on another body.

I made counter-drawings and took measurements from the life-size photographs which were placed at my disposition by M. Vignon and Father d'Armailhac. On these very fine proofs one can clearly see the protrusion of the pectoral muscles and one can even distinguish the nipples without difficulty. The inner end of the wound is 4 inches below and a little to the outside of the nipples, on a horizontal line running just under 4 inches below it. But the nipple is not a fixed point of reference. In a body, only the parts of the skeleton can be definitely located. I have, therefore, made my researches on the side of the breast-bone.

At the base of the neck, a series of spread-out stains can be seen, of which the mesial one certainly represents the sub-sternal hollow; the others, which are lateral, correspond to the sub-clavicular hollows (commonly known as the salt-boxes). The lower edge of the mesial stain thus obviously marks the upper edge of the breast-bone.

In the epigastric hollow there is a vertical stain, an irregular rectangle in shape, divided and vaguely marked in its lower part, which discloses fairly clearly the hollow situated between the two great pectoral muscles, and of which the base rests on the xyphoid process. The upper edge of this stain is thus the lower end of the breast-bone. Lower down, one can see the impression of the umbilicus (navel): the hands are crossed below this again, and in this *ensemble* the proportions seem to be absolutely correct and harmonious. One can even, on the sides, discern the costal borders which overhang the hypochondrium. The base of the stain on the right side comes down below the costal margin, reaching the abdominal wall.

The breast-bone is thus fixed at a height of just over 7 inches, which is not at all exaggerated in a man about 6 feet high. All that remains to be done is to locate the wound in relation to the mesial line and the point of the breast-bone (the lower end), which can easily be worked out on another body.

Now, the lower and inner extremity of the wound runs horizontally about two-fifths of an inch below the point and is just under 2½ inches from the mesial line. The upper and outer extremity runs horizontally one-fifth of an inch below the point and is about 6 inches from the mesial line. We thus have the wound located; we now only have to apply this to a live body, taking radiographs, and to dead bodies, experimenting by dissection. Before starting these experiments let us have one more glance at the shroud, which shows on this side two abnormal images that at first sight would appear to be errors; we shall come to see that they are the most instructive.

It has been noticed for a long time that the right arm was not in the same position as the left. The elbow is clearly lower and further out on the right than on the left. Attempts have been made to explain this anomaly by the fact that the right shoulder is itself a little lower. This is certainly the case and different reasons have been suggested for it, from the dislocation (?) of the shoulder joint to the professional deformation to be found in right-handed workmen, whose right shoulder would normally be slightly lower. This last fact, which has been brought forward by Dr. Gedda, may well be true but it is certainly insufficient.

In fact, even taking it into account, the fact remains that the right arm is longer than the left and, above all, the right forearm is also longer than the left forearm. Furthermore, the protrusion of the great right pectoral muscle is clearly broader than that of the left. There is thus a displacement of the right elbow in the outward direction, with an apparent lengthening of the right arm and forearm. This is peculiar and would indicate considerable lack of skill in a painter of genius!

But there is more than this. When, as we shall soon do, we come to mark the wound of the heart on the thorax of a vigorous man 6 feet high, in accordance with our points of reference, we shall observe that this wound is to be found on the side of the thorax, clearly behind the forward sternocostal surface. If we stretch out a piece of linen on his chest we shall observe that it forms a bridge over this forward surface, resting on the protrusion of the right arm placed in the position of burial. It does not touch the wound of the heart, nor the clot lying directly below it. Stranger still, for unless there was direct contact the wound and the clot would have been unable to make a counter-drawing. Now, the counter-drawing is a very good one.

But supposing that a hand made the quite natural gesture of leaning on this stretched-out linen in order to lay it against the wound of the heart, in the brachio-thoracic hollow, this hand would forcibly draw inwards some of the material which was on the arm, and this would leave an impression on an area rather to the outside of the original one. Now stretch out the shroud once more, as we see it to-day. The impression of the right elbow is rather to the outside of where it ought to be, further out than the left elbow. The right arm, and especially the forearm, is longer than on the corpse, and at the same time there appears a magnificent counter-drawing of the clot of the heart.

I am once more indebted for this demonstration to my friend Antoine Legrand (*Dossiers du Saint Suaire*, Paris, Nov., 1939). What forger would have been astute enough to imagine these deceptive impressions? But let us return to our experiments.

1°. *On a Living Body—the Radiographs.*

I cut out a little metal plate of the same shape and size as the wound and I fixed this on certain of my pupils, whom I chose because they would have been of about the same height as the Christ, at the exact spot marked by the measurements which I have quoted. I then had teleradiographs made in the Hôpital Saint-Joseph (with a four metre ampoule) so as to obtain images which were perceptibly ortho-diagrammatical, of the same dimensions as the body which was being radiographed. I reproduced one of these radios by means of a diagram, only including the front part of the skeleton and of the visceral shadows for the sake of greater clearness.

As could be seen, the little plate stood out, fairly well to the outside, against the sixth rib, and extending beyond the fifth right intercostal space. The measurements gave much the same figures as on the shroud. Behind the breast-bone, which was only clearly visible in its upper part, one could see the cardio-pericardial shadow (the heart), with the shadow of the great blood-vessels rising above (the aorta and the superior vena cava). The right part of the heart extended noticeably beyond the right edge of the breast-bone. The heart rested on the hepatodiaphragmatic shadow (the liver). Below the left diaphragm the gaseous sac of the stomach was outlined. The right convexity of the heart was 8 centimetres away from the centre of the wound, following a somewhat oblique line going inwards and upwards. The wound was definitely above the mass of the liver.

The lance must then have entered above the sixth rib, have perforated the fifth intercostal space and penetrated deeply beyond it. With what would it then have met? The pleura and the lung. If St. John's soldier had given the blow with his lance in an almost vertical direction, he would, first of all, have scarcely been able to perforate the intercostal space; if he had, the point of his lance would have become lost in the lung, in which he would only have been able to draw blood from a few pulmonary veins. He might have caused a great deal of blood to flow, but no water. The pleural fluid, if there was any, would have been necessarily accumulated at the base of the pleural cavity, which was behind and below the level of the wound. What I have in mind, as will be understood, is hydrothorax or dropsy of the chest, the pleural fluid which would be transuded as the result of the death agony, which we shall find in the pericardium. The hypothesis which was put forward some time ago in *La Folie de Jésus,* that there was tuberculous pleurisy, was intended by its author to be blasphemous; it was in fact merely untenable. We shall come back to this shortly.

The blow with the lance was then oblique and not far off the horizontal, which is easy to understand if the cross, as I think, was not very high. If it was more than 6 feet high, which I think most unlikely, a horseman would have been needed to deal the blow. But the executioners and the guards, that is to say the soldiers who were probably sent by Pilate for the *crurifragium,* were all foot-soldiers; nor was the centurion a mounted officer. If the cross was less than 6 feet high, as I believe to have been the case, a foot-soldier had only to stand in the position of the challenge, as we used to say when doing bayonet drill, in order to deal the blow with his lance correctly.

This blow at the heart from the right was always mortal, and must have become classical and have been taught in the fencing-schools of the Roman armies; all the more so in that the left side was usually protected by the shield. I have also discovered, when re-reading Cæsar's Commentaries (*De Bello Gallico,* Lib. I, 25, 6—Lib. VII, 50, 1—*De Bello Civili,* Lib. III, 86, 3), that the expression "*latus apertum*—the side *being opened,*" were the classical words for denoting the right side. Farabeuf used to teach us that blows into the intercostal spaces on the right edge of the breast-bone do not allow of recovery, because they open up the very thin wall of the right auricle. And this is still true to-day, even when a surgeon can intervene quickly.

And then: the point moved naturally across the thin, forward part of the right lung and, according to the radiographs, after a course about 3 inches in length, reached the right border of the heart enveloped in the pericardium.

Now, *and this is the important side of the question,* the part of the heart which extends to the right of the breast-bone *is the right auricle.* And this auricle, which is prolonged upwards by the superior vena cava, and downwards by the inferior vena cava, is *in a corpse always filled with liquid blood.*

Jesus, as we read at the beginning in the text of the Gospel, was quite dead at the time of the blow with the lance. It would also seem that Saint John was thoroughly aware of the importance of this fact, for he continues, with an insistence that is significant, and which reminds one of the first lines of his Gospel: *Et qui vidit testimonium perhibuit, et verum est testimonium ejus. Et ille scit quia vera dicit, ut et vos credatis* "—" And he that saw it hath given testimony; and his testimony is true. And he (Jesus) knoweth that he saith true; that you also may believe " (Jn. XIX, 35).[1] Father Lagrange says that the Greek " *ekeinos* " for the second " he " refers to Our Lord, whom St. John cites as a witness to the truth of his testimony.

If the blow with the lance had been given from the left it would have pierced the ventricles, which in a corpse have no blood in them. There would have been no flow of blood but only of water, as we shall see. But the shroud tradition and reasoning would place the wound on the right. We now have only to experiment on a dead body, which has fresh surprises in store for us.

2°. *On a Dead Body.—The Experiments.*

(*a*). *The Blood.*—I have repeated various experiments on dead bodies on which I was conducting autopsies. First of all I took a long needle mounted on a large syringe. I made for the level of the wound and I rapidly inserted the needle into the fifth right interspace, while all the time I was drawing into the syringe; I was pointing upwards and slightly towards the back. At between 3.8 and 4 inches I entered the right auricle and as I drew into the syringe I filled it with liquid blood. As long as I was passing through the lung no liquid was drawn into the syringe, either blood or water.

I then, under the same conditions, thrust in a large amputation knife. At the same depth it opened the right auricle and the blood flowed down the blade through the tunnel which had been made in the lung.

I would recall at this point that Donnadieu, with his passion for denial, held that the blood could not flow outwards, as it would accumulate in the open pleura, owing to the contraction of the lung. However, he forgot one thing, which is that in a dead body (and Jesus was dead) the lung does not contract and the two pleural layers remain adherent if one opens the pleura. On the other hand, the pulmonary tunnel remains gaping open and the blood from the heart continues to flow after the knife has been withdrawn.

All my experiments, as will be understood, were followed by dissection and were performed on bodies which had been dead for more than twenty-four hours.

(*b*). *The Water.*—The blood then comes quite naturally from the heart and it could only come from there in such a quantity. But whence comes the water?

---

[1] Mgr. Knox translated this verse:—" He who saw it has borne his witness; and his witness is worthy of trust. He tells what he knows to be the truth, that you, like him, may learn to believe."

In my first autopsies I noticed that the pericardium always contained a quantity of serum (hydropericardium) sufficient for one to see it flowing on the incision of the parietal layer. In some cases it was most abundant.

I, therefore, took my syringe once again, but I pushed the needle *very slowly*, drawing into the syringe the whole time. I was thus able to feel the resistance of the fibrous pericardium, and as soon as I had perforated it, I drew out a considerable quantity of serum. Then, as the needle proceeded on its way, I drew out some blood from the right auricle.

I then took my knife, and, inserting it with the same precautions, I saw the serum flowing and then, as I pressed on, the blood.

Finally, if one inserts the knife vigorously, a large flow of blood is seen to issue from the wound; but on its edges one can also see that a lesser amount of pericardial fluid is also flowing.

The water was then pericardial fluid. And one may imagine that after an exceptionally painful death-agony, as was that of the Saviour, this hydropericardium would have been particularly abundant, so much so that St. John, who was an eye-witness, was able to see both blood and water flowing. He would have imagined that the serum was water, for it has that appearance. As there was no other water in the body than the serous fluid, it could not have been pure water. We ourselves use the word hydropericardium, which means the water contained in the pericardium.

These experiments on the heart were continued in 1937 by Dr. Judica, who was then *libero docente* in pathological anatomy in the Faculty of Milan, after he had read the first edition of my *Cinq Plaies* (Five Wounds). I remember that my first article on the subject appeared in the *Bulletin de Saint-Luc,* in March, 1934. My experiments took place with various intervals in 1932 and 1933.

My friend Judica, in his article in *Medicina Italiana* (Milan, 1937), fully confirms the results of my experiments, with which his own agree. He also found that the blood came from the right auricle and the water from the pericardium; this confirmation was made quite independently, as at that time we did not know each other, and it was all the more valuable to me, in that it came from such an eminent anatomopathologist.

We are, however, not fully in agreement as to the origin of this hydropericardium. I put forward the hypothesis of a hydropericardium produced by the death agony. But I must own that, without vanity as an author, I do not cling to this pathogenic explanation, if experiments should end by showing that Judica is right.

He holds that there was a " serous traumatic pericarditis "; this was brought on by the blows and the cudgelling, and the terrible scourging in which the chest was injured. Such violence could certainly cause pericarditis, which, after a short period of hyperhæmia, frequently not more than a few hours, would produce a *rapid and abundant* serous discharge.

A doctor can well imagine all the grave disorders which such a lesion would bring about: dreadful pains in the region of the heart, oppression, anguish, rigor, fever, and finally intense difficulty in breathing, which would be superadded to the asphyxia caused by the tetany of the inspiratory muscles. This explains His extreme weakness on the way up to Calvary. He was not even able to carry His cross, which was reduced to the *patibulum,* for the 600 yards separating the Prætorium from Golgotha, and Simon had to replace Him. This also partly explains His falls on the way of the cross.

Anyway, whatever the cause may have been, there was a hydro-pericardium, and here Judica and I are in full agreement.

(c) *The inferior Vena Cava.*—We have then explained, with reasonable chances of accuracy, the origin of the blood and water, *but that is not all.* On the dorsal image of the shroud one can see a largish trail at the base of the thorax, stretching the whole way across; on the right side it is fairly broad, and then divides up into little streamlets, as it nears the left side of the trunk. This trail is caused by a flow of blood, for I was able to observe its special colour, which is reddish in tint, by the light of day. Whence came this blood and why did it flow transversally? Once again, anatomy will give us the reason for this.

At the moment of the blow with the lance the dead body was attached to the cross in a vertical position. The right auricle was able to empty itself and probably also the superior vena cava, which is above it with its branches, the veins of the head and of the arms. The large flow is produced on the forward side of the chest vertically, below the wound. But the inferior vena cava, which lies below it, has remained full. It is long and broad and we know that when it is cut in an autopsy there is at once a regular flood of blood in the stomach.

Now, when Joseph of Arimathea returned, the feet would have been unfastened from the *stipes,* the *patibulum* would have been unhooked and both *patibulum* and body would have been carried, *horizontally,* to the tomb. The blood of the inferior vena cava would then have flowed back into the right auricle and, going through the tunnel made by the lance, which remained gaping open, would have flowed out. But as the dead body was horizontal this fresh flow would slip round the right side and would continue to flow transversally *on the back, going right across the lower part of the thorax.* We shall return to this image when dealing with the carrying to the grave (Chapter VIII).

3°. *The Coagulation of the Blood.*

As St. John reminds us, the prophet Zacharias had truly predicted: *" Videbunt in quem transfixerunt."*

At this point I would refer once again to some elementary notions about physiology which hold good in regard to all wounds, for I have often observed that they are not widely known, even by very erudite people who, however, are not doctors: *the blood remains liquid and never coagulates in a vessel that is still undamaged.* (The thrombus which appears in a vein attacked by phlebitis is an entirely different phenomenon.) It remains liquid, even in the veins of a corpse, and this for an almost indefinite period, till putrefaction or desiccation sets in. (See Chapter I, E, 1°.)

It remains *alive* for a period, and in Russia *blood transfusions have been made from a corpse.* The fact that this is not done in France is probably due to sentimental reasons. It is certainly also due to a lack of suitable subjects. It is necessary to have healthy people whose blood group has been ascertained beforehand and whose death, foreseen and legally caused, is due to a not too serious traumatism of the blood system, as, for instance, death by the guillotine (and in our day few people are guillotined). The revolver shot into the back of the head is therefore necessary.

The blood coagulates when it has emerged from the vessel. In the case before us it spreads out while still in a liquid state, flowing over the skin. And it is on this that the part of the flow which has not dropped to the ground coagulates progressively, forming a fibriorous clot, which is red because it retains red blood cells in its meshes. Secondly, this clot contracts, exuding its liquid part, the serum, which spreads out around it. Both clot and serum can stain the linen which is lying against the skin, the one in the centre, the other in the periphery. But one must not speak of flows of clots and serum. *Liquid blood flows; the clot forms on the skin,* adheres to it, dries there.

It is important to be precise about this, especially when studying the wound in the heart, which must on two occasions have emptied out all the blood in the great veins; this would mean a considerable volume, for in a corpse the arteries are empty. It is certain that a large part of this blood must have dropped to the ground. That which remained and formed the two stains, both in front and behind, was merely the small amount which coagulated on the skin, to which it adhered owing to its viscous quality, and to which the clot will remain attached.

4°. *Other Hypotheses.*

This brings me to two hypotheses, neither of which is, in my opinion, admissible.

(*a*) It is the view of Dr. Stroud and Dr. Talmage, who agree with an imaginative idea of Renan's, that the heart of Christ broke spontaneously. The blood would then have flooded the cavity of the pericardium and coagulated there. The blow with the lance which opened the pericardium, without reaching the heart (well aimed and well controlled!), would have caused clot and serum to emerge; this serum would have been the water mentioned by St. John. This thesis cannot be sustained, though it has its attractions on the pseudo-mystical side—excess of love having caused the heart of Jesus to break. But:—

(1) This would infer a serious disease of the muscular structure of the heart (infarct, a waxy degeneration). There is nothing in the Gospels to infer that Jesus suffered from such an ailment.

(2) A healthy serous pericardium will for a long time preserve the blood which has flown into it, free from coagulation. This is a fact which has been proved by experience. My friend René Benard informs me that if one takes some blood from the ventricle of a laboratory guinea-pig with a needle, and owing to a movement of the animal at the wrong moment the needle makes a tear in the heart, the guinea-pig dies of hæmopericarditis (the flow of blood into the pericardium). But if one conducts an autopsy, even a number of hours later, one always finds that the blood is *liquid.*

This coincides with an observation which I came across by chance in the *Archives de Médecine Légale* (Dec., 1936), alongside a very fine communication from Dr. Belot, on the subject of the shroud of Turin: Dr. Bardou (of Tunis), who was conducting the autopsy (this more than twenty-four hours after death) on a man who had been killed by contusion of the thorax, found a burst at the point of the heart, and the pericardium distended by perfectly liquid blood.

(3) The blow with the lance was given only a very short time after death; less than two hours, says Strood, and we agree with him. It is certain that *liquid* blood, and not serum and clots, would issue from this so-called hæmopericardium due to cardiac rupture.

(*b*) Another hypothesis, as we have mentioned, was put forward a long time ago, in a pamphlet which was as detestable as it was absurd. This book, which unfortunately bore the signature of a doctor, was called *La Folie de Jésus* (The Folly of Jesus) and set out to prove that Our Lord was both of unsound mind and suffering from tuberculosis. The water would then have come from the serum of tuberculous pleurisy. I will not give the author the honour or the posthumous publicity of quoting his name.

This idea of ambulatory pleurisy has recently been upheld by Dr. René Morlot (*Revue Médicale de Nancy*, August-September, 1949), a veteran in pathological anatomy; but this time with the complete love and respect that one would expect in a convinced Christian. He furthermore accepts all our other conclusions, such as that the blood issued from a wound in the right auricle. I should be ashamed not to try and argue with him in all justice and sympathy; we are both seeking for the truth.

He seems to believe that according to St. John first blood and then water issued from Our Lord's side. There is nothing to this effect in the Gospel, which says: "And immediately there came out blood and water—*Kai exèlthen euthus aima kai udór*," which would indicate that they came out at the same time. One could even translate it: "blood and also water."

Besides, even without reference to the Holy Shroud or to tradition, it is certain that the lance struck in front, for the back was protected by the cross; high enough to reach the heart; on the right, so as to open the right auricle, the only cavity of the heart which could give out blood (the left auricle is deep down, and would be out of reach).

Now, a pleural effusion first accumulates in the posterior part of the pleura, which stretched down a long way, in front of the eleventh rib. The pleural sac ascends from there on a steep slope, forwards and upwards, to rejoin the base of the pericardium. There would then have to be a considerable quantity of the pleural fluid for its level to extend beyond the place where the wound of the heart would be. Such a quantity is scarcely compatible with the active life led by Jesus during those last weeks.

But, besides, there is nothing in the Gospels that in any way suggests to a doctor that during His public life (of which we have abundant details), Jesus suffered from any such disease. On the contrary, having been a workman for thirty years, He was leading the life of a wandering teacher, which must have entailed much hardship and weariness. He had to endure hunger, thirst, heat and fatigue, yet we find no trace of illness. One would imagine rather that He must have been robust, with an excellent constitution; on the shroud we are shown a man 6 feet in height, with a splendid physique.

Dr. Morlot points out most correctly that according to the Catholic Church the body of Jesus was not impassible, but the Conciliar decrees which he quotes (Ephesus, 431, Florence, 1438) have in view the

Monophysite heresies, according to which the body of Jesus was only an appearance and was incapable of suffering.

St. Thomas Aquinas, to whom he appeals (IIIa, Q. XIV), says quite rightly that Jesus assumed (voluntarily and not owing to birth, since He was exempt from original sin) a human nature, with its *defectus corporis,* its bodily failings. But he enumerates these: hunger, thirst, death and other similar things. Illness is not mentioned. It would seem that He could have accepted illness if He had consented to it. But the majority of Catholic theologians hold that He did not do so as it was not fitting. In any case, the fact remains that there is not a trace of it in the Gospels. We would also point out that illness is a possibility and not an unavoidable necessity for human nature. On the other hand, a traumatism or a blow will always cause lesions.

All these arguments would seem to me to rule out the hypothesis of a tuberculous pleurisy and bring us back to our experiments and to hydropericardium.

Yes, St. John was certainly clear-sighted. What he saw was the blood from the auricle and the water from the pericardium. I also have seen them, *et verum est testimonium meum.*

Chapter Eight

THE DESCENT FROM THE CROSS, THE JOURNEY TO THE TOMB AND THE ENTOMBMENT

T HIS chapter was written for the doctors of the *Société de Saint Luc* (Bulletin of March, 1938). I apologise for its avowedly dry and didactic note, as in a scientific demonstration.

I have always been a little shocked by the slightly brutal way in which artists represent the descent from the cross. Even my old friend Fra Angelico, the most mystical and Catholic of painters, is not altogether guiltless in this matter; and yet God alone knows how often I have meditated in front of his moving triptych, which is nowadays in the pilgrim's hostel of San Marco, Florence. It is true that the poor disciples of Jesus—Joseph, Nicodemus and the others—show deep affection; yet they would seem to be reduced to actions more worthy of executioners, which must have made their grief, already so violent, become almost desperate.

Now, the study of the Holy Shroud has led me to an entirely different conclusion and one far removed from the usual traditional iconography. Indeed, it is my belief that these good men were able to take the body down from the cross and to bear it to the tomb with infinite delicacy, respect and tenderness. They can scarcely have dared to touch that adorable body.

Many Catholic colleagues, having read the first two editions of the *Cinq Plaies*,[1] have either said or written to me that this study was for them the finest meditation on the Passion. I, therefore, thought it would be useful, while keeping within the sphere of science, to outline for them this new subject for reflection, one which in my opinion is no less suggestive; after the sufferings of the Passion and the cruelty of the executioners we still have before us the majesty of that dead body, in which the Divinity still resides, and at the same time we can watch the tender piety of the disciples.

They will, however, be content with a scientific exposition, from which

[1] *The Five Wounds of Christ.* (Clonmore & Reynolds.)

they may draw their own ascetical conclusions, and reap the spiritual fruit.

A.—*It is certain that the body of Christ was borne horizontally, but as it was on the cross, from this to the neighbourhood of the tomb; it was not till then that it was placed on the shroud.*

In fact, if it had been otherwise, the back part of the shroud would have been drenched with the blood from the inferior vena cava, during the period of the journey. On the contrary, the journey lasted long enough for the inferior vena cava to be able to empty itself through the wound in the heart. One day, when I was explaining this question in the neighbourhood of La Villette, I met with the enthusiastic agreement of the officials from the abattoirs. They knew from experience that when they open up an ox, empty it and take out the liver, the section concerned of the lower vena cava gives out a flow of black blood. (" What's the reason, doctor? Well, one knows why!")

The greater part of the blood was then lost (or was collected before they came to touch the body). Only that remained which coagulated on the skin, to a limited extent, while it was flowing. After the body had been carried naked, and had been laid, after the journey, on the shroud, the latter received *only the impression of the clots of blood formed on the skin of the back during the journey.* Only these clots of blood have imprinted on the shroud what we call the dorsal transversal flow, because these clots are its mark.

B.—It is certain that the journey was carried out with a minimum of handling, in such a way that the clots remained in their place, unmoved. If there had been more handling, or had it been less delicate, they would have been wiped away and obliterated.

C.—*In what fashion, then, was Jesus Christ borne, so that His body was not touched?*

1.—We have demonstrated the two following facts (Chapters II and III):—

(*a*) The *patibulum* (the horizontal part of the cross) *was mobile;* the hands of Jesus were nailed on to the *patibulum,* while He was lying on the ground. This was then lifted with the body on to the top of the *stipes* which was permanently fixed in the ground on Golgotha.

(*b*) Death occurred, as Dr. Le Bec has written (*Le Supplice de la Croix,* Paris, March, 1925), and as has been finally established by experiment and observation, by Dr. Hynek (*La Passion du Christ,* Prague, November, 1935), following tetanic contraction of all the muscles. This has no connection with tetanus (I stress this for the sake of those who are not doctors), an infectious disease which produces similar cramps. This tetanisation ended by reaching the respiratory muscles, thus causing asphyxia and death. The condemned man could only escape from asphyxia by straightening himself on the nail of the feet, in order to lessen the dragging of the body on the hands; each time that he wished to breathe more freely or to speak, he had to raise himself on this nail, thus bringing on further suffering. This hypothesis, which, as I have said, is based on the observation of a form of corporal punishment (by Dr. Hynek), which in Hitler's deportation camps was increased to the point of murder, is a most probable one; it is confirmed on the shroud by the jutting forward of the thorax and the concavity of the epigastrium.

We have also seen how the double flow of blood from the wrist corresponds with this double position, with its two slightly divergent angles.

Under these conditions *the rigidity of the corpse would be extreme*, as in the case of those who have died of tetanus: the body was rigid, fixed in the position of crucifixion. They would be able to raise it without its sagging, merely by holding the two extremities, as with a body in a state of catalepsy.

2.—This being so, it would be possible: (*a*) to free the feet by drawing out the nail from the *stipes*; (*b*) to lower the *patibulum* with the body still rigid; (*c*) to carry the whole without using any contrivance; two men could hold the two ends of the *patibulum* and another could hold the feet or maybe only the right foot (the rear one) at the level of the Achilles tendon and the heel. This part of the body would thus be *the only one to be touched during the journey.*

3.—Now, in the impression of the right foot on the shroud one can see precisely that: (*a*) the rear part of the heel is poorly marked in contrast with the rest of the impression of the sole, which is very clear; at first sight it even makes the foot appear shorter than it actually is, as we have already observed; (*b*) the flow of blood which has descended (during the carrying horizontally) from the wound in the sole towards the heel does not reach the rear part of this, which is the part which is poorly marked on the shroud. And this is easy to explain if this was the part which was covered by the hands of the bearer; his hands would have supported the heel and would have prevented the blood from flowing that far.

D.—It is probable that there were *five bearers* and not three, for they had to carry a body weighing approximately 200 lbs. and the heavy *patibulum*, which would have weighed another 110 lbs. at least. The two extra men would have supported the trunk by means of *a sheet, twisted so as to make a band, and placed across under the lower part of the thorax.*

In fact: (1) The blood of the inferior vena cava, of which a part has been congealed transversally on the back during the journey, has with considerable difficulty managed to *reascend* (even when the body was leaning towards the left side) from the mesial line to the left edge. This edge, in the horizontal position, was in fact higher than the mesial line. (2) The flow of blood, which has coagulated transversally on the back, consists of *irregular windings* which bifurcate several times and then come together again (Fig.); this would be unlikely in a regular flow of blood on skin which was touching nothing. (3) On the other hand, if one supposes there to have been a sheet, twisted irregularly and supporting the lower part of the thorax, this sheet would inevitably have been completely impregnated with blood during the journey; a small part of this has coagulated irregularly on the surface of the skin where it could reach it directly, *amidst the folds of the material.*

E.—The rigidity of the corpse, which made it possible to carry the body without it bending forward on account of its weight, would not prevent *the arms being brought back from the position of abduction to that of adduction,* and the hands being crossed, once the body had been laid on the shroud, the hands unnailed and the *patibulum* removed. We know from experience that there is no degree of cadaveric rigidity which cannot be brought to an end by the use of a little force, even if it has been sufficiently intense to resist the weight of the body.

F.—One may then conclude that everything is likely to have taken place in the following way:—

(1) The feet are unnailed from the *stipes.* Only one nail has to be removed from the wood.

(2) The *patibulum* is lowered with the body without unnailing the hands. The whole is then carried, without using any contrivance, by five bearers, of whom one alone touches the body, at the level of the heels; two others support the back with the sheet twisted to form a band, which becomes impregnated with blood. The two last carry the ends of the *patibulum.*

(3) This body is only placed on half the shroud at the end of the journey, during which a small amount of blood from the lower vena cava has coagulated transversally in the folds of the band on the skin of the back. These clots, in the form of irregular windings, will produce the "back transversal flow" by making counter-drawings, while still fresh, on the shroud.

(4) The body is placed on the shroud (probably on what is known as the stone of anointing). At the last moment it would have been necessary to support the back with the band, which, being completely impregnated with blood, would have made considerable stains on the shroud.

(5) The hands are unnailed; the *patibulum* is removed and they bend the arms forward, crossing the hands.

(6) They then fold back the other half of the shroud over the head (*epi tèn kephalén*) and the front part of the body.

G.—THE LAYING IN THE TOMB

Finally, once more owing to the extreme rigidity of the corpse, it has been easy to lay the body in the tomb, although the sepulchral stone was placed transversally at the end of the cave, occupying the whole breadth. It would have been carried in sideways, and held from underneath, all the bearers being on the outer side. This is how one lays an unconscious body in bed, after an operation; and the rigidity must have made the body far easier to carry. One might think that the body would have been laid temporarily, not on the stone at the end, but in an antechamber which has now disappeared, while waiting for the final embalming, after the Sabbath. This hypothesis is worthy of a fuller discussion, but it is outside the limits of this scientific work.

Chapter Nine

THE BURIAL

THIS chapter started by being a talk which I gave to the Paris doctors of the *Société de Saint Luc*, on June 16th, 1947. I said to them:

I wrote my first book, my dear colleagues, about all that Jesus did and suffered during His bitter Passion, till the hour when He decided to die, and gave back His soul to His Father. But since many have undertaken to give an account of the deeds accomplished after His death, according to the things which have been told us by those who from the beginning were eye-witnesses and servants of the Word, it seemed good to me, to me also, who for a long time had set myself to know everything exactly, to speak to you in order, O Théophiles, so that you may know the truth of the instruction which you have received.

This time it is clearly no longer a question of anatomy, and you will perhaps accuse me of mounting *supra crepidam*. My excuse is that philology and exegesis have for forty years been my violins of Ingres.[1] If I dare put forward any hypothesis or to come to any conclusions, please be ready to believe that I am relying on those who are deeply versed in the subject and on unquestioned authorities. In this matter, which some people seem to have taken pleasure in making confused, everything rests on the study of the Gospels, and we shall follow these word by word, seeking for the lights that we need in other passages of Scripture and at times looking to other sciences for the help that they can give us. The essential basis of our study is the synopsis of the four Gospel books, in the original Greek, in Latin and in English (in the French edition the author naturally says French); the Aramean may also have a surprise in store for us.

The first fact to strike one in this harmonised reading is that each

---

[1] This is a French term meaning that the author is much interested in subjects other than his own. There is a not very reliable legend that Ingres the painter was more proud of his performance on the violin, which was quite ordinary, than of his painting, which had made him famous. Trs.

one describes the events in a different way, in conformity with his own plan and his particular genius; different words are frequently used, and the same details are not always stressed. They are complementary to, but do not contradict each other. We know that they are all inspired by the Holy Spirit, and possess the gift of inerrancy. Should we seem to see any opposition between them, it is because we have failed to understand them. I do not think that in laying down this principle I am falling into the errors of concordism, and you will see how we shall be forced to conclude that they are in perfect agreement. These are mere details, if you will, since it is the Passion and the Resurrection which matter most to us, but details which may agitate wayward spirits.

The other fact, with which we will start, emerges clearly from the combined accounts. This is the shortness of the time at the disposal of the disciples for the burial of Jesus. Let us re-read our synopsis: we are on Golgotha, at nones, that is to say about three o'clock, on the 13th day of the month Nizan, probably in the year 30.

Jesus has bowed His head, right forward on His chest, at the moment chosen by Him, and He has given back His human soul to His Father, "et inclinato capite emisit spiritum." Now, the Sabbath will begin at about 6 o'clock, at the appearance of the first star, when one will no longer be able to distinguish a white thread from a black. And what a number of things are going to take place during these three hours! "The Jews then," says St. John, "(because it was the parasceve), that the bodies might not remain on the cross on the Sabbath day (for that was a great Sabbath day), besought Pilate that their legs might be broken and that they might be taken away."[2] Remember that it was 600 yards from Calvary to the Prætorium, along uneven roads, and that there was to be much going to and fro. Pilate is certainly not in the mood to be in a hurry to receive the Jews, who, by playing on his fears, have forced on him an unjust condemnation; he will have kept them waiting. Nevertheless, he consents to send soldiers equipped with the necessary iron bars. The Roman custom was to leave the condemned on the cross till they were dead, but the instructions from Rome were to conform to local conditions. "The soldiers, therefore, came; and they broke the legs of the first, and of the other that was crucified with Him." As we have already said, this *crurifragium* would prevent them from raising themselves, using their legs as a support, so as to lessen the dragging on the hands. Tetany would thus finally overpower them and would cause asphyxia. They will be in their agony. Jesus is already dead.

---

[2] Mgr. Knox gives a somewhat different translation:—"The Jews would not let the bodies remain crucified on the Sabbath, because that Sabbath day was a solemn one; and since it was now the eve, they asked Pilate that the bodies might have their legs broken, and be taken away."

At this point comes the tragic gesture of one of the soldiers; a tradition has it that he was the centurion of the guard on Calvary and that his name was Longinus, which is merely a play on the Greek name for the lance, "lonchè." Why should this centurion, who had been watching the martyrdom of Jesus with sympathy and had just proclaimed Him to be just and the Son of God, perform such a cruel act? In any case St. John writes "one of the soldiers." We have already seen (Chapter II, C.6) that it was merely a regulation act which was necessary before the body could be given back to the family.

The afternoon is already fast drawing onwards when Joseph and Nicodemus arrive, who will take charge of the burial. "When it was evening," says St. Matthew, "when evening was now come," says St. Mark, Joseph of Arimathea arrives first and foremost. He was a decurion, a good and just man and a disciple of Jesus, so the synoptics tell us. And though a counsellor, "he had not consented to their counsel and doings," we are told by St. Luke. When he sees that Jesus is dead, that the thieves are in their last agony, and the Jews are about to take them down, he decides to go and find Pilate so as to beg for the body of his Master; "he was a disciple of Jesus," says St. John, "but secretly for fear of the Jews." "*Audaciter introivit ad Pilatum,*" St. Mark insists, "went in boldly to Pilate." This was to compromise himself once and for all, and he must have experienced some hesitation. But Pilate, who was exasperated by the members of the sanhedrin, would be only too glad to comply with his request so as to have his revenge on his persecutors. One can read in St. Matthew how haughtily he would receive them on the following day when they came to reveal to him their fears that the body would be removed and to ask him to have it guarded: "You have a guard; go, guard it as you know."[3]

He would thus be in the mood to give Joseph's request a friendly welcome; one thing, however, astonishes him—that Jesus should already be dead; the crucified do not usually die so rapidly, and Joseph must have told him that the legs had not been broken. "*Pilatus autem mirabatur si jam obiisset*" (Mk.). He, therefore, sends an orderly to fetch the centurion of the guard, who has remained on Calvary. The latter arrives a little later and gives confirmation of the death to his chief, who delivers the body of Jesus to Joseph. It was the usual custom, as we know, to deliver the bodies of those who had been executed to their families when they asked for them.

But a shroud is needed. St. Luke says: "He wrapped Him in fine linen," while St. Matthew is a little more precise and says that "Joseph,

[3] Mgr. Knox brings this out with far more definiteness:—" You have guards; away with you, make it secure as you best know how."

taking the body, wrapped it up in a clean linen cloth." St. Mark, however, goes further and says that Joseph went and bought a shroud after
he had left Pilate: "*Joseph autem mercatus sindonem* ";[4] this means
one more step to be taken and further delay. Then he returns to Calvary
and the work still remains to be done.

I have said exactly what my ideas are as to the taking down from the
cross and the carrying to the tomb. The body was not wrapped in the
shroud till after it had been carried to the tomb; during the journey the
blood from the inferior vena cava and the lower limbs flowed out through
the wound in the side; otherwise the blood would have drenched the
shroud. After death from tetany the rigidity of the body is both sudden
and extreme; it becomes like an iron bar. May I repeat what the method
would have been: The nail of the feet would be removed, which would
not be altogether easy; then the *patibulum* would be unfixed, two men
holding the ends, while another upholds the right heel, which is behind
the left. Finally, as the combination of the body and the beam of wood
is too heavy, two others twist a sheet so as to make a band to support
the loins. The rest of the venous blood coming out of the heart, in the
horizontal position, drenches this sheet and coagulates in its folds in
irregular windings. (All these details, as we have seen, are verified on
the shroud of Turin, and they are not details which a forger would
have imagined.)

Fortunately, the sepulchre is quite near, and that is why it has been
chosen. This sepulchre " was hewed out of a rock," writes St. Mark—
" wherein never yet any man had been laid," adds St. Luke; St. Matthew
states precisely that it was Joseph's " own new monument, which he
had hewed out in a rock." St. John is yet more explicit: " Now there
was in the place where He was crucified, a garden; and in the garden
a new sepulchre, wherein no man yet had been laid. There, therefore,
because of the parasceve of the Jews, they laid Jesus, because the
sepulchre was nigh at hand." Their haste could scarcely be more
clearly stressed, so that they should be finished before the opening of
the Sabbath. St. Augustine writes (*Tr. in Joann.*, CXX, 19): " *Acceler-
atam vult intelligi sepulturam ne advesperasceret*—He wishes to make it
understood that the burial was in haste, for fear that the evening should
come on."

Having been carried there, the body is laid on a flag-stone placed in
the ante-chamber of the sepulchre, which is traditionally known as the
stone of anointing. For it has to be freed from the *patibulum*. The nails

---

[4] Mgr. Knox uses the word " winding-sheet " in his translation of all three
Gospels.

can now be removed from the hands, and we can imagine with what pious and loving precaution. The work is easier on the flat, but all the same it takes time and strength to draw the nails from the wood; once this is done, the nails can be removed from the wrists without difficulty. Then, these arms, which were spread out at an angle of 65°, must be brought back in front of the body. Much strength must be exerted in order to overcome them, the shoulders have to be made supple, and the arms brought down and crossed in front of the body: " and the Sabbath drew on," says St. Luke—" *et sabbatum illucescebat* "; the lamps of the Temple were being lighted, and the trumpets would soon sound, announcing the opening of the great day. How, then, were the burial rites to be performed in their completeness?

Before we continue with the study of our texts, it will perhaps be of value to find out how the Jews bury their dead. One thing seems to be certain, that it had nothing in common with the embalming practised by the Egyptians. In the whole of the Bible, we only find two examples of mummification, those of Jacob and of Joseph; this was in Egypt, for they had become half Egyptian. Neither was it ever the custom to enclose with bands, to use natron, or to disembowel. In the Jewish catacombs, mummies are extremely rare (there are, in fact, two) and these probably are of Jews belonging to the Egyptian diaspora. All the other bodies are clothed as we shall see. Maïmonides, the Jewish doctor of Cordova, in the 12th century, writes: " After the eyes and the mouth of the dead person had been closed, the body was washed, it was anointed with perfumed essences and then rolled up in a sheet of white linen, in which aromatic spices were placed at the same time " (Lévesque, article on embalming in *Dict. Bible*). La Michna (*Chabbath*, XXXIII, 5) tells us in regard to the same subject: " Everything is performed that is owing to the dead, both the anointing and the washing " (Note by Father Lagrange in his St. Mark). I suppose, then, that Our Lord had to be washed first.

Alfred Lévy, a Rabbi in Lunéville, writes (*Deuil et cérémonies funèbres chez les Israelites*):[5] " Once death was established, they would wait for a quarter of an hour, during which light feathers were placed in the nostrils of the deceased, and he was watched with great attention to make sure there were no movements to show that breathing had begun again. After this short wait, the eyes and mouth of the deceased were closed, his limbs were placed in an ordered position, he was wrapped in a shroud and laid on the ground, while the words were pronounced: ' Dust thou art and unto dust thou shalt return.' " It would seem, then, that this was a preliminary ceremony, after which they would have time

[5] Mourning and funeral ceremonies among the Israelites.

to prepare for the burial strictly so called. Alfred Lévy continues: "Before proceeding to the funereal clothing, the corpse was purified, it was washed with tepid water, and in the old days (this is of interest to us) it was perfumed with diverse essences. After that it was dressed in normal clothes. This clothing, however, became more and more luxurious, and shortly before the time of Jesus became such a charge on the heirs that Gamaliel the Elder, with the intention of preventing this, decreed that a corpse should only be dressed in simple clothing. This reform, which looked back to the ancient simplicity, was most successful, and continued in practice throughout the ages." We find the same account in a series of documents collected in Israelite circles by my friend, the late M. Porché, who was a fervent believer in the shroud. Several Rabbis who were interrogated by him in France and in Palestine confirmed all this; they only knew of one case when bands were used for the hands and the feet: it was that of Lazarus, in St. John's Gospel! And they had no explanation for this anomaly.

The custom of the first Christians, which must have been inspired by that of the Jews, is confirmed for us by the *Acta Martyrum,* where we always find references to shrouds, linen fabrics, plain linen garments or others more or less ornamented, " *in sindone novo, mundo linteo, mundis sindonibus, in sindone biblea, cum linteamentibus mundis et valde pretiosis dignissimis pannis, sindosin kainis, esthèti polutélè* " (Dom Leclerc, *Dict. Arch.*). In the *loculi* of the catacombs one finds linen cloths, cloths dyed purple, figured and ornamented fabrics and silks, cloth of gold and precious garments, such as those in which St. Cecilia is clothed in the cemetery of Domitilla.

Thus, having been first wrapped in a shroud, the body was usually clothed after the final anointing, and of this we even find confirmation in the Scriptures. I do not speak of the daughter of Jairus, who had just died when Jesus raised her from the dead. But the son of the widow of Naim (Lk. VII, 14) was being carried to the grave, when Jesus said to him: " Young man, I say to thee, arise. And he that was dead, sat up, and began to speak." In the case of Tabitha, who was raised from the dead by St. Peter at Joppa (Acts IX, 40) it stands out even more clearly: "Whom when they had washed, they laid her in an upper chamber." They then went to fetch Peter at Lydda, which would have taken at least ten hours. And Peter, "turning to the body, said: Tabitha, arise. And she opened her eyes; and seeing Peter, she sat up. And giving her his hand, he lifted her up." Both these dead persons must then have been dressed.

From the historical point of view it seems quite clear: in the first phase the body was wrapped in a shroud, and they then prepared for the burial. The latter consisted of washing with warm water, followed by anointing with perfumed essences, such as the ointment of precious spikenard of Mary Magdalene at the meal in Bethany, or the aromatic spices which she took to the tomb on Easter day. This anointing was done by rubbing. The verb *aleiphein,* used by St. Mark (XVI, 1) in describing this last scene, denotes a friction with balm and oil; the same verb is used in regard to the anointing of athletes before the contests in the stadium; there was more than a mere sprinkling.

Once the corpse was dressed it was carried into the sepulchre. The latter was sometimes a grave hollowed out in the rock (as, perhaps, in the case of Lazarus), into which they would go down by steps, and which would afterwards be covered by a flag-stone. Nearly always it was a cavern hollowed out by the hand of man, consisting of an ante-chamber and an inner cell in which the body would be laid down on a rocky ledge. The entrance would be closed in by a disc-shaped stone which rolled into a groove: " *Et advolvit lapidem ad ostrum monumenti*—And he rolled a stone to the door of the sepulchre." It was the custom to visit the dead every day for at least three days, for the Jews had a great dread of death being merely apparent. This was why Martha was able to say with full knowledge to Jesus, referring to Lazarus: " Lord, by this time he stinketh, for he is now of four days."[6] And when Mary, summoned by Martha, rose up to go and join the Lord, the Jews who had come to console her, thought she was going once more to the grave. (Jn. XI.)

Let us now turn once more to our texts and we shall see that there is no mention of washing or anointing in connection with this first burial, either in the Synoptics or in St. John. The fact was that time was short, and they had no hot water and no balm for the anointing.

Now, the Synoptics say that Joseph " wrapped Him up in the fine linen." St. Matthew and St. Luke say " *énétulixen*," and St. Mark " *éneilèsen*," but there can be no doubt as to what they mean, and St. Jerome translates all three with the word " *involvit.*"

The Greek " sindôn " (sindon in St. Jerome), which we translate as shroud, was a long piece of linen, much longer than it was broad, which they first placed round the head and then over the body; one may compare it to the " *himation* " of the Greeks, the Roman " *peplum,*" or better still, the " *palla*" worn by women. It could be worn as undercloth-ing or at night, or be used as a shroud for the dead. In Aramean it was called the *soudarâ,* but we shall return to this later. We find in St. Mark that when they were leading Jesus away after His arrest (XIV, 51), " a

---

[6] Mgr. Knox translates:—" Lord, the air is foul by now; he has been four days dead."

certain young man followed Him, having a linen cloth cast about his naked body—(*péribéblèménos sindona épi gumno*); and they laid hold on him. But he, casting off the linen cloth, fled from them naked."[7] This young man was no doubt John Mark himself, the son of a good Jerusalem family; his mother's house was to be one of the chief centres of primitive Christianity (Acts XII, 12). We come across the "*sindôn*" again in the Old Testament: Samson (Judges XIV, 12) promises his companions, if they can solve a riddle, that he will give them "thirty shirts[8] and as many coats—*dabo vobis triginta sindones et triginta tunicas.*" The "*sindon*" would be wrapped round under the coat or tunic, and thus he would be giving them a complete outfit. In Jeremias XIII, 1, the "*sindon*" reappears in the Greek of the Septuagint, and St. Jerome here translates as "*lumbare lineum,*" which would indicate the same kind of garment.

In ancient French the word used is sometimes "*sídoine.*" But the word "*linceul*" was used at the same time, from "*linteolus,*" which, like "*linteamen,*" is a derivative of "*linteum*" (linen cloth). In Italian we have "*lenzuolo,*" which means a linen sheet. But we shall return to this point later when dealing with the "*sudarium.*" To conclude, according to the Synoptics, the body of Jesus was wrapped in a shroud, and they do not speak of aromatic spices.

Let us now turn to St. John, and we shall find that he definitely mentions these. Joseph "came, therefore, and took away the body of Jesus. And Nicodemus also came (he who at first came to Jesus by night), bringing a mixture of myrrh and aloes, about an hundred pound weight" (Jn. XIX, 38, 39). Myrrh is a form of resin extracted from an umbelliferous plant, the balsamodendron; it has a fragrant scent and mild antiseptic qualities. The aloes, whatever may have been said about it, has no connection with aloes wood, or agallock; the latter, which is sold in chips, has very little scent, except when burnt; it has no antiseptic qualities. It was, furthermore, rare and very expensive at that time, as it came from the Far East.

What was in fact placed on the body of Jesus was a resin extracted from the aloes or agave, which, with its long, thick, sharp-edged leaves, can be seen all along the Mediterranean coast. Soccotrine aloes, from the island of Soccotra in the Red Sea, is still used in pharmacy. It has a scent of balsam, half-way between that of myrrh and that of saffron. And it has always been used when treating corpses. Dioscorides, St. John Chrysostom, the Arab doctors and the *Romance of the Rose* all tell of it. Even our old French codex, according to my friend M.

---

[7] Mgr. Knox translates:—"a linen *shirt*".

[8] In this case the Douay version and Mgr. Knox are in agreement.

Volckringer, contained a formula for powder for embalming, consisting of myrrh and aloes in equal parts, along with other drugs. In spite of everything, the mixture brought by Nicodemus would not suffice for embalming the whole body; it could only postpone the putrefaction of the surface, covered as it was with infected wounds. The very super-abundance of the mixture (100 pounds or 32 kilograms), shows that the disciples only aimed at temporary preservation.

They had to wait for thirty-six hours before they could perform the ritual burial on the Sunday morning, washing the body and anointing it with the balms; this was the work of the women, to which they were already giving much thought. " There was there Mary Magdalen," says St. Matthew, " and the other Mary (the mother of James and Joseph, whom he describes as present on Calvary) sitting over against the sepulchre." And St. Mark: " Mary Magdalen, and Mary the mother of Joseph, beheld where He was laid." St. Luke, who had certainly received his information from the holy women (*sicut tradiderunt nobis qui ab initio ipsi viderunt*—according as they have delivered them unto us, who from the beginning were eye-witnesses), goes into further detail: " And the Sabbath drew on. And the women that were come with Him from Galilee, following after, saw the sepulchre, and how His body was laid. (This surely means that they were making their plans for the anoint-ing). And returning, they prepared spices and ointments; and on the Sabbath day they rested, according to the commandment. And on the first day of the week, very early in the morning, they came to the sepulchre, bringing the spices which they had prepared." Can one not hear these wonderfully devoted women telling Luke of these memories, so dear to them, which must have been positively embalmed in their minds? St. Mark also tells us: " And when the Sabbath was past, Mary Magdalen, and Mary the mother of James (he singles her out, first by one son and then by the other), and Salome, bought sweet spices, that coming, they might anoint Jesus." It was indeed to be the ritual and final burial. We have already stated the precise meaning of the verb " *aleiphein*." Aromatic spices would be used, similar to the ointment of precious spikenard, poured out by the Magdalen at Bethany. The myrrh and the aloes were only used for purposes of temporary preservation.

Starting with the myrrh and aloes of St. John, we have ended up with the sweet spices of the Synoptics. This anticipation was necessary so as to establish what were the details of the burial. But we must return to St. John, in order to arrive at the meaning of the famous little sen-tence, which has worried so many orthodox exegetists, and has caused so many Protestants and modernists to lose their way. Let us start by turning to the Vulgate of St. Jerome: " *Acceperunt ergo corpus Jesu, et ligaverunt illud linteis cum aromatibus, sicut mos est Judaeis sepelire.*"[9]—" With the spices," with the myrrh and the aloes; the Greek text runs " méta tôn arômatôn," with *the* spices and not with *some* spices; there can be no doubt it is to these he refers. The fact that the Synoptics are silent about them presents no difficulty; they are not bound to tell everything.

"*Sicut mos est Judaeis sepelire.*" Father Lagrange and Canon Crampon both agree to translate this " as the manner of the Jews is to bury (*selon la manière d'ensevelir des Juifs*)." Let us admit this for the moment and do not accuse me of presumption; it is not I who will rectify it. But as regards " *ligaverunt cum linteis* "? Here there is a divergence: Lagrange says " they bound it with bandlets (*le lièrent de bandelettes*)," and Crampon " they wrapped it in linen cloths (*l'enveloppèrent de linges*)." The second translation seems to be the traditional one, for I have found it in a New Testament of Père Amelotte, of the Oratory, in 1758. And Gerson translates " *de linceulx* (with shrouds or winding-sheets)" (*La Passion de Notre-Seigneur*, Good Friday, 1403). We have seen that bandlets would not be used among the Jews. Besides, these bandlets, unless they were completely unrolled, would prevent the anointing which it was intended to perform on the Sunday. And why should they go to the pains of binding Him in this way when they had the anointing in view?

But the Greek text has " *othonia* " which St. Jerome translates very well as " *linea*." Now the dictionaries give us for " *othonion*": " small fine linen cloth; a garment or veil of fine linen " and even " veiling, veils," and finally " a bandage; in the plural, linen cloths." For " *linteum* " we find in the dictionaries: " linen cloth, a piece of cloth —by extension of the sense, the sail of a ship (Virgil, Ovid)." Thus in the plural, we have the same thing, linen cloths. Let us slightly anticipate the Sunday morning: Peter and John ran to the empty tomb, and there they found " *ta othonia* " as St. Luke and St. John tell us. St. Jerome translates this as " *linteamina*," which our dictionaries render as " linen cloths." Now, in his St. John, Father Lagrange remains faithful to his idea of the burial, and translates it as the " bandlets "; but in his St. Luke the same eminent exegetist says " the linen cloths " (*les bandelettes, les linges*). Furthermore, when St. John (XI), describing the resurrec-

---

[9] It will be of value, I think, to give here the three Catholic translations of this verse in English:—
DOUAY: " They took therefore the body of Jesus, and bound it in linen cloths, with the spices, as the manner of the Jews is to bury."
WESTMINSTER: " As the manner is with the Jews to prepare for burial." (The rest as above.)
MGR. KNOX: " They took Jesus' body, then, and wrapped it in winding-cloths with the spices; that is how the Jews prepare a body for burial."

tion of Lazarus, tells us that his hands and feet were held by bandlets, he uses the word " *keiriai*," which St. Jerome translates " *instita*." These two words mean in fact bandlets, bandages or straps. We may bring the debate to an end by calling in a high authority, for I find in the book by Mgr. Paleotto, which I have already mentioned (he was Archbishop of Bologna in 1598), the following quotation from St. Augustine, which will perhaps satisfy even the most exacting: " *Licet Joseph involverit eum in sindone, propterea non prohibteur intelligi quod et abia lintea postea addita fuerint a Nicodemo. . . . Unde etsi una sindon fuerit, verissime dici potuit: ligaverunt eum linteis.* If Joseph wrapped Him in a shroud, one is not forbidden to believe that other linen cloths were brought by Nicodemus. . . . Thus even if there was one shroud, he (John) was quite well able to say: they surrounded Him with linen cloths." St. Augustine then gives us his own view: " *Lintea quippe generaliter dicuntur quæ lino texuntur*—In fact, all things are generally called linen cloths which are woven from flax." And Paleotto adds, following Bede who had read it in the *Annales Pontificales*, that St. Sylvester ordered, out of regard for the linen cloths used in the burial, that the corporal of the Mass should be made of fine linen and of no other material. I have been able to trace both these texts: St. Augustine, *De consensu Evangelistarum*, Lib. III, cap. 23.—St. Bede, *In Marci evangelium expositio*, Lib. IV (in Patr., Tome XCII, col. 293).

We now come to the " *ligaverunt* " of the Vulgate; this is the translation of St. John's " *edesan*." The verb " *déô*," like the Latin " *ligare*," means essentially to bind, to make fast. If, however, we read over again St. John's account of the raising of Lazarus (XI), we find that " *facies illius sudario erat ligata*." St. Jerome uses the same " ligare " to translate a compound of " *déô*," which would tend to exaggerate the idea of winding in bandlets, " péridéô." (The dictionaries give " to surround, to fasten around.") But we are here concerned with a winding-sheet, and Father Lagrange translated " *péridein* " and " *ligare* " as " to envelop (*envelopper*)." Might I, so as to preserve the strength of *edesan*'s meaning, suggest as a translation " they surrounded it with linen cloths (*ils l'enfermèrent dans des linges*)"? These linen cloths would, as St. Augustine suggests, include among other things the shroud, which would closely surround the body in its full length and breadth, being folded above and below it; it would be quite permissible to say that the body was enclosed in it.

Let us turn once more to " *sicut mos est Judaeis sepelire*." The Greek original says: " *Kathôs étos éstin tois Ioudaiois éntaphiazein*." Now, M. Lévesque, the exegetist and philologist, who is as modest as he is learned, of whom I had the honour to be both the surgeon and the

friend under very serious circumstances, translates this (*Dict., Bible*):
" According to the manner of preparing for burial as is the custom
among the Jews—*Selon la manière de préparer l'ensevelissement en
usage chez les Juifs.*" Bailly's dictionary also gives us " preparing for
burial." Numerous Hellenists who were consulted by my friend Father
Aubert, O.P., have confirmed this sense: the suffix " *azein* " indicates
an action which has been begun but not completed, but which is still
being carried out. One of them writes that " *entaphiazein* " can be
translated as to " prepare for burial " (R.P. Aubert, O.P., *L'ensevelissement de N-S Jésus-Christ, d'après les Saintes Ecritures*. Publ., Rivoire,
18, rue Nicolaï, Lyons, and Librairie du Carmel, rue Madame, Paris).

We find the same verb used elsewhere in connection with the meal
at Bethany, the town of the palms, and it has been the occasion of
some rather embarrassed translations. Mary Magdalen has poured a
pound of ointment of precious spikenard over the feet of Jesus, and
Judas, the thief, reproaches her because she has not sold it and given
the money to the poor; St. John writes coldly that the money would
have gone into his pocket. Jesus reproves Judas and the detractors of
the Magdalen. St. John and St. Mark only use the noun " *éntaphias-
mon* " which is easier to translate: " That she may keep it against the
day of my burial " (Jn. XII, 7); " she is come beforehand to anoint my
body for the burial " (Mk. XIV, 8),[10] which is much clearer. But St.
Matthew writes: " *Pros to éntaphiasaï mé épiosèn* " (Mt. XXVI, 12),
which the Vulgate gives as " *ad sepeliendum me fecit,*" while Father
Lagrange translates this: " She has done it to give me a service of burial
—*Elle l'a fait pour me rendre un office de sépulture.*" It is clearly a
symbolic anointing; Jesus predicts that Mary will not be able to perform
this anointing on His body, because He will have risen again. If, however, one translates it as M. Lévesque suggests when speaking of the
burial of Jesus, the sense becomes clear, for Jesus said: " She has done
it to prepare for my burial."

And so everything becomes clear; the disciples have only performed
the first act of the Israelite customs, that which preceded the burial
proper, and this was because they have neither the time nor the materials.
They have wrapped Jesus in a shroud, surrounding this with linen
cloths which have been impregnated with the mixture of myrrh and
aloes, and this will act to a certain extent as an antiseptic; the final
anointing, following on the washing, will be performed by the women
on the first day after the Sabbath. We may then translate St. John, if

[10] Mgr. Knox translates these two passages:—
" Enough that she should keep it for the day when my body is prepared for
burial."
" She has anointed my body beforehand to prepare it for burial."

what I say carries conviction: "They wrapped it in linen cloths with the spices, according to the custom among the Jews of preparing for burial." The largest of these linen cloths (woven from flax) was the shroud of which the Synoptics speak, a long and broad piece of linen. St. John does not expressly refer to it, but he will do so, as we shall see, on the Sunday morning.

"*Vespere autem sabbati, quæ lucescit in prima sabbati*"—you know the rest, and with what joy it is chanted in the short vespers of Holy Saturday. At an early hour, then, on Sunday morning, Mary Magdalen (Jn.), with the holy women (Synoptics), bring their spices (Mk., Lk.), in order to anoint the body (" *aleiphein*," Mk.); they go to the sepulchre and find it both open and empty. I will pass over the details, the apparition of the angels, the fright and flight of the women. They run to tell the news to the apostles, who treat it as *deliramentum*, an absurdity; our holy colleague, Luke, uses here the technical term " *léros*," which is the delirium caused by a fever; let us make a note of this as we pass on.

Magdalen specially addresses herself (Jn.) to Peter and John who, without waiting for the opinion of the others, start out quickly for the tomb. Luke only mentions Peter: "But Peter rising up, ran to the sepulchre, and stooping down, he saw the linen cloths laid by themselves."—"*Blepei ta othonia mona.*" It should be noticed that on the Friday Luke only speaks of the shroud. It thus seems certain that this shroud forms part of these "linen cloths," and, in company with St. Augustine, we have already come to this conclusion when studying St. John's text.

St. John, who is the last to write, here, as is often the case, gives the finishing touch to his forerunners the Synoptists, just as he passes over in silence what he is aware must already be well known through their catechising. Peter and John, then, ran to the tomb, but John being the younger, arrived first. "And stooping down, he sees *linteamenta posita* —*Keiména ta othonia*—the linen cloths laid by." (The linen cloths laid on the ground, says Crampon; the bandlets lying, says Father Lagrange, who has, however, made the translation in his St. Luke, " he saw only the linen cloths.") "But yet he went not in." Note this deference to the chief of the Apostles, which is already to be seen. " Then cometh Simon Peter, following him, and went into the sepulchre, and saw the linen cloths lying, and the napkin that had been about his head, not lying with the linen cloths, but apart, wrapped up into one place. Then that other disciple also went in, who came first to the sepulchre; and he saw, and believed."[11] St. Jerome writes: " *Vidit linteamina, posita, et sudarium*

---

[11] Mgr. Knox writes of the " veil which had been put over Jesus' head "; he translates the end of the quotation " and learned to believe ".

quod fuerat super caput ejus, non cum linteaminibus positum, sed separatim involutum in unum locum." The question seems to be settled as regards the *linteamina* or *othonia;* these words refer to all the linen cloths, among which St. Luke has included the shroud, since he only mentions it on the Friday, and he does refer to it specifically on the Sunday. We now arrive at the last difficulty, which, as we shall see, is purely philological.

St. John writes: *" Kai to soudarion o èn èpi tès képhalès autou, ou meta tón othoniôn keiménon, alla chôris éntétuligménon eis éna topon."* (*Sudarium,* from *sudare,* to sweat, is, in classical Latin, a small linen cloth, like a handkerchief, used for wiping away sweat—*soudarion* is a transposition from the Latin into the Greek.) Since then it has always signified winding-sheet in the sense of the shroud; we shall return to this shortly.

" There is no sign in Jewish habits till the fall of Jerusalem and even later," writes M. Lévesque (*Revue pratique d'Apologétique,* 1939, Vol. I, p. 234), " of the use of the *sudarium,* a simple veil for covering the face, having been a regular custom. It would seem rather that they were content to lay the shroud over the face and the front of the body. This custom still exists in the East, and is to be found among the Druses and among the ancient inhabitants of the country. The body is wrapped in a shroud, and is carried, with the face uncovered, as far as the tomb, and part of the shroud is laid over the head to reach as far as the feet. The shroud is held by three or four bandlets, which bind the feet, fix the arms alongside the body or crossed on the chest, and are tied tightly in the region of the neck, so that the shroud completely surrounds the head.

" It is thus that the burial of Lazarus would seem to us to have been performed (Jn. XI, 44): ' And presently he that had been dead came forth, bound feet and hands with winding bands; and his face was bound about with a napkin.' St. John here uses the Greek word *keiriai,* in Latin *instita,* which in fact means bandlets or straps, and is different from *othonia, lineamenta.* One can picture Lazarus wrapped in the shroud, of which part was folded back over his face and fastened to the neck by a bandlet, with his arms alongside his body, also wrapped in the shroud, while outside this shroud there were bandlets holding the legs together and binding the arms to the body. A living man, who was bound in this way and lying on the ground, could no doubt by a vigorous effort get on to his feet, and move one foot in front of the other, but he would not be able to free his arms or his face. And Jesus said: ' Loose him, and let him go '!"

If I stand firmly by this conclusion of M. Lévesque's, it is solely because I believe it to be true, and not because the question of the sudarium-handkerchief worries me at all in regard to the formation of the imprint of the face. The objection has for a long time been made and is still being made that this veil, when laid over the face of Jesus, would have prevented the formation of this imprint on the shroud when placed over it. Volckringer's discovery (Chapter I, E, 2°) makes nothing of this objection. He verified that plants imprinted their negative image, not only on the sheet of paper which was bearing them, but *through this*, on the enveloping paper underneath. This second lower image, which was produced in spite of the supporting sheet of paper coming in between, is almost as beautiful as the first.

Now, in each case we are concerned with a dead body, the cells of which are, however, as I have said, still living; in a man this would be till putrefaction sets in, in a plant till it becomes dried. If one remembers that these vegetable imprints are the only ones known to have the perfection of the negative lights and shades on the shroud, it is surely not rash to conclude that the Holy Face could have left its imprint on the shroud, even through the veil left in between. But let us now return to St. John.

One can already, though with some difficulty, imagine this little handkerchief; it is rolled up apart in its corner, and it attracts our attention. But why should the meaning of its name have changed in ecclesiastical Latin, and in all the Romance languages, till it came to refer exclusively to the shroud? These are puzzling questions, even apart from the exegetical difficulty. But it is here that M. Lévesque, in the article quoted above and in Note I of his " *Abrégé chronologique de la Vie de N-S Jésus-Christ* " (Beauchesne, 1941), is able in a few words to throw a very clear light on to the problem. His conclusions seem to me to be irrefutable.

The whole aim of St. John, in this section, is to prove that Jesus rose from the dead, the basic dogma of our religion, and the first element in the apostolic preaching. Now, the presence of the shroud in the empty tomb seems to provide a very valuable proof. (Had the body been stolen from the tomb, it would not have been removed from the shroud, which would be very useful for carrying it.) They would thus be able to bring to nothing the clumsy calumny of the Jews that it was taken away while the guards were asleep. (Mt. XXVIII, 11.) " *O infelix astutia*," says St. Augustine, " *dormientes testes adhibes; vere tu ipse obdormisti!*"—" O clumsy cunning, you bring forward witnesses who were asleep; it is really you yourselves who were asleep." (*Tract.*, *super psalmos*. Ps. 63.) Would St. John not be certain to refer to the shroud?

One finds in the Aramean Bible of the Targums the word " *soudarâ*," which expresses exactly what we have seen that the "sindon" was. In the book of Ruth (III, 15), the great cloak, the "Mitfahah," in which Ruth wrapped herself when about to sleep at the feet of Booz, and into which, in the morning, the latter poured six measures of barley, was a long piece of material, a great veil which was placed over the head, and which was wrapped round the body and came down to the feet. Like the sindon, it reminds us of the Greek "himation," the "palla" of the Romans, and the "schauzar" worn by Arab women, except that it is an undergarment and one worn at night. St. Jerome translated it "pallium." Now, the Aramean Targum calls it "soudarâ," a shroud; one cannot pour six measures into a handkerchief. St. Ephrem, commenting in the 4th century on the passage in Jeremias XIII, 1, which we have already quoted in connection with the sindon, uses the word "soudoro" for the linen girdle which the prophet wound round his loins; the Hebrew word for this is "êzôr," and it was wound round the upper part of the thighs and the waist. The same function was performed by the sindon, which was wrapped round the body and was used as an undergarment beneath the tunic. (See Judges XIV, 12.) Elsewhere St. Ephrem uses the word of the Syriac version of the Bible, the "peschitto," which takes us back to the 2nd century of our era, and perhaps to the 1st century before Jesus Christ.

There is thus in Eastern tradition, before the days of the New Testament, the word "soudarâ," which has not the same meaning as the classical Latin "sudarium" and its Greek transcription "soudarion," but refers to a full linen garment, which is placed over the head and comes down to the feet. This is surely the "sindon," the "sudarium quod fuerat super caput ejus." Now, St. John was a pure Galilean; his Greek is deeply impregnated with Semitism, we might even say Arameism. When he thinks of a shroud he says the word "soudarâ" in his native tongue. It is, therefore, quite natural for him to write "soudarion" in Greek.

From now onwards, everything becomes quite clear. He found all the linen cloths in the tomb, and among them the shroud rolled up and set apart, which he calls the "soudarion." It was the largest of the "othonia," and one can easily understand how a piece of linen 12 feet long and 3 feet broad would be rolled up and would attract attention in the corner where it was placed.

Furthermore, St. John has achieved his aim; he has the proof he needs; the body was not stolen. Jesus, risen from the dead, has left His shroud in the empty tomb.

In the course of the centuries the words "sudarium" or "soudarion," as we have said, continue to be synonyms for the shroud. In the year

640 A.D. the monk Arculphus, who was on a pilgrimage in the Holy Land (*Acta Sanctorum Ordinis Benedictini, edit., Mabillon*), venerated the "*sudarium Domini quod in sepulchro super caput ipsius fuerat positum*—the shroud of the Lord which, in the sepulchre, had been placed over His head." This can have been no mere veil, but a long piece of material, which would give the impression of being about 12 feet long. In the 7th century once more St. Braulion (*Patr., Lat., LXXX*) speaks of the "*sudario quo corpus Domini est involutum*—the shroud in which the body of the Lord was wrapped." Neither of these was using the word "*sudarium*" for lack of a Latin word corresponding with the Greek "*sindôn*"; even apart from St. Jerome, one finds the Latin word "*sindon*" in the epigrams of Martial, where it means a long piece of linen: "*Sindone cinctus olente,*" he writes of Zoïlus, "wrapped in a perfumed sheet." In all the centuries and in all the Romance languages *sudarium* retains its meaning of shroud, and we find this oral tradition echoed in the beautiful sequence of the Easter Mass, "*Sudarium, et vestes.*" Were there, perhaps, among these linen cloths, these "*vestes,*" the linen garments in which the corpse would have been dressed, after the washing and anointing on Sunday morning?

We may then conclude, after this rather dry study, that the four Gospels, while complementary to each other, are completely in agreement. Because time was so short the body of Jesus was laid in the sepulchre on the Friday evening, after a simple preparation for burial which was merely intended to postpone putrefaction. The disciples, without washing or anointing the body, wrapped it in a shroud surrounded with linen cloths impregnated with a large quantity of myrrh and aloes. The final burial, which would consist of washing and anointing with sweet spices of a quite different kind, was to be performed by the holy women on Sunday morning. In the empty tomb, Peter and John found the linen cloths and the shroud rolled up separately.

Chapter Ten

VILLANDRE'S CRUCIFIX

AFTER I had submitted my researches for the approval of my colleagues of the Société de Saint-Luc, I was delighted to hear of their unanimous agreement in support of my conclusions. I have the greatest respect for all departments of knowledge, while at the same time submitting absolutely to the authority of my Mother the Church. But I should no more expect anatomical precision from a theologian or a paleographer than I should ask a doctor for a dogmatic definition or for an explanation of some exegetical or historical point. To speak the truth, it seems to me essential that we should collaborate, and that each one should tell what he knows. Now, learned exegetists have told me that nothing in my conclusions is contrary to the precise statements contained in the Scriptures and that, on the contrary, they develop these to a remarkable extent. Keeping, therefore, strictly to my own domain, I feel quite satisfied, while I do not wish to claim that my opinions are the last word, which would be far from scientific.

Among the anatomists who have encouraged me, and whose opinion I have specially valued, is my dear friend, Charles Villandre, who was surgeon in the Hôpital Saint-Joseph. As he was a past-master in sculpture as well as in surgery, I asked him to make a crucifix, according to the precise information I had given him; this is the crucifix which appears in the photograph. When this has been studied, and better still, when the original has been contemplated, there will be no need for me to add that he has not only put all his anatomical knowledge and all his artistic talent into this work, but also his faith. I am sure his crucifix will continue to be widely distributed among the faithful, for it seems to me that by keeping to what we believe to be historical reality, he has reached a depth of religious emotion, such as the mere imaginations of artists have never been able to realise. (Fig. XII.) (Librairie du Carmel, 27 rue Madame, Paris, 6.)

His *Crucified in Death* well represents the synthesis of the researches which I have described in the course of this work, and I thank him for it with much affection. He left us in the year 1943, to join his model in the Father's House. May he rest in peace.

Chapter Eleven

LAST THOUGHTS

THE reader who has come to the end of this book will have, I hope, the impression of a solid construction, one that is homogeneous and has the ring of truth. I am quite certain of this, as long as he is a reader who knows how to read, for, being naturally concise, I am not afraid of those who study it carefully; I am only worried about those people who are always in a hurry, who jump out of trains and buses at breakneck speed, and who gallop through a book with seven-league boots. To these I would say: read it over again at your leisure, or else leave the question alone! A thorough grasp of such a problem can only be obtained by a minute examination of the details.

It will have been noticed how this examination, with its anatomical experiments and its physiological considerations, its archæological and philological researches, seems to have carried me far away from the Holy Shroud of Turin, which I set out to examine; but it was only so that I might come back to it with fresh weapons. The fact is, that my thought was dominated from the beginning with the idea of reconstructing the Passion of Our Saviour in its smallest details; of exploring all the physical circumstances of the central drama of our Redemption, which dominates our brief earthly existence and finally settles the course of our eternal destiny.

It thus happened that I often came to forget the original object of my researches. My fervent quest was left with but one objective: Jesus died for me; how then did He die? This question, as will be understood, is deeply disturbing, when one is at the same time a Christian and a surgeon.

To speak frankly, the authenticity of the shroud was from the start a matter of secondary importance in my mind. It would have been as serious an error to rank me among its passionate partisans as among its frenzied adversaries. Even now my attitude is still as impartial; for, as Pope Pius XI used to say, that sacred strip of linen is surrounded by many mysteries, and I am far from certain that the learned men of the future (I do not say Science, for I am never quite sure who that lady is) will ever be able to solve the problem correctly.

I certainly hold that to describe these imprints as the work of a forger is an attitude which is now absurd, and which it is impossible to uphold. It is my firm personal opinion that this shroud has contained the dead body of Jesus and also His Divinity. I believe in this, just as I believe in the law of gravitation and in the fact of weight. I believe in it in the same way that one accepts a scientific truth, because this belief is in agreement with everything that we know. I am, therefore, quite ready, as one should be in scientific matters, to give up or to modify the details of this belief, if new and incontestable facts should be produced which can be reasonably said to contradict it. God alone knows the absolute truths, that is to say, the Truth; He and those to whom He has been pleased to reveal small parts of them.

As for the shroud, when I first heard of it, I remained sceptical; but as I studied the facts, they impressed me as being genuine and reliable, even when at first sight they were rather puzzling. And then, little by little, I came to have a special fondness for it; as for some fine type of man giving evidence, who, being at the same time candid and astute and hard to understand, may start by confusing one, but who is, one is sure, thoroughly honest.

I have heard this same fondness spontaneously expressed by a man whose previous historical formation made him sceptical of its authenticity, but who was deeply moved after studying the images, so much so that he now holds the forgery hypothesis to be quite without foundation. He was, however, fully aware, as I am, that it is extremely difficult to produce scientific proof of its authenticity.

May I, therefore, in bringing this (I hope) objective account to an end, try and state exactly how much we do know.

We know, without any doubt, that the imprints on the shroud were not made by the hand of man, but that they have formed spontaneously. We definitely do not know, with scientific certainty, *how* and even *when* they were produced and became visible, certainly in the case of the bodily impressions. In the case of the bloodstained images, I think I can from now onwards affirm that they are reproductions by direct contact, the counter-drawings of the clots of blood which formed naturally on the flesh of the Crucified.

We have already studied this sufficiently in all its details, so that there is no need for me to stress this any further. I would only sum up the facts which have impressed me most, as forcibly sponsoring the authenticity of the shroud. Some are of a general and especially of a photographic nature; others belong to the spheres of anatomy and physiology.

It will be easily understood that it is these latter by which I have been most affected. What is more, it is my special duty to make them stand out even more clearly, for the benefit of those unversed in the subject.

The first group can be summed up quite simply. The body imprints have the character of *a perfect photographic negative*. Now, the very idea of a negative was unknown and even inconceivable in the XIVth century. Even modern painters have never succeeded in making an exact copy of the shroud. As for the foolish hypothesis of the inversion of a positive and a negative, it will not stand up to examination.

There is no trace of painting, even in the photographs which have been made by direct enlargement; the whole scale of lights and shades has been obtained by the simple individual staining of the threads of the linen. The use of dyes, however, has been found incapable of obtaining such subtle variations of colour. Nature alone can produce them, as for example, in the phenomenon of photography. If more details are required, Enrie's valuable conclusions should be read over again, in Chapter I (E, 2°).

We may add that the body and especially the face as seen on the shroud have no relation with any known style of painting. In particular, there is no painter of the XIVth century whose work even remotely recalls them, or approaches anywhere near to their perfection.

From the artistic point of view, I would strongly recommend the study of Vignon's fine work (*Le Saint Suaire*, Paris, éd., Masson, 1938) on the probable influence of the Holy Face of the shroud on the ancient painters, especially the Byzantines. It contains a wealth of very suggestive documents which have been reproduced by Cechelli of Rome, after Vignon.[1] Finally, let us remember that the dead body in the shroud is completely naked; no painter has dared to portray it thus. To go further, would a forger have had the audacity to do this, on a shroud which was to be produced for the veneration of the faithful?

Let us now look at the bloodstained images. We shall notice first of all that most of them seem to be abnormal, strange, different from the traditional iconography, which indeed they usually contradict. Now, experiments have proved for me that they are all in strict conformity with reality. It is artistic custom, the fruit (in its place quite legitimate) of the imagination, which is always in error. A forger would naturally have been obedient to this tradition and would have avoided any such dangerous innovations, which might have made for the failure of his fraud. Let us now have a quick glance at these revolutionary anomalies.

The wounds of the scourging have an abundance and a realism, a

---

[1] A very fine English edition was produced by Archibald Constable & Co., of London, in 1902.

conformity with the findings of archæology, which are in curious contrast with the poverty of imagination to be found in the painters of every age.

The trickles from the crown of thorns, the clots which they have formed, are unimaginably genuine. Have a glance once more at the description of one of these clots on the forehead, in Chapter IV, D.

The carrying of the cross has left marks of excoriation which are in perfect conformity with the observations I was able to make. Who has ever thought of this, apart from one or two mystics? And what artist would ever have imagined those contused wounds on the face, and that fracture of the dorsal cartilage of the nose?

The hand is pierced at the level of the wrist, the only place where the nail could hold firmly. Before the shroud became known, it was always placed in the palm.

The thumb is bent back into the palm. Experiment has proved that it cannot remain stretched out.

A painter would probably have portrayed the four holes in the two hands and the two feet. Only two are to be seen on the shroud.

The blood flows from the wrist, vertically, and, which would have been a discovery of genius by any forger, there are two flows diverging at an acute angle; this is essential, when one takes into account the two alternatives of sagging and straightening of the body, in the course of the struggle against asphyxiating tetany.

The wound of the heart is placed on the right. This is also the most usual representation (although it corresponds with reality!). But neither tradition nor the forger knew the reason why, and how a blow from the left into the ventricles would not have produced the amount of blood, which is only to be found in the auricle. And above all, there was the false idea that there is no liquid blood in a dead body. Was it then a miracle? Indeed, a very great miracle, to account for that enormous forward clot, which would require an abundant flow of blood.

And then, why did this flow of blood leave a clot of irregular shape, with indented edges? Was the forger a trained anatomist, and did he think of the digitations of the serratus muscle?

Did he also foresee, when he was painting the back transversal flow, that, when in the horizontal position, the blood of the inferior vena cava would flow back into the heart, and would then flow out transversally on to the back, whilst the body was being borne to the grave? His imaginative efforts met with no reward, for in 1598 Mgr. Paleotto interpreted this curious image as the mark of a chain which had rubbed the skin off the poor loins!

But we must return to the front. Why has he placed the right elbow farther out than the left, thus lengthening the right arm and forearm? Was his intention to explain the contact of the shroud with the wound of the heart, which is behind it?

In any case, this painter must have witnessed the death of those who were crucified, from tetanic asphyxia, with forced inspiration, so as to be able to give us so impressive a picture: this over-distended thorax, with the pectoral muscles contracted and standing out; the ribs at the sides raised as far as they will go; the epigastric hollow made more hollow yet by the lifting up of the sides and not, as Hynek says, by the contraction of the diaphragm (which is also an inspiratory muscle); and then there is a protrusion of the lower abdomen, pushed out by the viscera, which are compressed precisely by the contraction of the diaphragm. An excellent painting, in which there is not one single blunder!

We need pay no attention to the minute details of the two successive flows on the right sole, the one towards the toes, the other towards the heel. We need not discuss whether the painter, by means of a few details, wished to give us a picture of death from tetanus, with a bending inwards in the front of the body (in *emposthrotonos*), and many minor points of which I will leave you to complete the catalogue.

We have studied these details one by one; they are exact, and experiments have confirmed their genuineness. The opponents of the shroud's authenticity say that they are, however, " marks which are too uncertain," over which " we shall deliberately spend no time." " There are none so blind as those who will not see."

We can then conclude that this forger, who is as good an anatomist and physiologist as he is an outstanding artist, in whatever age he is expected to have lived, is evidently a genius of such high quality that he must have been made to order!

Let us now return to the formation of all these bloodstained images. I think I have been able to demonstrate a certain number of facts. It is impossible to obtain such fine images, with such distinct outlines as those on the shroud, with any colouring liquid, even with liquid blood.

On the shroud there is practically no image of a flow of blood, as depicted by the painters. Besides, we should take into account that the dead body, having lost so much blood during the journey to the tomb, would not have been able to emit any considerable quantity of blood within the shroud. All the bloodstained images on the shroud are then the counter-drawings of fresh clots, or clots softened by the steam, which normally issues from a corpse for a fairly long time.

These portraits of clots have about them a natural, indeed most striking effect of genuineness, down to the smallest details. Only nature could have produced them, forming them on the skin and making their counter-drawings on the linen. They are perfect reproductions of natural clots. No artist would even have been able to imagine them in all their minute details, and he would have drawn back before the insurmountable difficulties of excuting them.

We may say, then, that a crucified body has lain in the shroud. Could it have been anyone else than Jesus? We here come up against an improbability, and I shall not linger over it. It is true that most crucified bodies would have borne almost all these stigmata (these would include the regulation scourging, and in certain cases, the blow with the lance). But this body must have been removed from its shroud at the end of quite a short time; the little that we know about the formation of imprints proves that too long an exposition, and in any case, putrefaction, would have diffused and dimmed these negative imprints. Furthermore, would the shroud have been so piously preserved in the case of any other crucified man?

But also, which crucified man was crowned with thorns, with an ironical pretence of royal honours? History only tells of one: That of the Gospels.

Finally, I would leave you to contemplate that wonderful Face, in which the Divinity shines out through the Semitic veil. Can you tell me of any artist who has painted one that approaches it, with its superhuman character?

It is also possible, as Vignon has tried to demonstrate, that the persistent tradition of this type of Christ among the artists goes back to ancient copies of the shroud, which interpreted it fairly well.

INDEED THIS MAN WAS THE SON OF GOD

Here, then, is the result of my anatomical and other researches on the subject of the Wounds of Christ. I hope I have given the impression that I have conducted them with full independence of mind and with all possible scientific objectivity. I started out with a certain scepticism, more or less with a Cartesian doubt, to examine the images on the shroud; I was quite ready to deny their authenticity, if they disagreed with anatomical truth.

But, on the contrary, the facts gradually grouped themselves into a bundle of proofs, which carried increasing conviction. Not only was the explanation of the images so natural and simple that it proclaimed them to be genuine; but, when at first they seemed to be abnormal, experiment demonstrated that they were as they should be, that they could not be different and as a forger would have portrayed them, following the current iconographic traditions. Anatomy thus bore witness to their authenticity, in full agreement with the Gospel texts.

We possess, then, the shroud of Christ, bearing the image of His body and the marks of His blood. It is the most noble relic in the world, a corporal relic of Our Lord. For him who can read and can reflect, it is the most beautiful, the most moving of the meditations on the Passion.

Before this image of Our Saviour, still adorned with all the flowers of the Redemption, still impregnated with the Divine Blood which was shed for our sins, we can truly repeat as after Holy Communion: " *Tua vulnera considero, illud præ oculis habens quod jam in ore ponebat tuo David propheta de te, O bone Jesu: Foderunt manus meas et pedes meos, dinumeraverunt omnia ossa mea*—I contemplate Thy five wounds, having before my eyes what David the prophet said long ago concerning Thee, O good Jesus, they have pierced my hands and my feet, they have numbered all my bones."

Chapter Twelve

THE CORPORAL PASSION OF JESUS CHRIST

A MEDITATION

ONE of the most deeply-rooted legends in human minds is that of the hard-heartedness of surgeons: we are given to understand that enthusiasm blunts our sensitivity, and that this habitual attitude, reinforced by the necessity of causing pain in order to achieve good, makes us into serenely insensible beings. This is not the case. Even if we set ourselves firmly against emotion, which must never be shown, and, even within us, must never interfere with the surgical act (just as a boxer instinctively contracts his solar-plexus muscles when expecting a blow), nevertheless, pity always remains alive in us, and even becomes purer as one grows older. When for many years one has been bending over the sufferings of others, when one has even experienced them oneself, one is certainly nearer to compassion than to indifference, because one is better acquainted with pain, because one knows better what are its causes and its effects.

Besides, when a surgeon has meditated on the sufferings of the Passion, when he has worked out its timing and its physiological circumstances, when he has methodically set himself to reconstruct all the stages of that martyrdom of a night and a day, he can, more than the most eloquent preacher, more than the most saintly ascetics (apart from those to whom was granted a direct vision, and who were overwhelmed by it), as it were *share* in the sufferings of Christ. I can assure you of a dreadful thing, I have reached a point when I no longer dare to think of them. No doubt this is cowardice, but I hold that one must either have heroic virtue or else fail to understand; that one must either be a saint or else irresponsible, in order to do the Way of the Cross. I no longer can.

And yet it is about this Way of the Cross that I have been asked to write, and I would not refuse to do so, for I am sure it should do good. *O bone et dulcissime Jesu*, come to my aid. You, Who had to bear them, make me able to describe Your sufferings. Perhaps, by forcing myself to be objective, in opposing emotion with my surgical "insensibility," perhaps I shall be able to reach the goal. If I should shed tears before the end, do you, my good friendly reader, do the same as me and not be ashamed; it will simply be that you have understood. Please follow me in what I say: for our guides we have the sacred books and the Holy Shroud, the authenticity of which has been demonstrated to me by scientific research.[1]

The Passion really begins at the Nativity, since Jesus, in His divine omniscience, always knew, saw and willed the sufferings which were awaiting His Humanity. The first blood shed for us was on the occasion of the Circumcision, eight days after Christmas. One can readily imagine what it must be for a man to be able exactly to foresee his martyrdom.

The holocaust was to begin, in fact, at Gethsemani. Jesus, having given to His own His body to eat and His blood to drink, leads them by night to that grove of olives where they were in the habit of going. He allows them to rest at the entrance, taking with Him a little further His three intimate friends, from whom He separates Himself about a stone's throw, in order to prepare Himself in prayer. He knows that His hour is come. He has Himself sent on the traitor of Carioth: *quod facis, fac citius.*[2] He is eager to be finished with it, and it is His will. But as He has assumed, by incarnating Himself, this form of a slave which is our humanity, the latter rebels, and there is all the tragedy of the struggle between His will and human nature. *Cœpit pavere et tœdere.*[3]

This cup which He must drink contains two bitternesses: first, the sins of men which He must take on Himself, on Him the Just One, in order to ransom His brothers, and this was probably the worst: an ordeal that we cannot imagine, because it is the saints amongst us who feel most keenly their worthlessness and their baseness. We shall perhaps better understand His anticipation. The experience beforehand of the physical tortures, which He already suffers in thought; nevertheless, we have only experienced the retrospective shudder at those sufferings which are passed. It is inexpressible. *Pater, si vis, transfer calicem istud a me: verumtamen non mea voluntas sed tua fiat.*[4] It is His Humanity speaking . . . and which submits, for His Divinity knows what it wills from all eternity; the Man is caught in a blind alley. His three faithful friends are asleep, *præ tristitia,* as St. Luke says.[5] Poor men!

The struggle is terrible; an angel comes to strengthen Him, but at the same time, so it seems, to receive His acceptance. *Et factus in agonia,*

[1] Cf. *The Five Wounds of Christ,* by Dr. Pierre Barbet, translated by M. Apraxine. (Clonmore & Reynolds.)
[2] "That which thou dost, do quickly." (*Jn.* XIII, 27.)
[3] "He began to fear and to be heavy." (*Mk.* XIV, 33.)
[4] "Father, if thou wilt, remove this chalice from me: but yet not my will, but thine be done." (*Lk.* XXII, 42.)
[5] "For Sorrow." (*Lk.* XXII, 45.)

prolixius orabat. Et factus est sudor ejus sicut guttæ sanguinis decurrentis in terram.[6] It is the *sweat of blood* which certain rationalist exegetists, scenting some miracle, have treated as symbolical. It is strange to note what nonsense these modern materialists can talk in regard to scientific matters. Let us remember that the only evangelist to record the fact was a physician. And our venerated colleague, Luke, *medicus carissimus*,[7] does so with the precision and conciseness of a good clinician. *Hemati-drosa* is a very rare phenomenon, but has been well described. It is produced, as Dr. Le Bec has written, in " very special conditions: great physical debility accompanied by violent mental disturbance, following on profound emotion or great fear."[8] (*Et cæpit pavere et tædere.*) Dread and horror are here at their maximum, and so is mental disturbance. This is what St. Luke means by agonia, which in Greek signifies a combination of struggle and anxiety. " And His sweat became as drops of blood, trickling down upon the ground."

How can one explain this? There is an intense vasolidation of the subcutaneous capillaries, which burst on contact with the millions of sudoripary glands. The blood mingles with the sweat, and it is this mixture which forms into beads and flows over the whole body, in a sufficient quantity to fall to the ground. Note that this microscopic hæmorrhage is produced all over the skin, which thus already suffers a general injury, and becomes sore and tender while awaiting the blows to come. But we must move onwards.

Here are Judas and the temple attendants, armed with swords and staves; they have lanterns and ropes. As this criminal case must be judged by the procurator, they have with them a platoon of the Roman guard; the tribune of Antonia accompanies them, to make sure things are orderly. It is not yet the turn of the Romans; they are behind these fanatics, aloof and contemptuous. Jesus steps forward; one word from Him is enough to throw His assailants to the ground, the last manifestation of His power, before He abandons Himself to the divine will. Honest Peter seizes the opportunity to cut off the ear of Malchus and, His last miracle, Jesus has healed it.

But the yelling crowd have recovered, and have bound Christ; they lead Him away, without courtesy, one may well imagine, and the minor

---

[6] " And being in an agony, he prayed the longer. And his sweat became as drops of blood, trickling down upon the ground." (*Lk.* XXII, 43, 44.)

[7] " The beloved physician."—St. Paul's Epistle to the Colossians.

[8] Dr. Le Bec, *Le Supplice de la Croix* (The Torture of the Cross), a physiological study of the Passion, published some time ago, in which my former colleague at Saint-Joseph shewed astonishing foreknowledge. My experience has confirmed and more clearly defined most of his views. As for any fresh contributions of my own, he has received them enthusiastically, which I greatly value.

actors are allowed to get away. To all appearances He has been abandoned. Jesus knows that Peter and John are following Him *a longe*,[9] and that Mark will only escape arrest by running away naked, leaving with the guard the cloth which had been wrapped round him.

Here they are before Caiphas and the Sanhedrin. It is by now the middle of the night, and it is clear that they are acting, according to previous instructions. Jesus refuses to answer: as for His doctrine, He has taught it publicly. Caiphas is all at sea, furious, and one of the soldiers, expressing his vexation, gives the accused a hard blow in the face: *Sic respondes pontifici?*[10]

Nothing has been achieved; they must wait for the morning, till the witnesses can give evidence. Jesus is dragged from the hall into the courtyard. He sees Peter, who has denied Him three times, and with one look He pardons him. He is dragged into some underground room, and the rabble of attendants is going to enjoy itself to the full at the expense of this false prophet, duly bound, Who, a short time ago, was able to throw them to the ground by who knows what sorcery. He is beset with slaps and blows; they spit on His face, and as there will be no chance of sleep, they are going to amuse themselves a little. A cloth is tied over His head, and each one is going to have his turn; their slaps ring out, and these brutes are heavy-handed: "Prophesy; tell us, O Christ, who struck You?" His body is already full of pain, His head is ringing like a bell; He has fits of giddiness . . . and He is silent. With one word He could destroy them, *et non aperuit os suum*.[11] This rabble ends by growing weary, and Jesus waits.

In the early morning the second hearing takes place, and a wretched string of false witnesses files past, proving nothing. He must condemn Himself, by affirming His Divine Sonship, and this base second-rate actor Caiphas, proclaims the blasphemy by tearing his robes. Oh, you may be sure, the good, careful Jews, who are not given to wasting money, have a slit all ready and lightly sewn up, which can be used many times over. All that remains is to obtain from Rome the death sentence which she has reserved to herself in this protectorate country.

Jesus, already worn out with fatigue and bruised all over with blows, is now to be dragged to the other end of Jerusalem, to the upper town, to the tower of Antonia, a sort of citadel, from which the majesty of Rome keeps order in this city that is always too excited for her taste. The glory of Rome is represented by a miserable official, a little Roman of the knight class, a self-made man, who is only too ready to hold this

[9] "Afar off." *Mk*. XIV, 54; *Jn*. XVIII, 15.
[10] "Answerest thou the High Priest so?" *Jn*. XVIII, 22.
[11] "And he opened not his mouth." *Isa*. LIII, 7.

difficult command over a fanatical, hostile and hypocritical people; Pilate's great care is to keep his position, wedged between the imperious orders of Rome and the sly ways of these Jews, who are often very well in with the emperor. In short, he is a poor type of man. He has but one religion, if he has one at all, that of Divus Cæsar.[12] He is the mediocre product of a barbarous civilisation, of a materialist culture. One should not be too hard on him for this, for he is that which it has made him; the life of a man has little value for him, especially if he does not happen to be a Roman citizen. He has been taught nothing about pity, and he knows but duty, to maintain order. (In Rome this is considered very suitable!) All these quarrelsome Jews, with their lies and their superstitions, with their taboos and their mania for washing for no reason, their servility and their insolence, and those cowardly denunciations to the Ministry of a colonial administration which is doing its best. The whole thing disgusts him. He despises them . . . and he fears them.

With Jesus it is just the opposite (although in what a state does He appear before him, covered with bruises and spittle); Jesus impresses him, and there is something he likes about Him. He will do everything he can to rescue Him from the claws of these fanatics: *et quærebat dimittere illum.*[13] Jesus is a Galilean; let us pass Him on to that old blackguard, Herod, who is always playing at being a king, and thinks he is somebody. But Jesus despises that old fox and refuses to answer him. And now He is back, accompanied by this yelling crowd and these insufferable Pharisees, for ever whining on a high-pitched note and wagging their heads. They are hateful creatures! Let them remain outside, especially as they would consider themselves defiled merely through entering a Roman pretorium.

Pontius questions this poor Man, in whom he is interested. And Jesus does not despise him. He pities him for his invincible ignorance; He answers him gently, and even tries to teach him. If there was no more than this howling rabble outside, a sortie by the guard *cum gladio*[14] would quickly silence the more noisy and disperse the others. It is not so long that I massacred certain Galileans in the temple who were showing rather too much excitement. Yes, but these crafty Sanhedrin men are beginning to insinuate that I am no friend to Cæsar, and that is no laughing matter. And then, *mehercle,*[15] what on earth is all this talk about the King of the Jews, the Son of God and the Messias? Had he read the Scriptures, Pilate might, perhaps, have been another Nico-

---

[12] The Divine Emperor.
[13] " Pilate sought to release him." *Jn.* XIX, 12.
[14] Sword in hand.
[15] By Hercules.

demus, for Nicodemus also is a coward; but it is cowardice which is going to break down the dikes. This is a Just Man; I will have him scourged (oh, Roman logic!), and then these brutes will maybe have some pity.

But I also am a coward, for if I continue to delay, pleading for this wretched Roman, it is only to put off my own pain. *Tunc ergo apprehendit Pilatus Jesum et flagellavit.*[16]

The soldiers of the guard then take Jesus into the hall of the pretorium, and all the men of the cohort are summoned to the scene; there are few amusements in this occupied country. And yet the Saviour has often shown Himself to have a special sympathy with soldiers. He admired the trust and humility of the centurion and his affectionate care for the servant whom He healed. Later, it will be the centurion of the guard on Calvary who will be the first to proclaim His divinity. The cohort seems, however, to be seized by a collective frenzy which Pilate had not foreseen. Satan is there, breathing hatred into them.

But that is enough. Nothing is said, there are just blows; and let us try to follow to the end. They remove His clothes and bind Him, naked, to a column of the hall. The arms are held up in the air and the wrists are bound to the shaft.

The scourging is done with numerous thongs to which are fixed, at some distance from the loose ends, two balls of lead or small piece of bone. (Certainly, the stigmata on the Holy Shroud correspond to this type of *flagrum.*) The number of strokes is limited to thirty-nine by Hebrew law. But His executioners are legionaries without restraint, and they will go on to the point of making Him faint. There are, in fact, marks without number on the shroud, and they are nearly all on the back; the front of the body is against the column. They are to be seen on the back, on the shoulders and the loins. The lashes fall on His thighs and on the calves of His legs; and it is there that the ends of the thongs, beyond the balls of lead, encircle the limb and mark it with a furrow right round to the other side.

There are two executioners, one on each side of Him, of unequal height (all this may be deduced from the direction of the marks on the shroud). They alternate their strokes, with great zest. At first, the strokes leave long livid marks, long blue bruises beneath the skin. Remember that the skin has already been affected; that it is sore owing to the millions of little intra-dermic hæmorrhages brought about by the sweat of blood. Further marks are made by the balls of lead. Then the skin, into which the blood has crept, becomes tender and breaks under fresh

---

[16] "Then therefore Pilate took Jesus and scourged him." *Jn.* XIX, 1.

M

blows. The blood pours out; shreds of skin become detached and hang down. The whole of the back is now no more than a red surface, on which great furrows stand out like marble; and, here and there, everywhere, there are deeper wounds caused by the balls of lead. These wounds, shaped like a halter (the two balls and the thong between them), will make their marks on the shroud.

At each stroke, the body gives a painful shudder. But He has not opened His mouth, and His silence redoubles the Satanic rage of His executioners. It is no longer a cold-blooded, judicial execution; it is the unchaining of demons. The blood flows from His shoulders down to the earth (the large paving-stones are covered with it), and is scattered like rain by the lifted whips as far as the red cloaks of the onlookers. But the strength of the Victim soon begins to fail; sweat breaks out on His forehead; His head whirls with giddiness and nausea; shivers run down His spine; His legs give way under Him, and if He was not tied up by His wrists, He would slip down into the pool of blood. They have completed the count, even though they have not counted. After all, they have not received the order that He should die under the lash. Let Him recover a bit; there will be further chances for amusement.

And this great Fool claims to be a king, as if He held it under the Roman eagles, and what is more, to be King of the Jews; of all ridiculous things! He has had some trouble with His subjects; what matter, we will be His faithful supporters. Quick, a robe, a sceptre. He has been put to sit at the base of the column (not a very secure place for His Majesty!). An old legionary's cloak thrown over His naked shoulders confers on Him the royal purple; a reed in His right hand, and everything is complete, except for the *crown;* now for something original! (For nineteen centuries He will be known by this crown, which no other crucified being has worn). In the corner there is a bundle of faggots, cut from those little trees which thrive on the outskirts of the city. The wood is flexible and covered with long thorns, much longer and sharper and harder than those of the acacia. They plait with caution (ugh! it hurts!) something like the bottom of a basket, which they place on His head. They beat down the edges and with a band of twisted rushes they bind it on the head from the nape of the neck to the forehead.

The thorns dig into the scalp and it bleeds. (We surgeons know how much a scalp can bleed.) The top of the head is already clotted with blood; long streams of blood have flown down to the forehead, under the band of rushes, have soaked into the tangled hair and into the beard. The comedy of adoration has begun. Each in turn comes forward and bows the knee before Him, with a horrible grimace, followed by a great blow: " Hail, King of the Jews! " But He answers nothing. His poor face, so ravaged and pale, displays no movement. It really is not funny! In their exasperation His faithful subjects spit in His face. " You don't know how to hold the sceptre, give it here!" There, a blow on the crown of thorns, which makes it sink further in, and then fresh blows. I cannot remember, did He receive it from one of the legionaries, or from the gentlemen of the Sanhedrin? But I can see that a blow from a stick delivered from the side has made a horrible bruise on His face, and that His fine well-shaped nose has been disfigured owing to the septum being broken. The blood is flowing from His nostrils. Oh, my God, this is enough!

But now Pilate is back, rather worried about the prisoner—what have these brutes been doing to Him? Well, they have dealt with Him all right. If the Jews are not satisfied now!—He will show Him to them from the balcony of the pretorium, in His royal robes, and is quite astonished at the pity he finds himself feeling for this poor bedraggled creature. But he has underestimated their hatred. *Tolle, crucifige!*[17] What fiends they are! And then they put forward the argument that terrifies him: " If thou release this man, thou art not Cæsar's friend. For whosoever maketh himself a king speaketh against Cæsar."[18] The coward then surrenders completely and washes his hands. As St. Augustine would write later, however, " It is not thou, O Pilate, who didst kill him, but the Jews, with their cutting tongues; and when compared with them, thou art far more innocent."

They tear the cloak from Him, which has already stuck to His wounds. The blood starts to flow once more; He gives a great shudder. They replace His own clothes, which become stained with red. *The cross is ready, they place it on His shoulders.* By what miracle of strength does He remain standing beneath this burden? It is not in fact, the whole cross, but only the great horizontal beam, the *patibulum,* which He must carry as far as Golgotha, but still it weighs nearly 125 pounds. The vertical stake, the *stipes,* is already planted on Calvary.

And so *He starts on His journey,* with bare feet, along the rough roads strewn with stones. The soldiers pull the cords which bind Him, anxious to know whether He will last out till the end. Two thieves follow Him with the same equipment. The road is fortunately not very long, about 650 yards, and the hill of Calvary is just outside the gate of Ephraim. But the journey is a very chequered one, even inside the ramparts. Jesus painfully puts one foot before the other, and He often falls. He falls on to His knees which are soon all raw. The soldiers who form the escort

[17] " Away with him, crucify him." *Jn.* XIX, 15.
[18] *Jn.* XIX, 12.

lift Him up, and are not too brutal about it, for they feel He might easily die on the way.

And all the time there is that beam, balanced on His shoulders, bruising Him, and which seems to wish to force its way into His back. I know what it is like: in the time gone by, when serving with the 5e Genie,[19] I have carried railway sleepers on my back; they were well planed, and yet I can still remember how they seemed to force their way right into one's shoulders, even into my shoulders which were in excellent condition. But His shoulders are covered with raw places, which open up again and get larger and deeper with each step He takes. He is worn out. On His seamless coat there is a large patch of blood which gets ever larger till it reaches right down His back. He falls again and this time at full length; the beam falls off Him; will He be able to get up again? Luckily at this moment a man passes by, on his way back from the fields, one Simon of Cyrene, who is soon, along with his sons Alexander and Rufus, going to be a good Christian. The soldiers make him carry this beam, and the good fellow is willing enough; oh, how well I would do it! There is at last only the slope of Golgotha to be climbed, and they make their painful way to the top of the hill. Jesus sinks to the ground and *the crucifixion begins*.

Oh, it is not very complicated; the executioners know their work. First of all He must be stripped. The lower garments are dealt with easily enough, but the coat has firmly stuck to His wounds, that is to say, to His whole body, and this *stripping* is a horrible business. Have you ever removed the first dressing which has been on a large bruised wound, and has dried on it? Or have you yourself ever been through this ordeal, which sometimes requires a general anæsthetic? If so, you know what it is like. Each thread has stuck to the raw surface, and when it is removed it tears away one of the innumerable nervous ends which have been laid bare by the wound. These thousands of painful shocks add up and multiply, each one increasing the sensitivity of the nervous system. Now, it is not just a question of a local lesion, but of almost the whole surface of the body, and especially of that dreadful back. The executioners are in a hurry and set about their work roughly. Perhaps it is better thus, but how does this sharp, dreadful pain not bring on a fainting fit? How clear it is that from beginning to end He dominates, He directs His Passion.

The blood streams down yet again. They lay Him down on His back. Have they left Him the narrow loin-cloth which the modesty of the Jews has been able to preserve for those condemned to this death? I must

---

[19] 5th Regiment of Engineers.

own that I do not know: it is of little importance; in any case, in His shroud, He will be naked. The wounds on His back, on His thighs and on the calves of His legs become caked with dust and with tiny pieces of gravel. He has been placed at the foot of the *stipes*, with His shoulders lying on the *patibulum*. The executioners take the measurements. A stroke with an auger, to prepare the holes for the nails, and the horrible deed begins.

An assistant holds out one of the arms, with the palm uppermost. The executioner takes hold of the nail (a long nail, pointed and square, which near its large head is $\frac{1}{3}$ of an inch thick), he gives Him a prick on the wrist, in that forward fold which he knows by experience. One single blow with the great hammer, and the nail is already fixed in the wood, in which a few vigorous taps fix it firmly.

Jesus has not cried out, but His face has contracted in a way terrible to see. But above all I saw at the same moment that His thumb, with a violent gesture, is striking against the palm of His hand: *His median nerve has been touched*. I realise what He had been through: an inexpressible pain darts like lightning through his fingers and then like a trail of fire right up His shoulder, and bursts in His brain. The most unbearable pain that a man can experience is that caused by wounding the great nervous centres. It nearly always causes a fainting fit, and it is fortunate that it does. Jesus has not willed that He should lose consciousness. Now, it is not as if the nerve were cut right across. But no, I know how it is, it is only partially destroyed; the raw place on the nervous centre remains in contact with the nail; and later on, when the body sags, it will be stretched against this like a violin-string against the bridge, and it will vibrate with each shaking or movement, reviving the horrible pain—This goes on for three hours.

The other arm is pulled by the assistant, the same actions are repeated and the same pains. But this time, remember, He knows what to expect. He is now fixed on the *patibulum*, to which His shoulders and two arms now conform exactly. He already has the form of a cross: how great He is!

Now, they must get Him on His feet. The executioner and his assistant take hold of the ends of the beam and then hold up the condemned man Who is first sitting, then standing, and then, moving Him backwards, they place Him with His back against the stake. But this is done by constantly pulling against those two nailed hands, and one thinks of those median nerves. With a great effort, and with arms extended (though the *stipes is not very high*), quickly, for it is very heavy, and with a skilful gesture, they fix the *patibulum* on the top of the *stipes*. On the top with two nails they fix the title in three languages.

The body, dragging on the two arms, which are stretched out obliquely, is sagging a bit. The shoulders, wounded by the whips and by carrying the cross, have been painfully scraped against the rough wood. The nape of the neck, which was just above the *patibulum*, has been banged against it during the move upwards, and is now just above the stake. The sharp points of the great cap of thorns have made even deeper wounds in the scalp. His poor head is leaning forward, for the thickness of His crown prevents Him leaning against the wood, and each time that He straightens it He feels the pricks.

The body is meanwhile only held by the nails fixed into the two wrists —Once more those median nerves! He could be held fast with nothing else. The body is not slipping forwards, but the rule is that the feet should be fixed. There is no need of a bracket for this; they bend the knees and stretch the feet out flat on the wood of the *stipes*. Why then, since it is useless, is the carpenter given this work to do? It is certainly not in order to lessen the pain of the crucified. The left foot is flat against the cross. With one blow of the hammer, the nail is driven into the middle of it (between the second and third metatarsal bones). The assistant then bends the other knee, and the executioner, bringing the left foot round in front of the right which the assistant is holding flat, pierces this foot with a second blow in the same place. This is easy enough, and with a few vigorous blows with the hammer the nail is well embedded in the wood. This time, thank God, it is a more ordinary pain, but the agony has scarcely begun. The whole work has not taken the two men much more than two minutes and the wounds have not bled much. They then deal with the two thieves, and the three gibbets are arranged facing the city which kills its God.

Do not let us listen to these triumphant Jews, as they insult Him in His pain. He has already forgiven them, for they know not what they do. Jesus has at first been in a state bordering on collapse. After so many tortures, for a worn-out body this immobility is almost a rest, coinciding as it does with a general lowering of His vitality. But *He thirsts*. He has not said so as yet. Before lying down on the beam, He has refused the analgesic drink, of wine mingled with myrrh and gall, which is prepared by the charitable women of Jerusalem. He wishes to know His suffering in its completeness; He knows that He will conquer it. He thirsts. Yes, *Adhæsit lingua me faucibus meis*.[20] He has neither eaten nor drunk anything since the evening before, and it is now midday. His sweat in Gethsemani, all His fatigues, His loss of blood in the pretorium and at other times, and even the small amount now flowing from His wounds,

---

[20] ". My tongue hath cleaved to my jaws." *Ps.* XXI, 16.

all this has taken a good part of His sum-total of blood. He thirsts. His features are drawn, His pale face is streaked with blood which is congealing everywhere. His mouth is half open and His lower lip has already begun to droop. A little saliva has flowed down to His beard, mingled with the blood from His injured nose. His throat is dry and on fire, but He can no longer swallow. He thirsts. How can one recognise the fairest of the children of men in this swollen face, all bleeding and deformed? *Vermis sum et non homo.*[21] It would be horrible, if one did not see shining through it the serene majesty of God Who wishes to save His brothers. He thirsts. And He will soon say it, so as to fulfil the Scriptures. A great simpleton of a soldier, wishing to hide his compassion beneath a mocking jest, soaks a sponge in his acid *posca, acetum* as the Gospels call it, and holds it up to Him at the end of a reed. Will He drink only a drop of it? It is said that the fact of drinking brings on a mortal fainting fit in these poor, condemned creatures. How then, after the sponge had been held up to Him, was He able to speak two or three times? No, He will die at His own hour. He thirsts.

And that has just begun. But, a moment later, a strange phenomenon occurs. The muscles of His arms stiffen of themselves, in a contraction which becomes more and more accentuated; His deltoid muscles and His biceps become strained and stand out, His fingers are drawn sharply inwards. It is cramp! You have all had some experience of this acute, progressive pain, in the calves of the legs, between the ribs, a little everywhere. One must immediately relax the contracted muscle by extending it. But watch—on His thighs and on His legs there are monstrous rigid bulges, and His toes are bent. It is like a wounded man suffering from tetanus, a prey to those horrible spasms, which once seen can never be forgotten. It is what we describe as *tetanisation*, when the cramps become generalised, which is now happening. The stomach muscles become tightened in set undulations, then the intercostal, then the muscles of the neck, then the respiratory. His breathing has gradually become shorter and lighter. His sides, which have already been drawn upwards by the traction of the arms, are now exaggeratedly so; the solar plexus sinks inwards, and so do the hollows under the collar-bone. The air enters with a whistling sound, but scarcely comes out any longer. He is breathing in the upper regions only, He breathes in a little, but cannot breathe out. He thirsts for air. (It is like someone in the throes of asthma.) A flush has gradually spread over His pale face; it has turned a violet purple and then blue. *He is asphyxiating.* His lungs which are loaded with air can no longer empty themselves. His forehead is covered with sweat, His eyes are prominent and rolling. What an appalling pain

---

[21] " I am a worm and no man." *Ps.* XXI, 7.

must be hammering in His head! He is going to die. Well, it is best so. Has He not suffered enough?

But no, His hour has not yet come. Neither thirst, nor hæmorrhage, nor asphyxia, nor pain will be able to overcome the Saviour God, and if He dies with these symptoms, He will only die in truth because He freely wills it, *habens in potestate ponere animam suam et recipere eam.*[22] And thus it is that He will rise again.

What, then, is happening? Slowly, with a superhuman effort, He is using the nail through His feet as a fulcrum, that is to say He is pressing on His wounds. The ankles and the knees stretch themselves out bit by bit, and the body is gradually lifted, thus relieving the pressure on the arms (a pressure which was of very nearly 240 pounds on each hand). We thus see how, through His own efforts, the phenomenon grows less, the tetanisation recedes, the muscles become relaxed, anyway those of the chest. The breathing becomes more ample and moves down to a lower level, the lungs are unloaded and the face soon resumes its former pallor.

Why is He making all this effort? It is in order to speak to us: *Pater, dimitte illis.*[23] Yes, may He indeed forgive us, we who are His executioners. But a moment later His body begins to sink down once more . . . and the tetanisation will come on again. And each time that He speaks (we have anyway preserved seven of His words), and each time that He wishes to breathe, it will be necessary for Him to straighten Himself, to get back His breath, holding Himself upright on the nail through His feet. And each movement has its echo, so to speak, in His hands, in inexpressible pain (those median nerves once again!). It is a question of periodical asphyxiation of the poor unfortunate Who is being strangled and then allowed to come back to life, to be choked once more several times over. He can only escape from this asphyxiation for a moment at a time and at the cost of terrible suffering, and by an effort of the will. And this is going to last three hours. O my God, may You be able to die!

I am there at the foot of the cross, with His Mother and John and the women who attended upon Him. The centurion, who had been standing a little apart, is observing the scene with an attention that has already become respectful. Between two attacks of asphyxiation, He draws Himself up and speaks: " Son, behold Thy Mother." Oh, yes, dear Mother, you who adopted us from that day!—a little later that poor wretch of a thief manages to have the gate of paradise opened for him. But when, O Lord, are You at last going to die?

---

[22] " Having the power to lay down his life and to take it up again."—St. Augustine, *Treatise on the Psalms.* (Ps. LXIII, *ad vers.*, 3.)
[23] " Father, forgive them." (*Lk.* XXIII, 34.)

I know well that Easter awaits You, and that Your body will not decay as ours do. It is written: *Non dabis sanctum tuum videre corruptionem.*[24] But, O poor Jesus (forgive a surgeon for these words), all Your wounds are becoming infected; this was certain to happen. I can see clearly how a light-coloured transparent lymph is oozing from them, which collects at the deepest part in a wax-like crust. On the earliest wounds false membranes are forming, which secrete a serum mixed with pus. It is also written: *Putruerunt et corrupta sunt cicatrices meæ.*[25]

A swarm of horrible flies, of great yellow and blue flies such as one finds in abattoirs and charnel-houses, is whirling the whole time round His body, and they swoop down on the different wounds in order to suck at them and to lay their eggs. They set on His face and cannot be driven away. Fortunately, the sky has during the last moments gone dark, and the sun is hidden; it has suddenly become very cold, and these daughters of Beelzebub have one by one taken their departure.

It will soon be three o'clock. At last! Jesus is holding out the whole time. Every now and then He draws Himself up. All His pains, His thirst, His cramps, the asphyxiation and the vibration of the two median nerves have not drawn one complaint from Him. But, while His friends are there indeed, His Father, and this is the last ordeal, His Father seems to have forsaken Him. *Eli, Eli, lamma sabacthani?*[26]

He now knows that He is going. He cries out *consummatum est.*[27] The cup is drained, the work is complete. Then, drawing Himself up once more and as if to make us understand that He is dying of His own free will, *iterum clamans voce magna:*[28] " Father, into Thy hands I commend My Spirit " (*habens in potestate ponere animan suam*).[29] He died when He willed to do so. I wish to hear of no more physiological theories!

Laudato si Missignore per sora nostra morte corporale![30] O yes, Lord, may You be blessed, for having truly willed to die. For there was nothing we could do. With a last sigh Your head dropped slowly towards me, with Your chin above the breastbone. I can see Your face straight before me, it is now relaxed and calm, and in spite of its dreadful stigmata, it is illuminated by the gentle majesty of God, Who is always present there. I have thrown myself on my knees before You, kissing Your

[24] " Thou wilt not give thy holy one to see corruption."—*Ps.* XV, 10.
[25] " My sores are putrified and corrupted." *Ps.* XXXVII, 6.
[26] " My God, my God, why hast thou forsaken me?" *Mt.* XXVII, 46; *Mk.* XVI, 34; *Ps.* XXI, 1.
[27] " It is consummated." *Jn.* XIX, 30.
[28] " Again crying with a loud voice." *Mt.* XXVII, 50.
[29] *Lk.* XXIII, 46.
[30] " May you be blessed, O Lord, for our sister the death of the body."—*Canticle of the Creatures, St. Francis of Assisi.*

pierced feet, from which the blood is still flowing, though it is coagulating at the tips. The *rigor mortis* has seized You in brutal fashion, like a stag run down in the chase. Your legs are as hard as steel . . . and burning. What unheard-of temperature has given You this tetanic spasm?

There has been an earthquake; what is that to me? And the sun has undergone an eclipse. Joseph has gone to ask Pilate for Your body, and he will not be refused. The latter hates the Jews, who have forced him to kill You; that writing above Your head proclaims his rancour for all to see; "Jesus, King of the Jews," has been crucified like a slave! The centurion has gone to make his report, and the brave man has proclaimed You to be truly the Son of God. We are going to lower You, and it will be easy, once the nail has been taken out of the feet. Joseph and Nicodemus will unfasten the beam of the *stipes*. John, Your beloved disciple, will bear Your feet; with two others we will support Your loins, using a sheet twisted to make a rope. The shroud is ready, on this stone nearby, in front of the sepulchre; and there, taking their time, they will remove the nails from Your hands. But who is this?

Oh, yes, the Jews must have asked Pilate to clear the hill of these gibbets which offend the eye and would defile to-morrow's feast. A brood of vipers, who strain at a gnat and swallow a camel! Some soldiers break the legs of the thieves, giving them great blows with an iron bar. They now hang miserably, and as they can no longer raise themselves on the ropes binding their legs, tetanisation and asphyxiation will soon have finished them.

But this does not apply to You. *Os non comminuetis ex eo.*[31] Can you not leave us in peace? Cannot you see He is dead?—No doubt, they say. But what is this idea that one of them has? With an exact and tragic gesture he has raised the shaft of the lance and with one blow upwards on the right side, he drives it in deep. But why? "And immediately there came out blood and water."[32] John truly saw it, and I also, and we would not lie: a broad stream of dark liquid blood, which gushed out on to the soldier, and slowly flowed in dribbles over the chest, coagulating in successive layers. But at the same time, and specially noticeable at the edges, there flows a clear liquid like water. Let us see, the wound is below and to the outside of the nipple (the fifth space), and the blow from below. It is therefore the blood from the right auricle, and the water issued from the pericardium. But then, O poor Jesus, Your heart was compressed by this liquid, and apart from everything

---

[31] "You shall not break a bone of him." *Jn.* XIX, 36; *Ex.* XII, 46.
[32] *Jn.* XIX, 34.

else You had the agonising cruel pain of Your heart being held as in a vice.

Had we not already seen enough? Was it so that we should know this, that this man performed this odd aggressive act? The Jews might also have made out that You were not dead but had fainted; Your resurrection needed this testimony. Thank you, soldier, thank you, Longinus; one day you will die as a Christian martyr.

CONCLUSION

And now, reader, let us thank God Who has given me the strength to write this to the end, though not without tears! All these horrible pains that we have lived in Him, were foreseen by Him all through His life; He premeditated them and willed them, out of His love, so that He might redeem us from oùr sins. *Oblatus est quia ipse voluit.*[33] He directed the whole of His passion, without avoiding one torture, accepting the physiological consequences, without being dominated by them. *He died when and how and because He willed it.*

Jesus is in agony till the end of time. It is right, it is good to suffer with Him and to thank Him, when He sends us pain, to associate ourselves with His. We have, as St. Paul writes, to complete what is lacking in the passion of Christ, and with Mary, His Mother and our Mother, to accept our fellow-suffering fraternally and with joy.

O Jesus, You Who had no pity on Yourself, You Who are God, have pity on me who am a sinner.

Laus Christo.

DOCTOR PIERRE BARBET,
Surgeon at the Hôpital Saint-Joseph,
Paris.

---

[33] " He was offered because it was his own will." *Is.* LIII, 7.

APPENDIX I

Aufbinden in Dachau

The condemned man was hung up by his hands, either side by side, or separated. The feet were some distance from the ground.

After quite a short time, the difficulty in breathing became intolerable. The victim tried to overcome this by drawing himself up on his arms, which allowed him to regain his breath; he was able to hold himself up from thirty to sixty seconds.

They then tied weights on to his feet, to make the body heavier, and to prevent him doing this. Asphyxia then came on rapidly, in three or four minutes. At the last moment they would remove the weight, so as to let him revive, by allowing him to draw himself up once more.

The witness of this, who is not a doctor, was not able to ascertain whether this drawing himself upwards was a voluntary act or was due to contraction of the muscles. In any case, the respiration was greatly relieved.

After hanging for an hour, this drawing up became more and more frequent, but at the same time more and more feeble. Asphyxia set in, progressively and finally. This was evident from the fact that the thoracic frame was swelled out to its maximum, and the epigastric hollow was extremely concave. The legs were stiff and hung without movement. The skin became violet in colour. A profuse sweat appeared all over the body, dropping down to the ground and staining the cement. It was especially abundant, indeed to an extraordinary extent, during the last few minutes before death; the hair and beard were literally drenched. And this, though the temperature was at freezing point. The dying man must have had a high temperature.

After death the body had an *extreme rigidity*. The head fell forward in the axis of the body. Death occurred after about three hours; rather more slowly when the hands were separated.

APPENDIX II

By

P. J. Smith, M.B., B.Ch.

Under Constantine in 315, or, at latest, 330 A.D., death by crucifixion was abolished in the Roman Empire. This horrible form of death penalty was very general throughout the Empire in the early centuries, and, although by far the largest number of victims were slaves, still, it did not vary much, in form, for slave or senator.

Thus during the lifetime of St. Augustine there was nobody living who had ever seen a crucifixion and the horror of the early Christians at the infamy of the Cross resulted in its being concealed under various symbols for centuries. In the catacombs one is familiar with the anchor and the fish but actual representations of the Cross are said to number only about twenty. The story of Christ crucified was kept alive by word of mouth in the early Christian churches and homes. It was not until the fifth and sixth centuries that the first crucifix appears and, then, for a very long time, the figure of Christ on it was not Christ crucified but Christ risen from the dead. Actual devotion to the Passion of Jesus did not begin until the thirteenth century, after which, the subject of the crucifixion in religious art increases in frequency during the transition from the Sienese primitives to Giotto and the later Florentine schools.

Thus for over a thousand years there was hush and silence in the Christian world over the tragedy of the death of Jesus. And to-day millions of Christians feel similarly and they would be content to live with the symbols of the Cross, and to know, in reticence and simplicity, the awful story—" Pilate . . . having scourged Jesus, delivered Him to be crucified . . . and they crucified Him."

Nevertheless, the details set out in this book will serve a useful purpose in very many ways. They will be of interest to a section of the medical profession; to archaeologists; to theologians and to those interested in exegetics. Indeed, had it been written before the thirty odd years at the turn of the seventeenth century, it would have been of great value and help to those who were defending the Church's position during the ferment of European thought from Bossuet to Voltaire. And it is pleasant to note that the country which produced Renan, Bayle, and Simon, also produced the author of this book.

Only four of the sections of this work are of purely medical interest. The first is the section on the cause of death. Here the author finally decides that Christ, at the end of the three hours' agony on the Cross, died of asphyxia brought on by what he calls " tetany of His musculature." We apply the word tetany to describe a different clinical entity, but medical people will understand the author's meaning. In other parts of the book there are detailed descriptions of the savage and barbarous brutalities to which Christ was subjected. There was the Scourging at the Pillar with the flagrum, which had thongs loaded at the ends with lead. These thongs cut deeply into the flesh and caused extensive laceration of the back and legs, and to some extent the ventral aspect as well. As a result of this there was excruciating pain and considerable loss of blood. The Crowning with Thorns, which, apparently, was in the form of a cap rather than the circlet, also caused very extensive hæmorrhage, as the scalp is very vascular. There is also a description of grievous violence having been done to Jesus which resulted in a large haematoma on the right side of His forehead, and much bruising of the face. This violence was caused by the soldiers striking Him on the head with a form of club in order apparently to drive the thorns still farther into His scalp. The carrying of the Cross, whether it was the transverse section or patibulum only or the whole Cross, resulted in considerable bruising of His right shoulder and back, particularly when He fell. It is clear that He must have been *in extremis* when the Roman centurion ordered Simon of Cyrene to carry His Cross for Him so that He might not die before He came to crucifixion.

I am of the opinion that there is overwhelming evidence that Christ died from heart failure due to extreme shock caused by exhaustion, pain and loss of blood. Asphyxia, or respiratory failure as we prefer to call it, the author thinks was caused by the respiratory muscles becoming fixed in inspiration due to the falling forward of the trunk away from the vertical section of the Cross and the consequent inability to expire and so empty the lungs of carbon dioxide. This theory is not supported by some of the evidence set out in the book.

For instance he describes a scaphoid epigastrium which could be most easily explained by the diaphragm being in the elevated or expiratory position. To be fair, he also describes a protuberant lower abdomen which might be caused by the diaphragm in descent. But it is a small point and really does not matter much as the cause of the death of Christ crucified is clear enough.

The other sections which might be of interest to medical men are those in which he describes the probable position of the nails in the hands and feet. I think he is completely convincing when he says that the nail in the hand must have been driven through the wrist immediately above the flexor retinaculum or transverse carpal ligament between the two rows of carpal bones in an upward and backward direction. The median nerve was destroyed in whole or in part on the way and this explained the position of the thumb in the palm presumably by the pull of the adductor pollicis which is supplied by the intact ulnar nerve. It is useless to search for an adjective to describe the excruciating pain caused by the continuing trauma to this nerve. The position of the nail in the palm of the hand between the metacarpal bones is that which is usually depicted in the paintings of the crucifixion by most artists. The author rightly points out that in that position the weight of the body would pull the nail out through the flesh between the fingers.

The position of the nail in the feet which the author finally decides on would appear to be accurate. He gives the position as the proximal part of the second metatarsal interspace, and as this is just below the tarsal mass the nail would easily support the whole body. He considers, on the evidence of the markings of the Holy Shroud, that the sole of the right foot was flat on the stipes or vertical section of the Cross, and that the left foot was on top of the right and obliquely across it. There was no supporting platform or suppedaneum, as it was called, for the feet, which were nailed directly to the Cross.

The lance wound in the side which was inflicted after Christ was dead is generally thought to have been on the right side. The author places it in the fifth interspace just lateral to the right margin of the sternum. He considers the lance to have passed upwards and inwards through the pericardial sac to enter the right auricle. In this way he explains the issue of blood and water from the wound in Christ's side which is described in the Gospel of St. John. The right auricle of course always contains blood after death so that this description is convincing.

It is interesting to note that in the Pietà in the Hospital of St. John at Bruges painted by Memling, the wound in the chest is accurately placed on the right side, the thumbs are mesially adducted across the palms and the nail wounds in both feet are in correct position.

The remaining sections of this book will be of very much interest to the archaeologists, the historian, and to the general reader as well.

There are two forms of the Cross which are used in crucifixion; one shaped like the letter " T " and called the Tau cross after the Greek letter. It was simpler to assemble and cruder in type. The other, called the Latin Cross, was a little more difficult to make. It provided a space for the titulus or description of the victim at the top of the Cross.

Although the Fathers of the Church were of the opinion that Christ died on the Latin cross, still many early writers, but especially Tertullian, thought the Tau cross was used. Artists who painted prior to the late thirteenth century like Duccio and Cimabue and the

Byzantine School used the Latin cross. But Giotto, as is to be seen in the Arena Chapel, Padua, painted a Tau cross. So did the great Roger Van Der Weyden after 1400 as is seen in his Descent from the Cross in the Escorial. The early German painters, Dürer, Grünewald, and Cranach, also painted Christ crucified on a Tau cross with the titulus on the cross-beam over His head. But the Italian School, with some exceptions, nearly all used the Latin cross, e.g., Masaccio in 1420, and by the end of the sixteenth century the Latin cross was universal, as can be seen in the work of El Greco, Ribera and Velasquez. Most artists showed a suppedaneum or platform for the feet and nearly all when they crossed the feet placed the right foot above the left

And so this book will tell many details of the death of Jesus to a section of inquirers, but what will move the hearts of men always will be the old and simpler story:—

"Pilate . . . having scourged Jesus, delivered Him to them to be crucified . . . and they crucified Him."

Illustrations

The laying in the Shroud
Miniature by G. B. della Rovere (xviith century), in the gallery at Turin

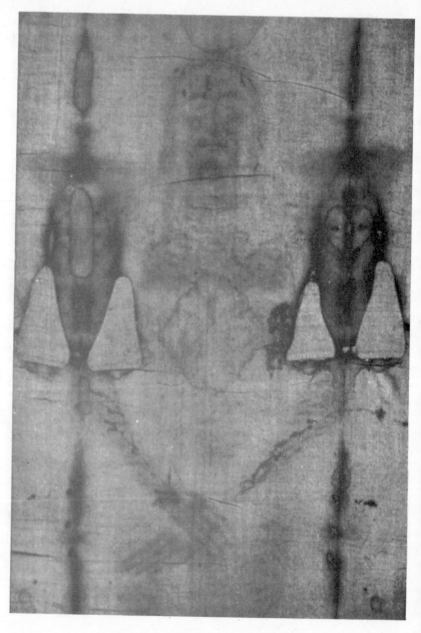

Fig. 1—*Frontal image on the Shroud (upper part)*
Photographic print

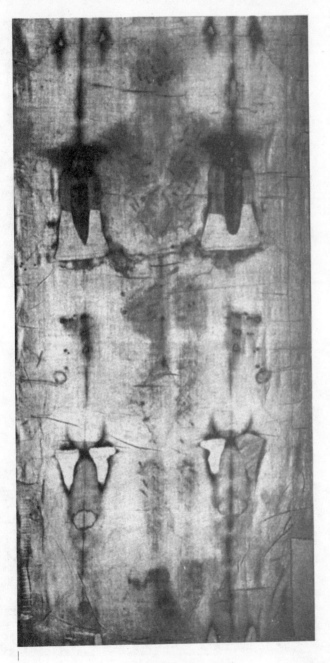

Fig. II—Rear image on Shroud
Photographic print

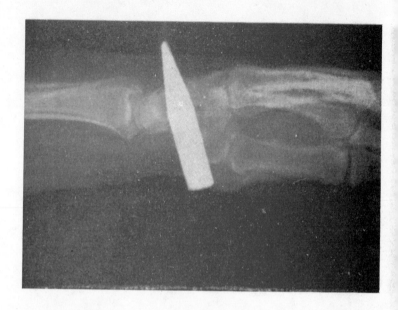

Fig. III

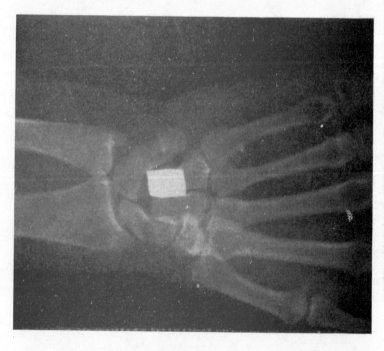

Fig. IV—Radiograph of a nailed hand

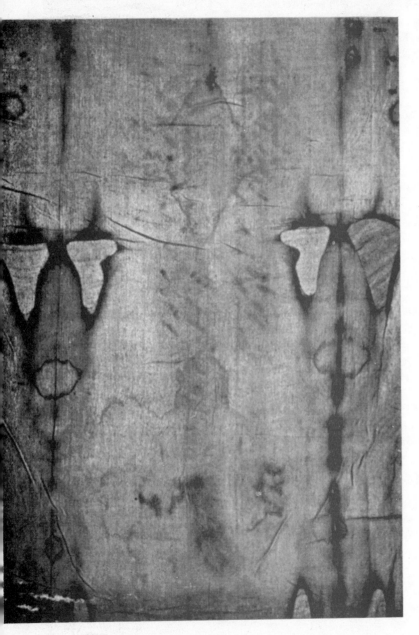

Fig. V—Rear image on the Shroud (lower members)

The lower members (*moving downwards: thighs, calves of legs, feet*). On the thighs and the calves there are the marks of the scourging. On the feet and on the outside of the feet there are flows of blood. On the right foot (to the left), which alone can be seen as a whole, there is the hole of the crucifixion.

Fig. VI—The nailing of the feet

Skeleton of right foot seen from above

The arrow indicates the direction of the interline of Lisfranc (articulation tarsometatarsal).

The cross marks the point of entrance of the nail at the crucifixion. (Posterior part of the 2nd interspace.)

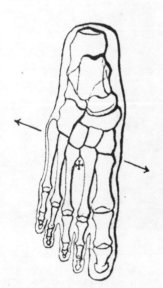

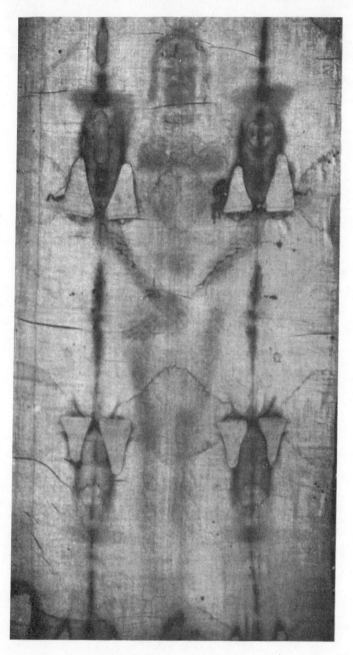

Fig. VII—Frontal image on Shroud
(Photographic proof)

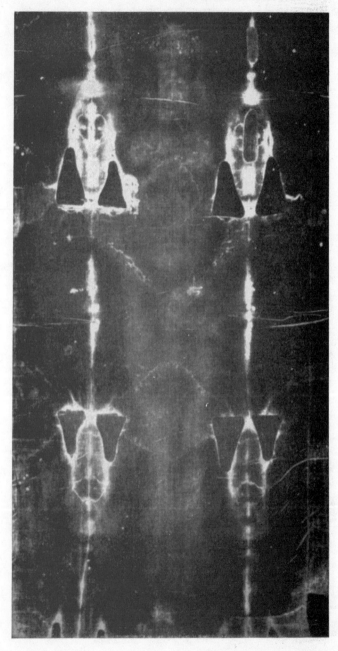

Fig. VIII—Frontal image on the Shroud
(Reproduction of negative)

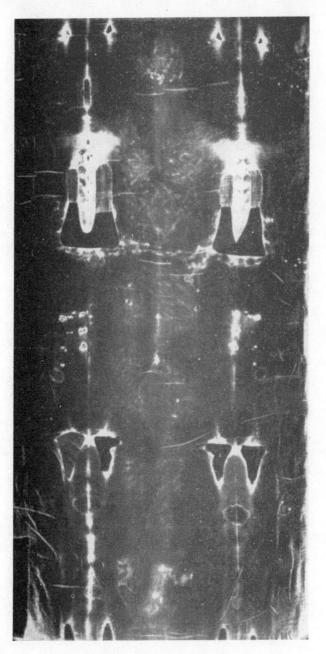

Fig. IX—Rear image on Shroud
(Reproduction of negative)

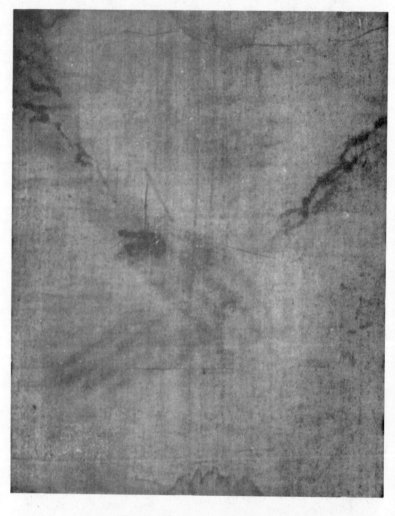

Fig. X—The Hands on the Shroud
Photographic print

Fig. XI—Volckringer—Marks left by plants in a herbal. Photographic print and negative

Fig. XII—The Villandre Crucifix

Of this crucifix Dr. Barbet writes :—
" As Charles Villandre was a past-master in sculpture as well
as in surgery, I asked him to make a crucifix, according to the
precise information I had given him; this is the crucifix which
appears in the photograph."